1200s

HEADLINES IN HISTORY

Books in the Headlines in History series:

The 1200s

HEADLINES IN HISTORY

Thomas Siebold, *Book Editor*

Bonnie Szumski, *Editorial Director*
Scott Barbour, *Managing Editor*

Greenhaven Press, Inc., San Diego, California

Every effort has been made to trace the owners of copyrighted material. The articles in this volume may have been edited for content, length, and/or reading level. The titles have been changed to enhance the editorial purpose.

Library of Congress Cataloging-in-Publication Data

The 1200s / Thomas Siebold, book editor.
　　　p. cm. — (Headlines in history)
　　Includes bibliographical references and index.
　　ISBN 0-7377-0532-9 (lib. bdg. : alk. paper)—
　ISBN 0-7377-0531-0 (pbk. : alk. paper)
　　1. Thirteenth century. 2. Civilization, Medieval—
13th century. I. Siebold, Thomas. II. Headlines in history
(San Diego, Calif.)

CB355 .A15 2001
909'.2—dc21

　　　　　　　　　　　　　　　　　　　　　　2001016035

Cover photos: Upper left: Kublai Khan gives his golden seal to the Polos, Art Resource; Upper right: King John signs the Magna Carta, North Wind Picture Archives; Lower right: Cahokia Mounds State Historic Site, painting by Michael Hampshire; Lower left: St. Thomas Aquinas, AKG Photo.
Bibliotheque Nationale, 122
Library of Congress, 185
North Wind Picture Archives, 206

Copyright © 2001 by Greenhaven Press, Inc.
P.O. Box 289009, San Diego, CA 92198-9009

Printed in the USA

CONTENTS

Chapter 1: Europe

1. The Decline of Empire and the Papacy in Europe

Both the Holy Roman Empire and the papacy lost
power and prestige during the thirteenth century. Internal dissension, struggles for control, costly military campaigns, and a growing decentralization of
power weakened both institutions.

2. Thomas Aquinas and High Medieval Philosophy in Europe

In his major work, *Summa Theologica*, philosopher
Thomas Aquinas not only draws a distinction between revelation and reason; he also fits both within
one religious truth. The work of Aquinas allowed humans to find truth both in faith and in observation of
the natural world.

3. Thomas Aquinas's Proof of God's Existence

Employing the elements of logic, Thomas Aquinas
presents a proof of God's existence. His philosophical approach reflects the burgeoning desire among
thinkers to find truth through reason and intellect.

4. The Magna Carta

In an attempt to combat the excesses of King John of England, rebellious barons drafted a document, the Magna
Carta, that limited the power of the English monarchy. In
essence, the historic Magna Carta asserted that all people,
including the king, are accountable to the law.

to second-class status. Zhao Mengfu and other members of the esteemed Chinese literati were able to keep some of the arts alive even though they were required to do administrative work and state-sponsored teaching.

3. The North American Indians of Cahokia

The great earthen pyramids of Cahokia distinguish the thriving thirteenth-century Cahokian Indians of the Mississippi River. Their location, which was accessible by numerous waterways, allowed them to establish a vibrant trading empire.

FOREWORD

hronological time lines of history are mysteriously fascinating. To learn that within a single century Christopher Columbus sailed to the New World, the Aztec, Maya, and Inca cultures were flourishing, Joan of Arc was burned to death, and the invention of the printing press was radically changing access to written materials allows a reader a different type of view of history: a bird's-eye view of the entire globe and its events. Such a global picture allows for cross-cultural comparisons as well as a valuable overview of chronological history that studying one particular area simply cannot provide.

Taking an expansive look at world history in each century, therefore, can be surprisingly informative. In Headlines in History, Greenhaven Press attempts to imitate this time-line approach using primary and secondary sources that span each century. Each volume gives readers the opportunity to view history as though they were reading the headlines of a global newspaper: Editors of each volume have attempted to glean and include the most important and influential events of the century, as well as quirky trends and cultural oddities. Headlines in History, then, attempts to give readers a glimpse of both the mundane and the earth-shattering. Articles on the French Revolution, for example, are juxtaposed with the then-current fashion concerns of the French nobility. This creates a higher interest level by allowing students a glimpse of people's everyday lives throughout history.

By using both primary and secondary sources, students also have the opportunity to view the historical events both as eyewitnesses have experienced them and as historians have interpreted them. Thus, students can place such historical events in a larger context as well as receive background information on important world events.

Headlines in History allows readers the unique opportunity to learn more about events that may only be mentioned in their history textbooks, or may be ignored entirely. The series presents students with a variety of interesting topics that span cultural, historical, and political arenas. Such a broad span of material will allow students to wander wherever their curiosity will take them.

INTRODUCTION

*H*eadlines in History: The 1200s focuses on the years 1200 to 1300, highlighting the major events, figures, and cultural patterns of the age. The goal is to present a global perspective of the ever-changing nature of the historical process as it unfolds through the century. To this end, *Headlines in History: The 1200s* is divided into four general geographical areas: Europe, Asia, the Islamic States, and Africa/the Americas. The areas were chosen because they include civilizations that experienced significant change, represented trends of the age, or played a key role in shaping or defining the century.

The articles for each geographical area concentrate on appropriate historical themes relevant to the thirteenth century: the conflict between nomadic people and sedentary cultures; a move to secularization; the growing role of commerce and trade; shifts in power; the changing role of institutions; and expanding intellectual patterns. Moreover, when possible, the articles have been selected to provide different perspectives illustrating one or more of seven cultural domains: social, economic, religious, political, intellectual, military, and artistic. Cultures within each of the four geographical areas did not remain isolated; they intermingled and interacted through trade, conversion, diffusion, adoption, exchange, and conquest. The Chinese, for example, were conquered by the Mongols; the North Africans converted to Islam; the Indians at Cahokia adopted crop products of Mesoamerica; and the Mali traded gold with the Europeans.

Headlines in History: The 1200s is designed to help students gain a greater appreciation of a time period that students often find difficult or inaccessible. Each of the articles is readable, manageable in length, and focused on concepts suitable for a beginning exploration into the century's key events. The inclusion of a primary source appendix provides readers with "you-are-there" immediacy. With this diverse overview of the century, students will have at their disposal a wealth of material for writing reports, designing oral presentations, or enriching their understanding of history.

The editors hope that with this book readers will gain a finer appreciation for the malleability and interconnectedness of world civilizations as they rise, change, adapt, and weaken through time. The joy of history is to witness patterns in the flow of historical events, recognizing that cultures not only have vast differences but also share many similarities. The articles included in this anthology emphatically reinforce the historical assertion that power is fickle, that conquest occurs both externally and internally, that events often have global ramifications, and that the survival of a civilization depends on its ability to respond to the challenges that it faces. *Headlines in History: The 1200s* explores civilizations at different stages in their growth: the Aztecs as they are coalescing into a powerful civilization, the Arab-Islamic world as it passes out of its golden age, the Mongols as they burn bright and fade quickly, the Europeans as they mold the intellectual and economic conditions for a major burst in creativity and progress, and the Chinese who are conquered and patiently work to restore their place internally.

The thirteenth century, then, is characterized by motion, when major civilizations rooted in customary historical patterns face the challenges of significant change.

An Overview
of the 1200s

The English historian Arnold J. Toynbee argued that cultures and civilizations are subject to a growth and decline process similar to that of human beings. He advanced the premise that they undergo a natural historical evolution in which they emerge, grow, flourish, peak, weaken, and finally fall. Their fate, indeed their very existence, depends on how they respond to internal and external challenges. All cultures must face the turmoil of change; they must learn to view themselves or their world differently, to confront threatening conflicts from the outside, to assimilate new ideas and inventions, to reconstruct old ideas in new ways, and, at times, to conceptualize a fresh worldview. History then is movement, and the dominant cultures of the thirteenth century were constantly in motion as they struggled with change through conquest, change through intellectual revelation, and change through political and power shifts.

Virtually all of the world's major cultural groups were transfigured in the thirteenth century. In Europe ideas once rigidly held prior to 1200 began to evolve, paving the way for a new mindset that would establish the intellectual groundwork for modern Western civilization. The once powerful and expansive empire of Islam experienced a crushing blow when the Asian Mongols destroyed Baghdad, the center of the Islamic world. Similarly, the Chinese were conquered by the Mongols and placed under the leadership of a foreign dynasty. The Mongols themselves experienced a mercurial rise to world domination, only to see their influence diminish by the end of the century. In Africa and the Americas three different cultures responded to the challenges of their own environments to form energetic and prosperous societies: the Indians at Cahokia in North America, the Aztecs in Mexico, and the Mali in western Africa. The story of the thirteenth century is transformation.

Europe and Christianity

Europe in the thirteenth century witnessed a transformation in medieval culture. This century, often called the High Middle Ages, produced social and economic changes that placed greater emphasis on human interests, reason, and values. This transformation from an otherwordly, nonsecular worldview to an increasingly worldly and secular mindset hinged on four forces of change. First, commerce exploded and the merchants who transformed the economy wielded new commercial and political power. Second, traditional power institutions, the church and royal authority, caught in petty power struggles and corruption, began to lose authority. Third, universities evolved and altered not only what people knew but the questions they asked and how they approached problem solving. Finally, theologians and philosophers altered the way people viewed their world by synthesizing the realm of God with the intellectual study of everyday life. As the century ended, Europeans suspected that they were forging a new world, that their civilization was maturing with a transfigured identity based on progress and strength.

Perhaps the most potent force for change in Europe was the expanding economy. Along vital trade routes and rivers, towns and cities prospered through commerce, manufacturing, and trade. A new mercantile freedom emerged and merchants, feeling a newly sprung sense of status and influence, banded together in guilds to protect their interests. Merchants in Germany, for example, formed a business association between eighty cities and towns called the Hanseatic League. The initial purpose of this organization was to secure and protect trade, but it soon gained political and military power as well. No longer isolated, these merchants of a growing middle class found that by organizing they could cut losses and survive better in a hostile world. By the middle of the thirteenth century merchants had instituted a revolutionary system of transaction with the introduction of credit through bills of exchange. The new wealth, the contact with many parts of the world through trade, and the celebratory freedom that comes with prosperity stimulated the arts and added to the secular notion that life here on earth could be infused with comfort and joy.

Throughout most of the Middle Ages political power was fragmented between feudal lords, kings, and the church. Both the church and the feudal nobles controlled vast lands on which they maintained their own courts, armies, and monetary systems. Despite the fact that nobles were technically vassals of kings, the monarchs had little real political, military, or legal power. However, throughout the thirteenth century this power distribution shifted as monarchs began to centralize their authority. Townspeople and particularly the merchant class

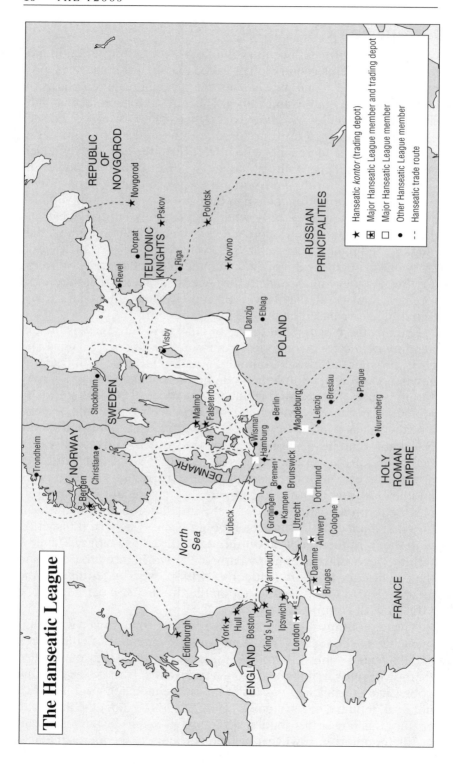

The Hanseatic League

REPUBLIC OF NOVGOROD

Novgorod

TEUTONIC KNIGHTS

Pskov

Dorpat

Polotsk

Revel

Riga

Kovno

RUSSIAN PRINCIPALITIES

Danzig

Elblag

POLAND

Visby

Breslau

Prague

Stockholm

SWEDEN

Malmö

Falsterbo

Berlin

Leipzig

Magdeburg

Nuremberg

Wismar

Hamburg

Trondheim

NORWAY

Christiana

Bremen

Brunswick

HOLY ROMAN EMPIRE

Bergen

Groningen

Kampen

Dortmund

DENMARK

Utrecht

Lübeck

Antwerp

Cologne

North Sea

Damme

Bruges

FRANCE

Yarmouth

King's Lynn

Ipswich

Edinburgh

York

Hull

Boston

London

ENGLAND

★ Hanseatic *kontor* (trading depot)

⊞ Major Hanseatic League member and trading depot

□ Major Hanseatic League member

• Other Hanseatic League member

-- Hanseatic trade route

generally supported the kings, believing that a powerful centralized authority would reduce the frequent feudal wars, curtail inconsistent and excessive taxes on trade routes, and standardize the monetary system. With an increase in trade, the economy slowly shifted from a land-based system to a money economy. Now the kings could tax wealthy towns and use the money to build and maintain their own powerful and professional armies with paid knights. As royal power gained momentum, the nobles sought concessions before they pledged their allegiance. In England, for example, the nobility, outraged at the king's excessive taxation program, forced a revolutionary legal charter in 1215 called the Magna Carta, which asserted that the king needed the nobility's consent before he raised taxes. In one key phrase, the nobles established the right of representatives to control taxation: "No scutage [a levied tax] or aid, save the customary feudal one, shall be levied except by the common consent of the realm."[1] Furthermore, the Magna Carta established that all people must obey the law, including the king.

The redistribution of power in the thirteenth century also altered the role of the church. At the outset of the century, Pope Innocent III, concerned about the shifting tide of power, reacted by exerting tight control over his bishops and exercising full papal authority against secular rulers, even to the extent of excommunicating King John of England in 1209. In the church's attempt to tighten control, its leaders ruthlessly attacked anyone who disagreed with their teachings, often charging them with heresy. In 1231 a chronicler for Frederick II, king of Sicily, described heretics as "bad angels, sons of perversity, appointed by the father of lies and deception to mislead the simple minded. They are serpents who deceive the doves. Like serpents they creep stealthily abroad; with honeyed sweetness they vomit forth their virus."[2] The Jews were one target of the church's crackdown on dissent. Early in the century the papal directives that offered official protection to Jews were modified or abandoned altogether. The Jewish holy book of law, the Talmud, was condemned as heretical and blasphemous. Jews lost their right to own land and were ousted from most trade guilds, required to wear identifying badges, and accused of witchcraft and sorcery. As a result, they were frequently expelled from Europe.

Through the course of the thirteenth century the church's efforts to solidify papal power eventually worked against itself. Critics began to see the church as overly political and medieval kings, resentful of the church's extensive tax-free lands and a court system that often conflicted with royal courts, targeted it as an obstacle to their growing power and worked to limit its role. Internally, the church was further weakened by the weight of a bureaucracy that grew cumbersome and top-heavy, governed by some leaders perceived by many as corrupt, worldly, and preoccupied with self-interest.

Late in the thirteenth century two new influential orders worked to redefine the church: the Dominican order of monks, founded by a Spanish priest, Dominic; and the Franciscans, founded by Francis of Assisi. Francis and his followers rejected worldly goods and sought converts among the poor. When asked by the bishop of Assisi why he renounced property, Francis replied, "My Lord, if we possessed property, we should have need of arms for its defense, for it is the source of quarrels and lawsuits, and the love of God and of one's neighbour usually finds many obstacles therein; that is why we do not desire temporal goods."[3]

Europe and the Growth of Knowledge

Thirteenth-century European society was also transformed by the accelerated growth of knowledge. As early as the twelfth century scholars began to recover and study the works of the ancient writers and thinkers, particularly the Greek philosopher Aristotle. The excitement generated by the recovery of ancient texts stimulated a revival of learning that steadily gained momentum throughout the thirteenth century. Scholars at the time were expected to present their studies in the form of a summa, a learned work that systematically and thoroughly presents a specific subject through a series of propositions, each one developed with pro and con arguments. In 1252 the most notable thirteenth-century intellectual and theologian, Thomas Aquinas, revolutionized Christian thought when he presented his *Summa Theologica.* In this work Aquinas argued that both reason and faith were elements of one truth. In an attempt to prove that the revelations in Scripture do not contradict conclusions drawn from logic, Aquinas wrote:

> The light of faith that is freely infused into us does not destroy the light of natural knowledge [reason] implanted in us naturally. For although the natural light of the human mind is insufficient to show us these things made manifest by faith, it is nevertheless impossible that these things which the divine principle gives us by faith are contrary to these implanted in us by nature [reason]. Indeed, were that the case, one or the other would have to be false, and, since both are given to us by God, God would have to be the author of untruth, which is impossible. . . . It is impossible that those things which are of philosophy can be contrary to those things which are of faith.[4]

The significance of this position is the justification it gives reason and the credibility it provides for serious scientific study of this world. Aquinas successfully infuses the Christian universe with reason, making it coherent and not dependent solely on revealed truth. Aquinas glorifies the individual thinker and the body of knowledge that will come from the collective scholarly community:

> That which a single man can bring, through his work and his genius, to the promotion of truth is little in comparison with the total of knowledge. However, from all these elements, selected and co-ordinated and brought together, there arises a marvelous thing, as is shown by the various departments of learning, which by the work and sagacity of many have come to a wonderful augmentation.[5]

With Aquinas's synthesis of faith and reason, Western thought is transformed by rationality. By providing a justification for reason, Aquinas opened the door for the growth of science. Ultimately, individuals began to see their world, their bodies, and their ability to think as gifts from God rather than attributes to be spurned.

Knowledge and the love of learning spread throughout Europe during the thirteenth century as universities grew in number and authority. Students who attended universities were taught a curriculum of the liberal arts that included such subjects as rhetoric, mathematics, music, astronomy, and Latin. The schools produced scientists, like Roger Bacon, who extolled the efficacy of rational experimentation and physicians who attempted to dispel the commonly held belief that illness was the product of sin or the work of evil spirits. Graduates of the university system grew in number to form a new medieval secular influence, an educated class.

An educated class, trade guilds, universities, cities, contact with foreign cultures, and wealth nurtured a demand for beauty and art. Cathedral building, which had reached its height in the twelfth century and continued into the thirteenth, was a major outlet for artistic expression. Artists enhanced the architecture with sculpture, textiles, and stained glass windows. Painters of the late thirteenth century began to paint much more humanistically, emotionally, and realistically. Cimabue, Duccio, and the greatest of all medieval painters, Giotto, experimented with pictorial space, creating the illusion of greater depth and volume to replicate nature as people really saw it. The notable Renaissance artist Lorenzo Ghiberti wrote that "Giotto saw in art what others had not attained. . . . He was extremely skillful in all the arts and was the inventor and discoverer of many methods which had been buried for about six hundred years."[6] Writers made literature more accessible to the bulk of readers by turning away from Latin and writing in the vernacular, the everyday speech of the people.

The thirteenth century in Europe was a time of transformation from the more traditional, faith-centered worldview to a more mercantile, reason-based mindset. Traditional centers of power were under assault from a society that was becoming increasingly secular.

Islam

While Europe experienced a transformation to greater secularization, the Islamic empire in the thirteenth century confronted a different kind of change—the collapse of its center and the end of a golden age.

As the thirteenth century began the religion of Islam remained the dominant rival force to Christianity in Europe. For centuries the two religions had contested for lands, allegiance, and world prestige. Muhammad (A.D. 570–632), a member of the ruling clan in Mecca, founded the Islamic religion. Muhammad attacked the polytheism of his fellow Arabs and preached that there was only one God, called Allah. Muhammad's goal was to clarify God's revelation and unify the diverse tribes of Arabia into a community of the Islamic faithful. By 630, Mecca accepted Islam and positioned Muhammad as its prophet and leader. The Islamic call to prayer opens: "There is no God but Allah, and Muhammad is the prophet of God."

During the seventh and eighth centuries the clear message of Islam spread remarkably fast, across North Africa and into Spain and across the Middle East to the Indus Valley. When dedicated Muslim soldiers moved into conquered lands they brought with them not only the teachings of Islam but also a stable, relatively honest and workable government. The majority of people conquered by the Arabs willingly converted and merged their past and native way of life into Arabic-speaking Islam. The Islamic empire was headed by a successor to the prophet Muhammad, called a caliph, who served the dual roles of religious leader and political head. It was the caliph's duty to see that the world of Islam adhered to the teachings

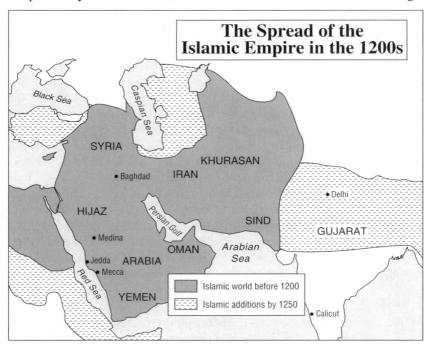

The Spread of the Islamic Empire in the 1200s

Black Sea

Caspian Sea

SYRIA

KHURASAN

● Baghdad   IRAN

● Delhi

HIJAZ

Persian Gulf

SIND

GUJARAT

● Medina

OMAN   Arabian Sea

● Jedda   ARABIA

● Mecca

Red Sea

YEMEN

Islamic world before 1200

Islamic additions by 1250

● Calicut

and laws of the Qur'an (or Koran), a collection of revelations transmitted from God to the prophet Muhammad. This holy book not only became the basis of Muslim ethical behavior but also established the foundations for government and the legal system.

By the thirteenth century the capital of the Islamic empire was located in Baghdad. From this religious focal point, the Arabs were well situated to control major trade routes between three continents: Africa, Asia, and Europe. As a result, the Arabs thrived, commanding tremendous wealth and riches through manufacturing, farming, commerce, and trade. Baghdad was one of the most cosmopolitan cities in the world, with

> bazaars containing goods from all over the known world. There . . . [one] would find spices, minerals, and dyes from India; rubies, fabrics, and slaves from central Asia; honey, wax, and white slaves from Scandinavia and Russia; ivory, gold dust, and black slaves from Africa. One bazaar in the city specialized in goods from China, including silks, musk, and porcelain. The merchants were a wealthy and respected group, as were the professional men and scholars.[7]

Muslim intellectuals, who translated Greek works, made huge leaps in science, philosophy, medicine, and mathematics. Muhammad established a cultural tone for learning and scholarship when he preached that the written word of the scholar was holier than the blood of the warrior. Additionally, artists, particularly poets who held an honored place among Arabs, produced works of art that were in demand throughout the world.

The spread of Islam posed a threat to the Christians of Europe. When the advancing Arabs reached parts of France and Italy in the eleventh century, the Christians halted them, regrouped, and counterattacked with holy crusades, beginning in 1095 and lasting late into the thirteenth century. The First Crusade was initiated by Pope Urban II to retake the Holy Land from the heathens. Although the crusaders were told that the crusade was a holy war in which the fighters could be assured a place in heaven, the reasons men throughout Europe participated were diverse: Some believed it was a test of their faith; some saw it as an opportunity to gain land, riches, and access to trade; other simply sought the excitement of a new adventure. During subsequent centuries of hostilities Christians and Muslims fought bitterly, each feeding off misconceptions and misrepresentations of the others. Ironically, the two religions have a great deal in common. The Islamic scholar Bernard Lewis writes that both the Christians and the Muslims

> shared the inheritance of the ancient civilizations of the Middle East; both had adopted the Jewish religious tradition of ethical monotheism, prophetic mission, and revelation preserved in scripture; both were dis-

ciples of Greek thought and science and heirs, in different ways, of the societies and institutions that had grown up in the Middle East and around the Mediterranean under the rule of Alexander, his successors, and the Romans.[8]

Nevertheless, many differences in their approaches to law, religious leadership, the interaction of religion and politics, religious organization, and religious mission kept them very much apart. But as the thirteenth century progressed, enthusiasm for the interminable Christian holy war against the Muslims and the Islamic jihad (struggle for the faith) against the Christians waned, and both sides grew weary of the bloody and inconclusive battles.

The bloody ebb and flow of the Crusades took its toll on the resources and energy of the Islamic empire. Weary of war, the Arabs had to confront another foe in the thirteenth century, the Mongols, fierce warriors from the steppes of central Asia. The Mongol invasion was a turning point in Islamic history that dramatically transformed and weakened the once glorious empire. By 1258 the Mongols had captured Arab lands and destroyed the caliphate. Mongol dominance was not lasting, however, because a combination of Arabs and Turks in Egypt counterattacked and ousted the advancing Mongols. Despite regaining their territory, the Arabs never regained their strength and glory because the real power transferred into the hands of the Turks who took control after the war.

The Mongols

The Mongol quest for world domination during the thirteenth century is a story of civilization transformed by barbarism. Unlike most of the peoples they conquered, the Mongols were a simple nomadic, clan people who lived by hunting and tending their livestock. Throughout the thirteenth century the Mongols, dedicated to a religious conviction that they were destined to rule all peoples, were a seemingly irreversible force that ruthlessly and mercilessly conquered much of the European, Asian, and Islamic world.

The nomads of the steppes were organized into contentious tribes who fought each other incessantly. Along China's border one powerful group called the Tatars battled the Chinese. By 1200 a rebellious Tatar tribe, after years of infighting, broke from the Tatars and began referring to themselves as Mongols. A ruling chieftain's son, Temujin, later called Genghis Khan, used his skill as a fighter and his cunning as a leader to consolidate and organize the Mongols. By 1206 Genghis Khan had successfully conquered the territory of Mongolia and created one mighty empire with himself the Great Khan, or supreme ruler. In an anonymous Mongolian history written in 1240 Temujin's investiture as the Great Khan was reported to be finalized when the

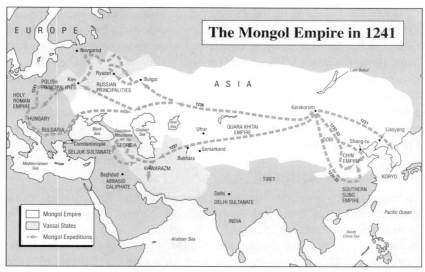

Mongol princes swore their allegiance: "We will make you khan! We will fight your enemies however numerous they may be. The fairest girls of conquered nations we will bring to you. If in war we disobey you, abandon us as felons in the pathless places."[9]

Genghis abolished the tribal system and organized his Mongol Empire under feudal rule with himself at the head and his kin commanding under him. Genghis demanded that all males serve in the military and that all his subjects submit completely to his will or face annihilation. To this end, he instituted strict laws supported by harsh punishments. Violators of laws were routinely sentenced to a violent, bloody death; the only exception was for convicted royalty, who could escape the ignominy of bloodshed by being clubbed to death rolled up in carpets. The Mongols feared the powerful khan, yet they respected his cunning, organization, and military genius. As a reward for their loyalty, his warriors enjoyed the booty of their conquests.

Mongol soldiers were horsemen who could travel light and fight murderously. The army charged in separate columns connected by messengers, each column moving in different directions and converging simultaneously at the point of attack. A Mongol assault typically consisted of three waves of aggression: an initial, lightly armed and rapid moving vanguard; an onslaught of expert archers; and a final blow of heavily armed cavalry. Because of their reputation for ruthlessness, the advance of the Mongol armies was preceded by great terror, unsettling the defending troops psychologically. The Mongols scored victories almost everywhere they attacked, including Europe. In world history, Genghis Khan ranks with Alexander the Great and Napoléon as a military conqueror and strategist.

When the threat of the Mongols struck Europe, the Christian leaders worked under the illusion that they could finesse the great Genghis Khan; indeed, they firmly believed that they could convert him. Pope Innocent IV sent diplomatic ambassadors to Genghis insisting that when the Mongol leader converted to Christianity the two peoples could enjoy a productive alliance. Angered and perhaps a bit bemused, Genghis Khan dismissed the Christian imperative and in return demanded that all the leaders of western Europe travel to Outer Mongolia to pay tribute to him, the Great Khan.

Mongol Conquests

Genghis and his successors scored staggering victories. He conquered northern China, Korea, India, and the powerful Turks in the Middle East. The fierce Turks of Bokhara, for example, fought bravely but were finally defeated and the survivors slaughtered; the Turks of Samarkand surrendered without a fight, yet they too were slaughtered. The Muslim historian Ibn al-Athir records an eyewitness account of a Mongol invasion:

> A man . . . told me that, being hidden in his house, he perceived through a peep-hole what was going on outside. Each time that the Mongols killed someone they would cry out *La Illaha il Allah*—"God, there is none but Him." After the massacre was over they pillaged the town and carried off the females. "I saw them," he said, "drunkenly swaying on their horses; they laughed; they sang in their own language, and shouted *La Illaha*." [10]

The Mongols pushed into Russia, overtaking Kiev and killing or enslaving all inhabitants. From Russia the Mongols moved into Poland and Hungary and swept along the Adriatic and into the Balkans. They stormed through the Arabic states and delivered a crushing blow to Islam by defeating the seat of its caliph in Baghdad.

The downfall of Baghdad in 1258 was orchestrated under the skillful leadership of Hülegü, a grandson of Genghis Khan. The Mongol leader sent an ultimatum to the Islamic caliph, who, believing that he was protected directly by God, ignored the advice of his advisers and rejected the Mongol directive to surrender. Hülegü was outraged and his army of 200,000 warriors stormed out of the Iranian mountains to meet the onrushing Muslim troops. Hülegü's engineers destroyed a dam on the Tigris River and flooded the plain behind the Muslim troops. The Mongols slaughtered more than 120,000 Muslim soldiers when they tried to retreat through the mud of the flooded plain. By 1258 the Mongols breached the city walls, killing the caliph's elite guard and then murderously slaughtering the reported 800,000 citizens who were rounded up after the collapse of the city. The Islamic chronicler Ibn Kathir wrote in 1351 that "[the Mongols] came down upon the city and killed all they could, men, women and children, the old, the middle-aged, and the young. Many of the people went into wells, latrines, and sewers and hid there for many days without emerging. . . . Baghdad, which had been the most civilized of all cities, became a ruin with only a few inhabitants, and they were in fear and hunger and wretchedness and insignificance."[11] After giving up the riches of the city, the caliph himself was trampled to death by Mongol horses.

With the advent of Mongol rule, trade routes opened between Europe and the East. Many merchants seeking the exotic goods of the East traveled to Mongol Asia. One of the most influential was the Venetian adventurer Marco Polo, who served the Mongol court of Kublai Khan for seventeen years. During a return visit to Europe Polo was arrested and placed in prison; it was there that he met a fellow prisoner and writer named Rusticiano who wrote down Polo's description of Mongol Asia and the wondrous sights that he saw there. The result was a manuscript, *Description of the World,* which became one of the most widely read books in Christendom. The popularity of Polo's travel accounts reflected the insatiable European curiosity about the exotic lands of the East.

The Mongols transformed the world through conquest, but they lacked a unifying religion such as had the Muslims, they could not convey a sense of progress such as the Europeans, nor could they inspire the cultural and social traditions such as those of the Chinese. Internal disputes and struggles for power, religious conversions, the introduction of firearms, and a general loss of enthusiasm for the nomadic warrior life gradually worked to weaken Mongol dominance. The distinguished historian Daniel J. Boorstin argues that the Mongols deserve a higher place in history than they are generally awarded, claiming that the Mongols "showed a combination of military genius, personal courage, administrative versatility, and cultural tolerance unequaled by any European line of hereditary rulers." He concludes:

> Without the peculiar talents and special achievements of these Mongol rulers and their people, the way to Cathay [city in China that epitomized Asian riches] would probably not have been opened when it was. When would there then have been a path for Marco Polo? Without Marco Polo and the others who stirred the European imagination with impatience to reach Cathay, would there have been a Christopher Columbus?"[12]

China and Japan

Like the Muslims, the Chinese in the thirteenth century were victims of Mongol conquest. When the Mongols stormed into China they subjugated and transformed a unified, cultured, and stable civilization.

From 960 to1279 the Song dynasty in China was experiencing a golden age; the economy was strong, the government was steadfast, and the arts flourished. China's canal and river system allowed for efficient commerce within the country and a strong navy helped protect foreign trade. The economy rapidly expanded, bolstered by a banking system that was the first to use paper money. Increased wealth helped support many technological advances such as movable type and printing, the abacus, blast furnaces, and the magnetic compass. Because education was highly prized, scholars served in government posts, giving them the social wherewithal to perpetuate the value of learning and culture. In the arts the Chinese were master carvers, painters, and textile artisans. Like the scholars, poets held a respected place in Chinese society and, consequently, poetry and literature flourished.

But cultural achievements could not stop the fierce Mongols as Genghis Khan moved into northwest China in 1209, pushing south from there. After the death of Genghis and his brother Mangu Khan, Kublai, a grandson of Genghis, became the Great Khan. In 1259 Kublai Khan began his campaign against the powerful Song of southern China. The final defeat of the Song was in 1279 and Kublai, after rebuilding the devastated city of Peking, established his headquarters there and proclaimed his own ruling dynasty, which he called the Yuan dynasty.

As the new overlords, the Mongols focused primarily on collecting tributes and, consequently, they were careful to allow the Chinese to continue generating wealth. This permitted the Chinese to preserve much of their national culture, including their advanced farming system, canals, roads, and some literature and art. Kublai Khan was particularly protective of foreign trade and opened his dynasty to merchants from Europe. Under the protection of the Mongols from 1260 to 1350 large caravans carried Eastern goods to Europe over the Silk Road, a fabled, all-land trade route from China across Asia. One scholar was so impressed by the open trade route that he wrote, "It was indeed marvelous that, through the protection of one man, an Italian trader could journey unmolested from the Black Sea to Peking and back again—a situation which had never existed before and which disappeared with the passing of Kublai Khan."[13] Kublai Khan was fascinated by Chinese culture and, consequently, he allowed selected Chinese scholars to serve as advisers and teachers. Hence, from inside the Mongol bureaucracy Chinese operatives could slyly effectuate some positive changes for their people. The Mongols ruled China for ninety years, but even during the long rule of Kublai Khan their hold began to weaken. By 1350 the Yuan dynasty had fallen to populist uprisings inspired to a large extent by the Chinese scholar-gentry. Perhaps it was inevitable that a few hundred thousand Mongols could not indefinitely control a tradition-unified civilization of 100 million.

Japan

Off the coast of northeast Asia, the sea protected the archipelago of Japan from invaders. But the waters could not stop the determined Mongols, who believed that all peoples, including the Japanese, must be subservient to them. They launched two massive sea attacks against Japan beginning in 1267. Although the Japanese survived the Mongol onslaught, its aftereffects contributed to civil war and an internal transformation of society.

Prior to the thirteenth century, Japan was organized with a feudal system in which large landowners protected their property with hired warriors called samurai. These fighters constituted a warrior class defined by an unwritten yet strict code, called the Bushido, that defined honor and chivalry. A civil war between powerful clans in 1156 opened the way for Minamoto Yoritomo, a samurai, to gain the title of shogun, or overall "general." Although an emperor remained head of the state, his responsibilities were relegated to religious rituals while the shogun exercised real political power. With a ruling shogunate, thirteenth-century Japan became a militaristic culture organized with a feudal system of large property owners and their hired samurai.

Throughout the thirteenth century, Buddhism was the most popular religion in Japan. In ancient times, prior to Buddhism, the ruling clans worshiped nature spirits and practiced ritual purification with a religion called Shinto, which literally means "way of the gods." But during the seventh century the Chinese introduced Buddhism, a religion that originated in India. As in Shinto, nature was an important element in Buddhism, teaching that one can best find enlightenment through an intuitive connection with nature. In both China and Japan this reverence for nature translated into art as artists attempted to capture a poetic, spiritual quality in landscape painting.

Although China influenced Japan, the island nation was, for the most part, isolated and rarely invaded by outsiders. This changed in 1267, however, when the Mongol leader, Kublai Khan, inspired by his belief in a divine mission to rule the world, sent an embassy to Japan demanding its subservience. The Japanese abruptly and emphatically rejected Kublai Khan's demands. Incensed, Kublai sent a fleet of nine hundred ships, fifteen thousand sailors, and ten thousand soldiers to Japan. They landed at Kyushu, Japan, and engaged in a fierce battle. In part because they were running out of arrows and provisions and in part because a huge and violent storm was raging, the Mongols headed back to their home port. In 1277 Kublai sent another envoy to the shogunate at Kamakura asserting that Japan was now a province under the direct rule of the Great Khan.

Not surprisingly, the Japanese had the Mongol envoy executed and summarily rejected the notion of becoming a province. This time Kublai mustered an even larger force of three thousand ships and a hundred thousand soldiers. After limited battle with the Japanese most of the ships were damaged or destroyed in a furious typhoon. Those vessels that could sail returned once again to their home base. The Mongol troops left in Japan, approximately thirty thousand, were slaughtered or enslaved by the Japanese.

The Mongol generals had planned a third campaign against Japan for 1286, but other interests intervened and it did not take place. Although the Mongol threat had subsided, the struggle had depleted the coffers of the Japanese regents and they could not adequately pay their samurai. The unpaid samurai began to question their loyalty and the beleaguered court, blind to social trends, retreated into a self-absorbed, trivial existence oblivious to growing national discontent. In the 1330s Japan lapsed into civil war.

Africa

As the Mongols were transforming much of the known world, three important civilizations were emerging in Africa and the Americas: the Mali in western Africa, the Indians at Cahokia in North America, and the Aztecs in Mexico. Each of the three civilizations enjoyed prosperous trade, proficient farming, and flourishing cities.

After a powerful West African empire in Ghana collapsed in the early 1200s, the kingdoms that survived struggled with one another for dominance and territory. One group of people, the Malinke, who were once part of the Ghanian Kingdom, gained control under the leadership of a military genius named Sundiata. Sundiata captured the gold-producing areas and the rich farming lands of the upper Niger River. The wealth from gold mining and the bounty of fertile soil provided the basis for one of Africa's great trading kingdoms, Mali. By the end of the thirteenth century and start of the fourteenth, Malian gold, farm goods, and other trade products were exchanged throughout Africa and the Mediterranean world, making the Malians rich.

The Aztecs

In the Americas the thirteenth century witnessed the rise of several important and powerful civilizations. Like the civilizations in the Old World the people of the Western Hemisphere developed complex societies, built cities, organized politics, stabilized commerce, created art, and constructed monuments. It is not correct to say, however, that the civilizations of the New World developed as did those of the Old; they did not evolve under the same notions of classical progress, science, and technology.

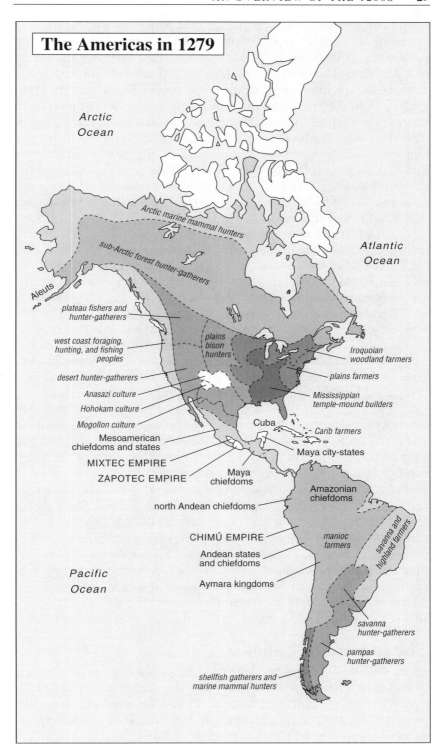

The Americas in 1279

Arctic
Ocean

Arctic marine mammal hunters

sub-Arctic forest hunter-gatherers

Atlantic
Ocean

Aleuts

plateau fishers and
hunter-gatherers

west coast foraging,
hunting, and fishing
peoples

desert hunter-gatherers

Anasazi culture

Hohokam culture

Mogollon culture

Mesoamerican
chiefdoms and states

MIXTEC EMPIRE

ZAPOTEC EMPIRE

plains
bison
hunters

Iroquoian
woodland farmers

plains farmers

Mississippian
temple-mound builders

Cuba

Carib farmers

Maya city-states

Maya
chiefdoms

north Andean chiefdoms

Amazonian
chiefdoms

CHIMÚ EMPIRE

manioc
farmers

savanna and
highland farmers

Andean states
and chiefdoms

Aymara kingdoms

Pacific
Ocean

savanna
hunter-gatherers

pampas
hunter-gatherers

shellfish gatherers and
marine mammal hunters

In Mesoamerica (Mexico and Central America) a nomadic people from the north called the Toltecs moved into the area when the previous civilizations of the Mayans and Teotihuacans weakened and declined. The nomadic Toltecs settled and became sedentary farmers, advancing a vast empire that extended across central Mexico. By 1150 the Toltecs were scattered by militaristic nomads from outside the region. These scattered Toltecs settled in the Valley of Mexico, surviving on the shores of the marshes, lakes, and rivers that characterize the valley. This was a very unstable period as various groups fought for territory and supremacy. At the outset of the thirteenth century, the Aztecs, people from Aztlan, a territory north of the Valley of Mexico, migrated into the area, adding yet another group to the volatile mix.

The thirteenth century then was a time of migration, settlement, and formation of one of the great civilizations in the Mesoamerica, the Aztecs. Like the Toltecs before them, the rugged Aztecs eventually settled into a sedentary farming existence with maize (an easily grown corn that may have been domesticated as early as 6,600 B.C.) as their primary crop. Their evolution to supremacy took nearly a century as the Aztecs struggled with the large number of population groups that had settled previously in the Valley of Mexico. Because of their skill at warfare and their fanatical devotion to their gods and their goal to settle, the Aztecs ascended to power. Their conquered neighbors quickly assimilated into the Aztec way of life, aided by the fact that they all spoke the same language, Nahuatl, and they all shared many common rituals, beliefs, and gods. Through the thirteenth century the people in the Valley of Mexico coalesced into a powerful empire and in the 1300s they built a magnificent Aztec capital, Tenochtitlan, on an island in Lake Texcoco.

Aztec religion was polytheistic, supporting a vast array of deities and gods that blended the natural world with the divine. The gods demanded offerings and worship to guarantee fertile land, victory in war, and world stability. To appease their gods, the Aztecs practiced ritual cannibalism, torture, and human sacrifice, frequently flaying the victims and using their skins as priestly robes. Aztec artists recurrently symbolized human sacrifice by depicting an eagle eating a heart. When adventurers from the Old World discovered the Aztecs they were shocked and outraged by the extensive practice of human sacrifice.

The Indians of Cahokia

As the Middle Ages was beginning in Europe around A.D. 450 Indians of the eastern woodlands in North America, a huge region stretching from Maine to the Gulf of Mexico, developed thriving cultures that depended on hunting, trading, and farming. One of the earliest known advanced groups was the Hopewell Indians, who established themselves along the Mississippi River Valley as great mound builders. The Hopewell Indians built their great pyramidal mounds for burials and fortification, some reaching heights of ninety feet. The Hopewells were also proficient traders, collecting goods from as far away as the far west, the Appalachian Mountains, and the Gulf of Mexico. When the Hopewell culture declined, a new group of Indians, the Mississippians, continued the Hopewell mound-building tradition. These eastern woodlands Indians also mastered the cultivation of new crops like squash, beans, and maize. With better agriculture, cities emerged as great ceremonial centers, the most magnificent being Cahokia, located near present-day East St. Louis, Illinois.

Cahokia peaked in the thirteenth century, reaching one hundred thousand inhabitants by 1250. Although little is known about the organization of their society, archaeological evidence indicates that powerful chieftains controlled all aspects of the culture. Some historians believe that the Mississippians had contact with the more advanced cultures of Mesoamerica because the agriculture of these North American Indians depended upon maize and other crops cultivated in Mexico. Moreover, artifacts uncovered in the Mississippian pyramids indicate that they, like the Mesoamerican people, practiced ritual sacrifice, usually of slaves or wives. Additionally, Monk's Mound, the largest pyramid at Cahokia, was decorated with a feathered serpent that closely resembles artwork from the Valley of Mexico. In an 1813 letter to Thomas Jefferson, Henry Brackenridge, an archaeologist and the first westerner to record the American West firsthand, describes the Cahokia site:

> There exists traces of a population far beyond what this extensive and fertile portion of the continent is supposed to have possessed, greater, perhaps, than could be supported by the present white inhabitants, even with the careful agriculture practiced by the most populous states of Europe. . . . There are certainly many districts on the Ohio and Mississippi equally favorable to a numerous population. When I contemplated the beauty and fertility of those spots, I could scarcely believe it possible, that they should never have supported a numerous population.[14]

By the end of the thirteenth century the people at Cahokia had mysteriously dwindled; perhaps most had moved south toward milder weather.

Although both the Aztecs and the Mississippian Indians at Cahokia developed respectable trading empires, they were essentially agricultural societies. The development of both groups, like that of other peoples in the Americas, was limited by a lack of technology. Unlike the millers of medieval Europe or the Mediterranean states, the American Indians did not have the wheel or animal power to process maize or grains. Moreover, the civilizations in the Americas supported beliefs and rituals not found in the Old World: human sacrifice, polygamy, and a nontechnological definition of progress. Nevertheless, the advanced cultures of the Americas shared the dimensions of all great civilizations: a high degree of organization; the ability to build, particularly cities and monuments; a sustainable economy; and a workable social structure supported by a unifying philosophical and religious view of their world, their environment, and their historical context.

Conclusion

The complexity and malleability of the historical process was very much in evidence during the thirteenth century. As different peoples interacted, the cultural dynamism within each civilization changed, shifted, and transformed: Europe initiated the intellectual mindset and the institutional framework to surge in technology and economics; the Arabs saw the end of their golden age; the Chinese too saw the end of an accomplished period and fell victims to foreign rule; the Mali of western Africa gained prominence by learning to take advantage of Western and Islamic tastes and traditions; the Indians of Cahokia and the Aztecs of Mesoamerica found their own cultural identity; and the bellicose Mongols rose through conquest but waned by the end of the century due, in part, to their inability to maintain a civilized cultural definition.

The thirteenth century witnessed the beginnings of one of the greatest transformations in history—the eventual triumph of sedentary town dwellers over nomadic military might. Throughout the century the Mongols sustained one of the last major military victories of nomadic warriors. Even the most sophisticated civilizations of the thirteenth century could not withstand the savagery, mobility, dedication, and unwavering military regimen of the rugged nomads. But as the century ended, the ongoing conflict between two different ways of life swayed in favor of sedentary civilization, particularly in Europe, with the benefit of newfound advantages: abundant wealth, a rapidly growing population, stronger centralized organization, medical advances, better metalwork, and powerful gunpowder and firearms. The noted historians Peter Stearns, Michael Adas, and Stuart Schwartz conclude that with the eventual downfall of the Mongols the

> age-old pattern of interaction between nomads and farming town-dwelling peoples was fundamentally transformed. This transformation resulted in the growing ability of sedentary peoples to first resist and then dominate nomadic peoples, and it marks a major watershed in the history of the human community. . . . The periodic nomadic incursions into the sedentary zones, which had reoccurred sporadically for millennia, had come to an end.[15]

Notes

1. Quoted in F. Roy Willis, *Western Civilization, Volume I: From Ancient Times Through the Seventeenth Century.* Lexington, MA: D.C. Heath, 1985, p. 357.
2. Quoted in Norton Downs, ed., *Readings in Medieval History.* Princeton, NJ: D. Van Nostrand, 1964, p. 185.
3. Quoted in R.H.C. Davis, *A History of Medieval Europe: From Constantine to Saint Louis.* London: Longman, 1970, p. 356.
4. Quoted in John P. McKay, Bennett D. Hill, and John Buckler, *A History of Western Society.* Boston: Houghton Mifflin, 1987, p. 339.
5. Thomas Aquinas, "Commentary on Aristotle's *Metaphysics*," in Douglas J.Soccio, *Archetypes of Wisdom.* Belmont, CA: Wadsworth, 1995, p. 282.
6. Lorenzo Ghiberti in *A Documentary History of Art*, Elizabeth Gilmore Holt, ed. in Daniel J. Boorstin, *The Creators.* New York: Random House, 1993, p. 382.
7. T. Walter Wallbank and Alastair M. Taylor, *Civilization: Past and Present.* Chicago: Scott, Foresman, 1942, p. 243.
8. Bernard Lewis, ed. and trans., *Islam: From the Prophet Muhammad to the Capture of Constantinople.* New York: Walker, 1974, p. xv.
9. Mongol-un Ni'ucha Tobchi'an, in Franklin Mackenzie, *The Ocean and the Steppe: The Life and Times of the Mongol Conqueror.* New York: Vantage, 1963, p. 55.
10. Ibn al-Athir, *Tarikh al-Kamil*, in Mackenzie, *The Ocean and the Steppe*, p. 285.
11. Ibn Kathir, *Al-Bidya wa'l-nihaya*, in Lewis, *Islam*, p. 83.
12. Daniel J. Boorstin, *The Discoverers.* New York: Random House, 1985, p. 126.
13. Quoted in Wallbank and Taylor, *Civilization*, p. 294.
14. Quoted in Roger G. Kennedy, *Hidden Cities: The Discovery and Loss of Ancient North American Civilization.* New York: Free Press, 1994, p. 184.
15. Peter N. Stearns, Michael Adas, and Stuart B. Schwartz, *World Civilizations: The Global Experience, Volume I, Beginnings to 1750.* New York: HarperCollins, 1992, pp. 469–70.

Europe

PREFACE

As the thirteenth century began, the European medieval view of life, in which humans are beset by the devil and drawn to evil, was in the process of change. Medieval thinkers were beginning to challenge old despairing values built on the suspicion of reason and temper them with a more hopeful and optimistic view of nature and human behavior and rationality. Motivated by better living conditions, increased trade, and the spread of knowledge, thirteenth-century thinkers redefined the relationship between faith and reason, divine revelation and secular observation, and nature and otherworldliness. In short, a synthesis was at work in which these dualities were bridged, opening the doors for greater enjoyment, exploration, and understanding of this life and this world.

The impetus for this synthesis found its most influential voice with Thomas Aquinas, arguably the greatest thinker of the century. In his work *Summa Theologica,* Aquinas argues that since God made man and the universe, then human reason must reflect aspects of the divine. Consequently, reason and worldly experience must not be discarded and mistrusted; rather, they should be celebrated as part of a larger religious truth. With Aquinas, then, it is legitimate for humans to find meaning and truth in the study and observation of the natural world—knowledge through the intellect is justified.

Even some monastic orders, which had withdrawn from the evil nature of this world, changed their focus and became involved in worldly affairs. St. Francis of Assisi, friar and founder of the Franciscan order, abandoned seclusion and moved into everyday life, glorifying all of God's creations and the natural world. His followers, armed only with the power of humility and simplicity, were committed to helping the poor and spreading the ideals of charity and love directly to the people. In both St. Francis and Thomas Aquinas there is new faith in the value of humankind.

With society's seemingly greater tolerance for the affairs of the here and now, two worldly institutions flourished: universities and commerce. The rapid growth of universities in urban areas reflected a revival of the intellectual life and the growing desire for learning. Thinkers and scientists asked new questions about nature and how things worked, deriving their answers through the detailed observation of nature. As new topics of inquiry were explored, more questions arose and the scope of knowledge expanded.

The thirteenth century also saw a virtual explosion of towns as centers for commerce. A dramatic increase in trade and trade routes between Europe, the Mediterranean states, and the Far East moved new and exotic goods from place to place: silks from the Far East, fine wines from France, textiles and gold from North Africa, and forest products from the Baltic. A new merchant class quickly became a powerful player in the shaping of society, demanding a greater role in politics, religion, education, and the arts.

Supported by the patronage of nobles and wealthy merchants, artists felt aesthetically liberated in the newly acquired freedom to probe and celebrate human nature and the world. Increasingly, artists worked to express issues and moral concerns in individual human terms.

As the thirteenth century progressed, the two institutions that dominated life in Europe during the previous centuries, the papacy and feudal monarchies, were unalterably changed. Although still very powerful, the papacy's spiritual prestige and influence was weakened by its overzealous acquisition of wealth and its long, bitter, and unbecoming struggle for control with lay rulers. Similarly, internal struggles and a push for the decentralization of power by local nobility weakened feudal monarchies. King John of England, for example, pushed his obsession to collect royalties so far that his subject vassals rebelled by drafting the Magna Carta, a document that held the king, like everyone else, accountable to the law.

However, despite an increased understanding of the world in which they lived, some medieval presuppositions and prejudices lingered throughout the century, perpetuating a dark side to the age. The Crusades continued, fueled by a misrepresentation of the Arabs and the ongoing quest for power. The Fourth Crusade, sponsored by Pope Innocent III, ended in a bloodthirsty rampage in which Constantinople was sacked, virtually subordinating the Eastern Church to the Western pope. Moreover, Jews continued to be targets of hatred and persecution. After the Fourth Lateran Council of 1215 Jews were stripped of civil rights and required to wear identification badges sewn on their clothing. Visibly different in their appearance and religious loyalties, Jews were accused of witchcraft, heresy, and sorcery.

The synthesis of Aquinas, the university system, the growth of commerce and trade, and the changing focus of power led to an increasing secularization of many aspects of thirteenth-century life. Indeed, the worldview of Europe in the thirteenth century expanded. Perhaps the growing excitement about living in and understanding the secular world is best represented by the adventurer Marco Polo, who traveled across Eurasia and observed many different cultures. Like the best of his age, Polo acted on a newly activated sense of inquiry and exploration.

The Decline of Empire and the Papacy in Europe

John E. Rodes

John E. Rodes argues that Europe's two most powerful institutions, the papacy and the Holy Roman Empire, reached their zenith and were eclipsed during the thirteenth century. The Holy Roman Empire, a confederation of German and Italian territories, began the century ruled by Emperor Frederick II. Frederick II was well educated, skilled in diplomacy, and a patron of learning. In his attempt to gain control of central Italy, he became embroiled in a long and unproductive struggle with the papacy. Rodes writes that after Frederick II died, the papacy supported the appointment of French leader Charles of Anjou as the ruler of the empire. According to Rodes, Charles's power eroded when the Italian city-states moved to greater autonomy, Italy and Germany splintered, and Germany selected its own ruler, Duke Rudolf of Hapsburg. Stability was shattered and the crown was weakened. Although the empire shrank in size in the south and west, it expanded in the north under the Hapsburgs. During this period of German expansion, two forces emerged as powerful influences: the Teutonic Knights, an order of crusading knights dedicated to fighting heathens, and the Hanseatic League, an association of north German trading cities organized to protect trade and business interests.

Rodes suggests that during the thirteenth century the papacy also lost power and control. Not only weakened by its long fight with Frederick

Excerpted from John E. Rodes, *A Short History of the Western World.* Copyright © 1970 Charles Scribner's Sons. Reprinted with permission of Scribner, a division of Simon & Schuster.

II, it also lost authority over the Crusades and faced growing dissension from some of its mendicant orders. Rodes reports that the papacy became increasingly secularized and hopelessly embroiled in national quarrels. Subsequently, its moral prestige was weakened and numerous and challenging demands were advanced for dramatic reforms.

John E. Rodes is chairman of the history department at Occidental College, Los Angeles, California. He has written a history of Germany and contributed numerous articles to professional journals.

In the thirteenth century, empire and papacy, the two institutions that aspired to universal recognition if not predominance, both passed their zenith. By the middle of the century, the Holy Roman Empire[1] began to disintegrate; even its slight recovery at the end of the century left it greatly reduced in power and prestige. The papacy, after an undulating course of power during the century, suddenly took a similar plunge after the pontificate of Boniface VIII (1294–1303).

Emperor Frederick II

Emperor Frederick II began his career as a ward of Pope Innocent III and came to the throne only after a prolonged period of civil wars. Half Norman and half Hohenstaufen by birth, Frederick was perhaps the best educated medieval emperor, skilled in diplomacy and a patron of learning. He spoke fluent Arabic, kept a harem, and was more interested in the Saracen culture of his native Sicily than in his German lands. His realm was larger and wealthier than that of other medieval emperors, since he also owned southern Italy and Sicily, and indirectly ruled the Kingdom of Jerusalem as well as East Prussia, which was conquered by the Teutonic Knights during his reign.

Since he was not much interested in his possessions north of the Alps, so long as they remained obedient and paid taxes, he ceded much power to the princes and bishops of Germany. By granting them authority to collect their own taxes and tolls, to control their own police systems, strike their own coins, and set up their own courts, Frederick accelerated the decentralization of the empire.

His desire to gain control of central Italy involved him in an interminable struggle with the papacy, a struggle which neither was able to win. As husband of the heiress to the Kingdom of Jerusalem, Frederick undertook a crusade (the Sixth, 1228–1229) to the Holy Land, although he was under the ban of papal excommunication. Instead of conquering the Holy Land by force of arms, he negotiated a settlement

1. confederation of German and Italian territories

with the Moslems and thereby gained for the Christians free access to Jerusalem, Nazareth, and Bethlehem. To see an excommunicated emperor obtain access to the Holy Land horrified devout Christian believers while delighting the antipapal factions. This ambivalence helps explain Frederick's reputation: with some he ranked as the greatest of emperors; others looked upon him as anti-Christ.

The Splintering of the Holy Roman Empire

After Frederick's death, the imperial structure collapsed. The popes waged a relentless struggle to keep Frederick's descendants from retaining control of southern Italy. To help extirpate the house of Hohenstaufen, the papacy invited the French Charles of Anjou (1226–1285), St. Louis'[2] brother, to seize the Kingdom of the Two Sicilies. The ambitious Charles complied gladly. He defeated the Hohenstaufen forces, had the last surviving male heir, Emperor Frederick's fifteen-year-old grandson (Conradin) beheaded in Naples, and assumed the Sicilian crown. But Charles of Anjou, who dreamt of creating a Sicilian Mediterranean empire at the expense of Byzantium, soon became as unwelcome a neighbor to the papacy as the Hohenstaufen had been. In 1282, the Sicilians themselves rose in rebellion, massacred their French masters, and awarded the Sicilian crown to the King of Aragon (Peter III, the husband of Frederick II's granddaughter). The Angevins succeeded in retaining only Naples. Thereafter, Sicily and Naples remained divided between Aragon and Anjou until the mid-fifteenth century.

Meanwhile, during the so-called Interregnum (1254–1273), there was no effective ruler for the Holy Roman Empire. The Italian city-states acted like sovereign bodies, and north of the Alps individual princes and bishops gained ever greater independence. The political splintering of Italy and Germany thus increased at a time when the French monarchy was growing more unified and centralized.

In 1273, the German electors ended the Interregnum by choosing as ruler Duke Rudolf of Hapsburg (1273–1291). The election had taken place under pressure of the papacy which recognized the need for re-establishing order in Germany and which was already casting about for a possible ally against the unruly Charles of Anjou who had barely established himself in Naples. Despite centuries of fighting between emperors and popes, the papacy realized that the two needed each other.

With the election of Rudolf of Hapsburg, the Holy Roman Empire entered a new era. Gone was the relative dynastic stability which before had left the crown in the same family for several generations at a time. For the next two centuries, the imperial crown was continu-

2. King Louis IX of France

The Excommunication of Frederick II

Although Pope Innocent IV was friendly to the emperor prior to his election as pope, he promptly excommunicated Frederick II when he gained power. Frederick's excommunication reflects the ongoing thirteenth-century struggle for power between the papacy, the Roman Catholic Church centered in Rome, and an increasingly powerful secular authority.

[Innocent recapitulates the efforts of the popes to maintain peace between the church and the empire and dwells upon the sins of the emperor. Then, after charging him with the particular crimes of perjury, sacrilege, heresy, and tyranny, he proceeds as follows:] We, therefore, on account of his aforesaid crimes and of his many other nefarious misdeeds, after careful deliberation with our brethren and with the holy council, acting however unworthily as the vicar of Jesus Christ on earth and knowing how it was said to us in the person of the blessed

ally passed from one ducal house to another. The center of the empire as well as of the royal domains that provided the primary income of the ruler shifted erratically from southern Germany (Hapsburg) to central Germany (Nassau), to western Germany (Luxemburg), to Bavaria (Wittelsbach), to the East (Luxemburgs of Bohemia), and to Austria (later Hapsburgs). As a result, the crown was seriously weakened while the territorial princes gained in strength.

Emperor Charles IV (1347–1378) of the Luxemburg-Bohemian dynasty sought to put some order into the electoral process. In the Golden Bull of 1356, Charles awarded sole rights to elect the king as well as the emperor to seven electors—four lay lords and three ecclesiastical princes—and stipulated that the lay electorates should be inherited by primogeniture and be indivisible. This scheme did not provide for greater stability but merely guaranteed more power to the seven electors. Meanwhile the German princes, aided by pamphleteers and antipapal ecclesiastics such as the Spiritual Franciscans, who believed in apostolic poverty and objected to the wealth of the Church and to the worldly possessions acquired by the Franciscan Order, had proceeded to secularize the imperial crown. Through edicts by the German imperial Diet they stipulated that the imperial crown was henceforth to be bestowed by the German electors without papal approval or intervention.

apostle Peter, *Whatsoever ye shall bind on earth shall be bound in heaven;* we announce and declare the said prince to be bound because of his sins and rejected by the Lord and deprived of all honor and dignity, and moreover by this sentence we hereby deprive him of the same since he has rendered himself so unworthy of ruling his kingdom and so unworthy of all honors and dignity; for, indeed, on account of his iniquities he has been rejected of God that he might not reign or exercise authority. All who have taken the oath of fidelity to him we absolve forever from such oath by our apostolic authority, absolutely forbidding anyone hereafter to obey him or look upon him as emperor or king. Let those whose duty it is to select a new emperor proceed freely with the election. But it shall be our care to provide as shall seem fitting to us for the kingdom of Sicily with the council of our brothers, the cardinals.

Norton Downs, ed., *Basic Documents in Medieval History*. Princeton, NJ: D. Van Nostrand, 1959.

During this period, the empire shrank in size and gradually shifted its center of gravity eastward. Control over Italy was lost despite occasional fruitless attempts to reclaim the peninsula. The Swiss cantons declared their independence; Provence, Burgundy, and the Low Countries slipped from imperial control. While the empire shrank in the south and west, its influence expanded in the east and north. Hungary, Bohemia, and Silesia became closely associated with it, and the Hapsburgs shifted their basis of operation from southern Germany and Switzerland to the newly acquired Austrian hereditary lands. Meanwhile German settlers, lay and ecclesiastic, noble and peasant, continued to push east along the Danube Valley and northeast along the shores of the Baltic, extending German commercial and cultural influence.

Two organizations were particularly active in this movement. During the thirteenth and fourteenth centuries, the Teutonic Knights acquired a vast principality, stretching from west of the Vistula River to the Gulf of Finland. Although these lands did not remain within the official imperial frontiers after 1250 and their extent shrank considerably after the Knights' several defeats by the Poles and Lithuanians between 1410 and 1466, the Teutonic conquests in Prussia formed the political basis for the later Kingdom of Prussia.

At the same time, the Hanseatic League extended German influence from Bruges and London in the west through the Scandinavian lands to Novgorod in Russia. The League was a loose association of north German trading cities for the purpose of protecting their trade, safeguarding common warehouses in foreign lands, and, if necessary, imposing favorable commercial settlements on other states through joint military action. By the late fourteenth century, the Hanseatic League had become so strong that it was able to defeat the Kingdom of Denmark.

Thus the Holy Roman Empire survived as a weak secularized state north of the Alps. Until the sixteenth century, most emperors still dreamt of reconquering Italy and some actually attempted it. But, in fact, the claim to universality had ceased to be meaningful with the end of the Hohenstaufen dynasty, with the rise of territorial states within the empire, and with the growth of more centralized monarchies elsewhere in Europe.

The Papacy

After the powerful pontificate of Innocent III, the papacy spent the first half of the thirteenth century in bitter fight against Frederick II; much of the second half of the century was taken up by the problems of Naples and of anarchy in Rome. Meanwhile the papacy lost control over the crusades. Even some of the mendicant orders, although organized to spread the faith and to combat heresy, complicated the work of the popes. The Spiritual Franciscans alarmed the prelates of the Church through their insistence on apostolic poverty, while the Dominican friars became embroiled in the scholastic quarrel over the relative importance of reason and faith.

During the late thirteenth century, the papacy became quite secularized. Noble Roman families, supported by outside forces, particularly the Angevins of Naples, fought to determine whom to make pope. Yet the papacy retained much prestige. Pope Boniface VIII (1294–1303) attempted once more to raise the papacy to the level of universal authority and to recapture the glory of the pontificate of Innocent III. His failure has been attributed to many causes: he was too tactless in his maneuvers and too much interested in the advancement of his own family; his opponents, Edward I of England and Philip IV of France, were much stronger than had been Innocent III's antagonists, John I and Philip II; moreover, the temper of the times no longer left room for claims of universal power.

Boniface's fight with the kings of England and France centered primarily on tax exemption of the clergy. The pope was unsuccessful, since the English and French clergy generally sided with their king. Finally Boniface issued the bull *Unam Sanctam* (1302), an anachronistic statement of papal supremacy over the rising national monarchies. "Outside this [Catholic and Apostolic] Church," the bull stated, "there is neither salvation nor remission of sins," and "both are in the power of the Church, the spiritual sword as well as the material." Such claims to superiority were clearly out of tune with the time. The papal bull aroused the wrath of the French monarchy. Confident in the support of public opinion—a strong term for this period, but perhaps justified—the French king dispatched agents who captured Boniface with the aid of local enemies of the papacy. Although they were supposed to bring the pope back to France for trial, the French had to release him after a few days, when the local populace rose in his support. Soon thereafter Pope Boniface died, and with his death ebbed the power of the medieval papacy.

For well over a hundred years after Boniface's death, the papacy floundered, embroiled in national quarrels, its political power low, its moral prestige in danger. Afraid of the anarchy in Italy, especially in Rome itself, and pressured by the kings of France, the popes took up residence at Avignon in southern France from 1309 to 1376. The Italian poet Petrarch (1304–1374) called this period "the Babylonian Captivity of the Papacy."

While at Avignon, the popes succeeded in centralizing papal administration and improving the tax collection system. At the same time, they unwittingly endangered papal power. Some unwisely continued to fight with the Holy Roman emperors at a time when they had lost the power to conduct such a struggle effectively. Moreover, the financial exactions and the pomp of the Avignonese court aroused the ire of kings and religious reformers—such as John Wyclif (1320?–1384). Above all, it was risky for the papacy to abandon its universal character and to become identified with national politics, particularly during the Hundred Years' War (1337–1453). For during this prolonged struggle against France, the English naturally distrusted a French pope, surrounded by French cardinals and residing in the confines of the French kingdom.

Papal Schism

Worse problems faced the papacy after 1378. The cardinals first elected an Italian pope who took up residence at Rome. Soon thereafter, some changed their support and chose a French pope to reestablish the Avignonese line. The resulting schism in the Church lasted until 1417. With Christians able to choose between two popes, obedience to, or rather support of, the one or the other depended heavily on political considerations. England, for example, still at war with France, sided with the Italian pope, whereas Scotland, as an ally of France, supported Avignon.

The papal schism further lowered the prestige of the papacy and stirred demands for reform both within and outside of the Church. As early as 1324, Marsiglio of Padua (1290–1343) in his book *The Defender of the Peace,* used in part by the emperor in his fight against the Avignon popes, had advocated the separation of church and state and had rejected the Petrine theory of apostolic succession. He had also urged that within the Church a general council should always be superior to the pope. This concept of conciliar supremacy within the Church, which harked back to the early centuries of Christianity before papal centralization, gained momentum after 1378, since the schism could only be ended if an authority *higher* than the popes determined which one was the legitimate pontiff. The conciliar movement was strongly supported by the theologians of the University of Paris and ultimately by various lay rulers, cardinals, lawyers, and reformers. Moreover it corresponded to a similar phenomenon in the secular world of the fourteenth century when corporate or representative bodies attempted to gain control over the monarchs.

When the conciliarists finally succeeded in forcing the convocation of a Church council (Pisa, 1409), the result was disastrous. The council deposed the two popes and chose one (Martin V); as no incumbents resigned, a triple schism resulted. A new council convened five years later at Constance (1414–1418). By then France was more than half occupied by English troops and was in no position to aid the Avignon pope. As in earlier centuries, the Holy Roman Emperor (Sigismund, 1411–1437) assumed control. The council then ended the schism by deposing all three popes and electing a new one. At the same time, the council of Constance passed several decrees which threatened the centralized, hierarchical structure of the Church. One (*Sacrosancta*) spelled out conciliar superiority over the papacy; the other (*Frequens*) asserted the right of Church councils to meet at regular intervals, without waiting to be convoked by a pope.

Thomas Aquinas and High Medieval Philosophy in Europe

C. Warren Hollister

C. Warren Hollister writes that although philosophers in the thirteenth century were churchmen they nevertheless were not apologists for the church. Their philosophical debates were intellectually adventuresome and provocative. Hollister maintains that the European philosophers drew upon the ideas of five early sources: the early Greeks, particularly Plato and Aristotle; Islamic translations of Greek scientific writings; early church fathers, namely Augustine; early medieval scholars; and Hebrew and early Christian religious traditions, using the Bible as the ultimate authority. Together, these influences shaped medieval scholasticism, a movement concerned with exploring the relationship between reason and revelation.

Hollister explains that the most influential philosopher of the age was Thomas Aquinas, who in his masterwork *Summa Theologica*, created a vast intellectual system of thought. Aquinas imposes formal analysis on philosophical questions, methodically arriving at logical "solutions" that are used to solve subsequent questions. Hollister writes that Aquinas worked to distinguish between revelation and reason and, simultaneously, to fit both within one religious truth. For Aquinas, knowledge resulted from the observation of the natural world, not divine illumination. Hollister explains that in Aquinas's philosophy God is at the center of a wide existential system in which humans are allowed to find truth both through revelation and through the intellect.

C. Warren Hollister is professor of history at the University of California, Santa Barbara. He has authored more than a dozen scholarly historical books and over forty articles on medieval history.

Although every important philosopher in the High Middle Ages was a churchman of one sort or another, ecclesiastical authority did not stifle speculation or limit controversy. Catholic orthodoxy, which would harden noticeably at the time of the Protestant Reformation, was still relatively flexible in the twelfth and thirteenth centuries, and philosophers were by no means timid apologists for official dogmas. If some of them were impelled to provide the Catholic faith with a logical substructure, others asserted that reason does not lead to the truth of Christian revelation. And among those who sought to harmonize faith and reason there was sharp disagreement as to how it should be done. Their shared faith did not limit their diversity or curb their spirit of intellectual adventure.

Philosophical Sources

The high-medieval philosophers drew nourishment from five earlier sources: (1) From the Greeks they inherited the philosophical systems of Plato and Aristotle. At first these two Greek masters were known in the West only through a handful of translations and commentaries dating from late Roman times. By the thirteenth century, however, new and far more complete translations were coming into Christendom from Spain and Sicily, and Aristotelian philosophy became a matter of intense interest and controversy in Europe's universities. (2) From the Islamic world came a flood of Greek scientific and philosophical works that had long before been translated into Arabic and were now retranslated from Arabic into Latin. These works entered Europe accompanied by extensive commentaries and original writings of Arab philosophers and scientists, for the Arabs came to grips with Greek learning long before the West did. Islamic thought made a particularly vital contribution to European science. In philosophy it was enriched by the work of Jewish scholars such as Moses Maimonides (1135–1204), whose *Guide for the Perplexed*— a penetrating reconciliation of Aristotle and Scripture—influenced the work of thirteenth-century Christian philosophers and theologians. (3) The early Church Fathers, particularly Ambrose, Jerome, and Augustine, had been a dominant intellectual force throughout the early Middle Ages and their authority remained strong in the twelfth and thirteenth centuries. St. Augustine retained his singular significance and was, indeed, the chief vessel of Platonic and Neo-platonic thought in the medieval universities. (4) The early medieval scholars themselves contributed significantly to the high-medieval intellectual revival. Gregory the Great, Isidore of Seville, Bede, Alcuin, Raban Maur, John the Scot, and Gerbert of Aurillac were all studied in the new universities. The original intellectual contributions of these men were less important, however, than the fact that they and their contemporaries had kept classical learning alive, thus creating the intellectual climate that made possible the reawakening of philosophical speculation in the eleventh century. (5) The high-medieval philosophers looked back beyond the scholars of the early Middle Ages, beyond the Fathers of the early Church, to the Hebrew and early Christian religious traditions as recorded in Scripture. Among medieval theologians the Bible, the chief written source of divine revelation, was the fundamental text and the ultimate authority.

Such were the chief elements—Greek, Islamic-Jewish, Patristic, early medieval, and scriptural—that underlay the thought of the scholastic philosophers. Strictly defined, "Scholasticism" is simply the philosophical movement associated with the high-medieval schools—the cathedral and monastic schools and later the universities. More interestingly, it was a movement concerned above all with exploring the relationship between reason and revelation. All medieval scholastics believed in God; all were committed, to some degree, to the life of reason. Many of them were immensely enthusiastic over the intellectual possibilities inherent in the careful application of Aristotelian logic to basic human and religious problems. Some believed that logic was the master key to a thousand doors and that with sufficient methodological rigor, with sufficient exactness in the use of words, the potentialities of human reason were all but limitless.

The Scholastics applied their logical method to a multitude of problems. They were concerned chiefly, however, with matters of basic significance to human existence: the nature of human beings, the purpose of human life, the existence and attributes of God, the fundamentals of human morality, the ethical imperatives of social and political life, the relationship between God and humanity. It would be hard to deny that these are the most profound sorts of questions that one can ask. Many philosophers of our own day are inclined to reject them as unanswerable, but the scholastics, lacking the modern sense of disillusionment, were determined to make the attempt. . . .

St. Thomas Aquinas's Logical System

St. Thomas was born of a Norman-Italian noble family in 1225. His parents intended him to become a Benedictine monk and to rise in due course to an influential abbacy. But in 1244 he shocked them by choosing a life of poverty in the new Dominican Order. He went to the University of Paris shortly thereafter and spent his ensuing years traveling, teaching, and writing. Unlike Augustine[1] he had no youthful follies to regret. Unlike Anselm[2] and Bernard,[3] he played no great role in the political affairs of his day. He persevered in his academic tasks until, late in life, he suddenly declared that all his books were rubbish and devoted his remaining days to mysticism. At his death, the priest who heard his last confession described it as being as innocent as that of a five-year-old.

In his copious writings—particularly his *Summa Theologica*—Aquinas explored all the great questions of philosophy and theology, political theory and morality. He used Aristotle's logical method and Aristotle's categories of thought but arrived at conclusions that were in harmony with the Christian faith. Like Abelard,[4] St. Thomas assembled every possible argument, pro and con, on every subject that he discussed, but unlike Abelard he drew conclusions and defended them with cogent arguments. Few philosophers before or since have been so generous in presenting and exploring opinions contrary to their own, and none has been so systematic and exhaustive.

St. Thomas created a vast, unified intellectual system, ranging from God to the natural world, logically supported at every step. His theological writings have none of the passion of St. Augustine, none of the literary elegance of Plato; rather, they have an *intellectual* elegance, an elegance of system and organization akin to that of Euclid's geometry. His *Summa Theologica* is organized into an immense series of separate sections, each dealing with a particular philosophical question. In Part I of the *Summa,* for example, Question 2 takes up the problem of God's existence. The *Question* is subdivided into three *Articles:* (1) "Whether God's existence is self-evident" (St. Thomas concludes that it is not); (2) "Whether it can be demonstrated that God exists" (St. Thomas concludes that it can be logically demonstrated); and (3) "Whether God exists" (here St. Thomas endeavors to prove God's existence).

In each *Article,* St. Thomas takes up a specific problem and subjects it to rigorous formal analysis. He always begins with a series of *Objections (Objection 1, Objection 2,* etc.) in which he sets forth as effectively as he possibly can all the arguments *contrary* to his final conclusion. For example, *Question 2, Article 3,* "Whether God exists," begins with two *Objections* purporting to demonstrate that God does not exist. One of them runs as follows:

> *Objection 1.* It seems that God does not exist, because if one of two contraries can be infinite, the other would be altogether destroyed. But the name "God" means that He is infinite goodness. Therefore, if God ex-

1. medieval Christian scholar, A.D. 354–430   2. archbishop of Canterbury, St. Anselm   3. St. Bernard of Clairvaux   4. theologian and philosopher, Peter

isted there would be no evil discoverable; but there is evil in the world. Therefore God does not exist.

Leaving the objections for the time being, St. Thomas subjects the problem to his own logical scrutiny and concludes that "the existence of God can be proved in five ways." Here is one of them:

> The fifth way is taken from the governance of the world. We see that things which lack knowledge, such as natural bodies, act for an end, and this is evident from their acting always or nearly always in the same way, so as to obtain the best result. Hence it is clear that they achieve their end not only by chance but by design. Now whatever lacks knowledge cannot move toward an end unless it be directed by some being endowed with knowledge and intelligence, as the arrow is directed by the archer. Therefore some intelligent being exists by whom all natural things are directed to their end; and this being we call God.

The analysis concludes with refutations of the earlier *Objections:*

> *Reply to Objection 1.* As Augustine says, "Since God is the highest good, He would not allow an evil to exist in His works unless His omnipotence and goodness were such as to bring good even out of evil." This is part of the infinite goodness of God, that He should allow evil to exist, and out of it to produce good.

Having completed his analysis, St. Thomas then turns to the next *Article* or the next *Question* and subjects it to precisely the same process of inquiry. As in Euclidian geometry so in Thomistic theology, once a problem is settled, the conclusion can be used in solving subsequent problems. Thus the system grows, problem by problem, step by step, as St. Thomas's wide-ranging mind takes up such matters as the nature of God, the attributes of God, the nature and destiny of humanity, human morality, law, and political theory. The result is an imposing, comprehensive edifice of thought, embracing all major theological issues.

As the Gothic cathedral was the artistic embodiment of the high-medieval world, so the philosophy of Aquinas was its supreme intellectual expression. Both were based on clear and obvious principles of structure. St. Thomas shared with the cathedral builders the impulse to display rather than disguise the structural framework of his edifice. Like the boldly executed Gothic flying buttress, the Thomistic *Questions, Articles,* and *Objections* allowed no doubt as to what the builder was doing or how he was achieving his effects.

Aquinas's View of the Physical World and the State

St. Thomas distinguished carefully between revelation and reason but endeavored to prove that they could never contradict one another. Since human reason was a valid avenue to truth, since Christian revelation was authoritative, and since truth was one, then philosophy and Christian doctrine had to be compatible and complementary. "For faith rests upon infallible truth, and therefore its contrary cannot be demonstrated." This was the essence of St. Thomas's philosophical position.

As against the Augustinianism of Anselm and Bonaventure,[5] Aquinas emphasized the reality of the physical world as a world of things rather than symbols. Embracing the moderate realism of Aristotle, he declared that universals were to be found in the world of phenomena and nowhere else—that knowledge came from observation and analysis, not from divine illumination. He shared with St. Francis and others the notion that the physical world was deeply significant in itself.

Similarly, the state, which previous Christian thinkers had commonly regarded as a necessary evil—an unfortunate but indispensable consequence of the Fall of Adam—was accepted by Aquinas as a good and natural outgrowth of humanity's social impulse. He echoed Aristotle's dictum that "Man is a political creature" and regarded the justly governed state as a fitting part of the divine order. Like John of Salisbury, St. Thomas insisted that kings must govern in their subjects' behalf and that a willful, unrestrained ruler who ignored God's moral imperatives was no king but a tyrant. Just as the human body could be corrupted by sin, the body politic could be corrupted by tyranny. But although the Christian must reject both sin and tyranny, he should nevertheless revere the body, the state, and indeed all physical creation as worthy products of God's will, inseparable from the world of spirit, and essential ingredients in the unity of existence.

Aquinas's Existential Unity

Aquinas sought to encompass the totality of being in a vast existential unity. At the center was God, the author of physical and spiritual creation, the maker of heaven and earth, who himself had assumed human form and redeemed all humanity on the cross, who discloses portions of the truth to his followers through revelation, permits them to discover other portions through the operation of the intellect, and will lead them into all truth through salvation. Ultimately, God *is* truth, and it is our destiny, on reaching heaven, to stand unshielded in the divine presence—to love and to know. Thus the roads of St. Thomas, St. Bonaventure, St. Bernard, and Dante,[6] although passing over very different terrain, arrive finally at the same destination. It is not so surprising, after all, that in the end St. Thomas rejected theology for mysticism.

Although Aquinas's thought has been studied across the centuries, many of his own contemporaries rejected it in whole or in part. Franciscans such as Bonaventure were suspicious of the intellectual *tour*

5. Franciscan theologian 6. poet, and author of *The Divine Comedy*

de force of this gifted Dominican. Bonaventure was a rationalist, but a cautious one, and his Franciscan successors came increasingly to the opinion that reason was of little or no use in probing metaphysical problems. The Scottish Franciscan Duns Scotus (d. 1308) undertook a subtle critique of St. Thomas's theory of knowledge. And in the philosophy of the astute English Franciscan, William of Ockham (*c*. 1300–1349), reason and revelation were divorced altogether. Christian doctrine, Ockham said, could not be approached by reason at all but had to be accepted on faith. The Thomist synthesis was a mirage; reason's province was the natural world and that alone.

Thomas Aquinas's Proof of God's Existence

Thomas Aquinas

The Dominican theologian Thomas Aquinas synthesized the role of faith with the role of reason when he outlined five ways to prove the existence of God using logic. The first way was the argument from motion. Aquinas stated that whatever is moved must be moved by another. If one thing moves another and that, in turn, moves another and so on, the chain of movement must ultimately arrive at a first mover, which is God. Similarly, the second argument, the nature of efficient cause, suggested that in our world of sensible things, nothing can be its own cause. Therefore there must be a first cause which Aquinas gave the name of God.

Aquinas's third proof was the argument of possibility and necessity. Since everything has the possibility to not be, then at one time there was nothing in existence. In order for anything to exist there must be one thing that has its own necessity, and this, he argued, is God. The theologian contended that the fourth way to prove the existence of God is the argument of gradation. Among beings there are some that are more or less good, honest, noble, etc. In short, they resemble, by degrees, a maximum or perfection, which is God. Finally, Aquinas argued that all things act for an end by design. The force that directs all things to their end is God.

Thomas Aquinas, c. 1225–1274, was an Italian scholastic theologian and philosopher. He wrote two great summaries of knowledge:

The Summa contra Gentiles, and his greatest work *The Summa Theologica*.

The existence of God can be proved in five ways. The first and more manifest way is the argument from motion. It is certain, and evident to our senses, that in the world some things are in motion. Now whatever is moved is moved by another, for nothing can be moved except it is in potentiality to that towards which it is moved; whereas a thing moves inasmuch as it is in act. For motion is nothing else than the reduction of something from potentiality to actuality. But nothing can be reduced from potentiality to actuality, except by something in a state of actuality. Thus that which is actually hot, as fire, makes wood, which is potentially hot, to be actually hot, and thereby moves and changes it. Now it is not possible that the same thing should be at once in actuality and potentiality in the same respect, but only in different respects. For what is actually hot cannot simultaneously be potentially hot; but it is simultaneously potentially cold. It is therefore impossible that in the same respect and in the same way a thing should be both mover and moved, i.e., that it should move itself. Therefore, whatever is moved must be moved by another. If that by which it is moved be itself moved, then this also must needs be moved by another, and that by another again. But this cannot go on to infinity, because then there would be no first mover, and, consequently, no other mover, seeing that subsequent movers move only inasmuch as they are moved by the first mover; as the staff moves only because it is moved by the hand. Therefore it is necessary to arrive at a first mover, moved by no other; and this everyone understands to be God.

The second way is from the nature of efficient cause. In the world of sensible things we find there is an order of efficient causes. There is no case known (neither is it, indeed, possible) in which a thing is found to be the efficient cause of itself; for so it would be prior to itself, which is impossible. Now in efficient causes it is not possible to go on to infinity, because in all efficient causes following in order, the first is the cause of the intermediate cause, and the intermediate is the cause of the ultimate cause, whether the intermediate cause be several, or one only. Now to take away the cause is to take away the effect. Therefore, if there be no first cause among efficient causes, there will be no ultimate, nor any intermediate, cause. But if in efficient causes it is possible to go on to infinity, there will be no first efficient cause, neither will there be an ultimate effect, nor any intermediate efficient causes; all of which is plainly false. Therefore it is necessary to admit a first efficient cause, to which everyone gives the name of God.

The third way is taken from possibility and necessity, and runs thus. We find in nature things that are possible to be and not to be, since they are found to be generated, and to be corrupted, and consequently, it is possible for them to be and not to be. But it is impossible for these always to exist, for that which can not-be at some time is not. Therefore, if everything can not-be, then at one time there was nothing in existence. Now if this were true, even now there would be nothing in existence, because that which does not exist begins to exist only through something already existing. Therefore, if at one time nothing was in existence, it would have been impossible for anything to have begun to exist; and thus even now nothing would be in existence—which is absurd. Therefore, not all beings are merely possible, but there must exist something the existence of which is necessary. But every necessary thing either has its necessity caused by another, or not. Now it is impossible to go on to infinity in necessary things which have their necessity caused by another, as has been already proved in regard to efficient causes. Therefore we cannot but admit the existence of some being having of itself its own necessity, and not receiving it from another, but rather causing in others their necessity. This all men speak of as God.

The fourth way is taken from the gradation to be found in things. Among beings there are some more and some less good, true, noble, and the like. But *more* and *less* are predicted of different things according as they resemble in their different ways something which is the maximum, as a thing is said to be hotter according as it more nearly resembles that which is hottest; so that there is something which is truest, something best, something noblest, and, consequently, something which is most being, for those things that are greatest in truth are greatest in being, as it is written in *Metaph.* ii. Now the maximum in any genus is the cause of all in that genus, as fire, which is the maximum of heat, is the cause of all hot things, as is said in the same book. Therefore there must also be something which is to all beings the cause of their being, goodness, and every other perfection; and this we call God.

The fifth way is taken from the governance of the world. We see that things which lack knowledge, such as natural bodies, act for an end, and this is evident from their acting always, or nearly always, in the same way, so as to obtain the best result. Hence it is plain that they achieve their end, not fortuitously, but designedly. Now whatever lacks knowledge cannot move towards an end, unless it be directed by some being endowed with knowledge and intelligence; as the arrow is directed by the archer. Therefore some intelligent being exists by whom all natural things are directed to their end; and this being we call God.

The Magna Carta

Bernard Schwartz

Bernard Schwartz contends that John Lackland, king of England from 1199 to 1216, excercised his feudal rights to the utmost to squeeze money from his vassals. John's various financial excesses and abuses of power led to a barons' rebellion, in the form not of a conspiracy to murder John but of forcing John to sign a document called the Magna Carta (or Charta), or Great Charter. Schwartz reports that the barons, in order to establish a precedent for reform, revived an earlier charter written during the reign of Henry I (1100–1135) that granted baronial rights and privileges. Unlike the charter of Henry I, the Magna Carta of 1215 was not granted by the king; rather, it was based on straight-forward demands by the subjects in order to guarantee continued obedience to the king. Schwartz characterizes the charter as a bargain struck between the king and the nation that directly limited the powers of government.

Schwartz argues that the charter itself is designed mostly to remedy feudal abuses and does not, as is often assumed, provide safeguards of Anglo-American liberty. But its language is broad enough that reformers in future centuries used it as an instrument to fight governmental oppression. Schwartz identifies two key provisions that support this use: The first allows the nation, not the king, the right to ordain taxation. The second guarantees a trial by jury for all men, prohibits arbitrary arrest, and demands a speedy trial that follows the due process of the law. Schwartz reasons that the greatest strength of the Magna Carta is its adaptability to fight governmental absolutism, making the king accountable to the law.

Bernard Schwartz is a professor of law at New York University. He is the author of *A Commentary on the Constitution of the United States* and *The Reins of Power.*

John's[1] constant need for revenue was the principal factor behind the exactions and abuses that were the primary cause of Magna Charta. There was no system of taxation, in the modern sense, by which the pecuniary exigencies of the Crown could be satisfied. The only fiscal machinery available to John was that connected with the feudal system: the recognized feudal incidents and aids, as well as knight's service, which had . . . come to mean so-called scutage—a money payment in commutation of the actual military service that had once been due.

King John's Financial Excesses

To obtain the needed revenue, it was necessary to increase the customary feudal obligations. During John's reign, according to William S. McKechnie's[2] standard treatise on Magna Charta, "the stream of feudal obligations steadily rose until the barons feared that nothing of their property would be saved from the torrent." This was particularly true of scutage, which John altered from a device reserved for emergencies into a regular source of revenue. The normal rate of scutage was raised and the frequency of its imposition increased, until, with the demand for a new scutage in 1214 at an unprecedented rate, the limit of the barons' endurance was reached and John was met with flat refusals to pay.

In addition, John sought to exercise his other feudal rights to their utmost limits, affecting his vassals on the point where they were most sensitive—their family interests—as well as to exact money by other means, such as efforts to impose a general property tax. His ingenuity in this respect is illustrated by the curious entry in the public record for Christmas 1204: "The wife of Hugh Neville promises the lord king two hundred chickens that she might lie one night with her husband."

At the beginning, John's efforts, extra-legal though they seemed to men bound by the customary feudal rules, may have appeared successful. Thus, the so-called Thirteenth [a tax on property] of 1207 brought in more than twice the ordinary revenue for a year. Yet, in the phrase of the papal legate in Shakespeare's *King John,*

'Tis strange to think how much King John
hath lost
In this which he accounts so clearly won.

John's financial excesses led directly to the barons' rebellion that resulted in the Great Charter. "He was a pillager of his subjects," says the annalist who wrote at Barnwell priory shortly after John's death, and, for that reason, "they foresook him and, ultimately, little mourned his death." Well might John plaintively declaim, in the Shakespeare play, when his acts had united the nation against him,

1. English king, 1199–1216   2. historian

Our discontented counties do revolt;
Our people quarrel with obedience. . . .

Influence of the Henry I Charter

What was it that converted the resistance to John from a petty attempt of the barons to preserve their feudal prerogatives into an epochal event in the history of freedom? The answer to this query is to be found in the very existence of the Great Charter itself. The end result of the rebellion against John was, not the mere death or deposition of a tyrant, but a written instrument laying down the fundamentals of good government as they were understood at the time. In this sense, Magna Charta is based directly upon the Coronation Charter of Henry I.

The derivation of Magna Charta from the Charter of Henry I is told dramatically in a famous tale of the contemporary chronicler Roger of Wendover. As he tells it, Archbishop Stephen Langton (whose role was crucial in the actual securing of the Great Charter), at a great service held in St. Paul's in 1213, made the theatrical gesture of producing the then-forgotten document of the first Henry, saying, "a charter of King Henry I has now been found by which you can, if you will, recover your long-lost liberties in their pristine condition." And, continues the chronicler, "when it had been read and understood by the barons, they rejoiced with exceeding great joy, and all swore, in the archbishop's presence, that they would fight for those liberties, if it were needful, even unto death."

Modern scholars consider this tale apocryphal. But it is clear that, some time in 1212, the emphasis of the opposition to John shifted from one of the king's deposition to one of a written document defining good government to be secured from the Crown. As W.L. Warren[3] puts it, "in place of the conspiracy to murder John and set up a new king, which had been their one policy in 1212, they were now waving a charter." This was the crucial development, and it could scarcely have occurred had there not been the precedent of Henry I's Charter: it furnished both a safe standing-ground (for men who deemed existing custom practically immutable) and a precedent for a deliberate scheme of governmental reform.

Yet, if the Charter secured at Runnymede in 1215 may thus be said to be derived from the Henry I Charter, its importance is to be found in the fact that it goes far beyond that earlier document both in its wording and implications. Most significant were the differing circumstances in which the two charters were secured. . . . Henry issued his Coronation Charter to obtain support for his accession to the throne; but the instrument itself was plainly a unilateral act on the part of the monarch—a promise by the king given as a matter of

---

3. biographer of King John

grace and not as the result of any external coercion.

John's Charter also, it is true, is in terms only a grant by a sovereign to his subjects. "John, by the grace of God," it starts, and, after listing his titles and his formal greeting to his subjects, goes on to state, "Know that we . . . have . . . granted to all freemen of our kingdom, for us and our heirs forever, all the liberties written below, to be had and held by them and their heirs, of us and our heirs forever." And, after listing the different liberties granted, it concludes, with the traditional words of royal grant: "Given by our hand, in the meadow which is called Runnymede, between Windsor and Staines, on the fifteenth day of June, in the seventeenth year of our reign." The actual giving, by John's hand, was effected by the imprint of his great seal.

But if the Magna Charta was thus cast in the form common to royal charters of the period—announcing in the pious legal language of the day that the king has been pleased to make certain unilateral grants, by the advice of certain counsellors who are named—how different was its reality! In actuality, John's Charter was anything but a unilateral act of grace on the part of that monarch. The promises made at Runnymede were exacted by the united arms of most of the kingdom. The reasons stated for the grant of the Charter were quaintly paraphrased by Lord Coke four centuries later: "Here be four notable causes of the making of this great charter rehearsed. 1. The honour of God. 2. For the health of the King's soul. 3. For the exaltation of holy church, and fourthly, for the amendment of the Kingdom." But the real reason, William S. McKechnie tells us, is to be found in the army of the rebels. The true *quid pro quo* which John received for the grants made by him was the renewal by his opponents of the homage and fealty that they had solemnly renounced.

Seen in this light, what can we say is the true legal nature of the Great Charter? Here, once again, is a question on which countless scholars have disagreed. As already indicated, the document's form as a unilateral grant—a mere act of grace—on the part of the Crown does not give the answer. Bishop Stubbs's famous characterization of Magna Charta as "really a treaty between the King and his subjects" has been rejected by more-recent historians. Yet it is not so far from the truth as they suppose—if we bear in mind that, unlike the usual treaty between independent States, this was a concord worked out between ruler and subjects of the same State.

From the point of view of the modern American, such an agreement, drawn up by the different estates of the realm, and accepted by the king as the price for their continued obedience—setting limits to the powers of government—has many of the earmarks of the constitutional documents with which he is familiar. Even the charter form—a grant of franchises freely made—does not seem out of place to one cognizant of the constitutional role played by documents cast in a similar form in the American Colonies.

What is clear is that there took place at Runnymede what was essentially a bargain struck between the king and the nation. The result of this bargain was a document enumerating what were deemed the basic liberties of Englishmen of the day. This enumeration may strike us as brief, contained as it is in sixty-three short chapters; for its date, nevertheless, it is a rather lengthy document. It was natural for the men of the day to resort to the legal form invariably used for all irrevocable grants—the feudal charter authenticated by the grantor's seal. The analogy was that of a grant of land and much of the language employed was actually that appropriate to such a grant. If the substance of Magna Charta is the establishment of a framework of good government, its form, as McKechnie puts it, "is borrowed from the feudal lawyer's book of styles for conferring a title to landed estate."

Strengths of the Magna Charta

In a provocative passage, [historian Frederick W.] Maitland asks, "Have you ever pondered the form, the scheme, the main idea of Magna Charta? If so, your reverence for that sacred text will hardly have prevented you from using in the privacy of your own minds some such words as 'inept' or 'childish,' etc." Certainly, Magna Charta is an unrewarding document for the nonspecialist. "If we set aside the rhetorical praise which has been so freely lavished upon the Charter," says Winston Churchill, "and study the document itself, we may find it rather surprising."

The Great Charter is drawn up as a feudal grant. It abounds in the technicalities of feudal law and, when these are out of the way, it seems to deal mainly with mundane and petty aspects of the relations between the king and his tenants in chief. There is in it no broad statement of principle or defined political theory. It is not what we would look for in a declaration of constitutional doctrine, but only a practical document to remedy current feudal abuses. Most surprising is that most of what we now consider the great safeguards of Anglo-American liberty are conspicuously absent from the first great charter of English liberties.

Yet if we analyze the Great Charter on its own terms, there is much that is notable. It is of great significance that the custom of feudal tenure is stated as a defined component of English law, with precise limits set to royal claims in strict terms of money, time, and space. The questions of scutage, feudal reliefs, wardship, and the like are regulated in legally enforceable terms against a king who had claimed to be all but a law unto himself. More important is the fact that, though Magna Charta is primarily a feudal document directed against specific feudal abuses committed by the king against his tenants in chief, its important provisions are cast in broader terms. This is of crucial consequence, for it means that the key chapters of the Charter have been capable of construction to fit the needs of later ages that sought precedents to justify establishment of the liberties we now deem basic.

The barons were concerned with their own grievances against John; but, when the original Articles of the Barons were being refined, the words "any baron" were changed, in important provisions, to "any free man" (*liber homo*). This change in phraseology may have seemed of minor significance at the time (certainly "free man" was a technical feudal term with a much more restricted meaning than we should assign to it), yet it turned out to be of momentous importance in giving the Charter the widest application in future centuries. The wrongs done to the barons may have been the direct cause of Magna Charta, but the language used was broad enough to protect the entire nation against governmental oppression.

Two Key Provisions of the Magna Charta

This was particularly true of what history came to consider the two key provisions of the Great Charter: (1) Chapter 12, under which "No scutage or aid shall be imposed in our kingdom, unless by common counsel of our kingdom"; and (2) Chapter 39, which declares, "No free man shall be taken or imprisoned or disseised or exiled or in any way destroyed . . . save by the lawful judgment of his peers and by the law of the land."

The first of these may have been intended by the barons only as an assertion of their right not to have their feudal obligations unilaterally altered by the king, but, without undue stretching, it can readily be construed as an admission of the right of the nation to ordain taxation.

In addition, Chapter 14 specifies how the consent of the nation is to be given. To obtain the common counsel of the kingdom to the assessing of an aid or scutage, it states, "we will cause to be summoned the archbishops, bishops, abbots, earls, and greater barons," as well as those who hold of the king in chief below the rank of the greater barons—all this on forty days' notice—and the action of those who obey the summons is to be taken to represent the action of the whole. Here we have a rough attempt, albeit in rudimentary form, to define what will become the national assembly for purposes of taxation. In it is at least the seed of the basic principle that no financial burden may be imposed upon the people without the consent of Parliament, as well as that of Parliamentary representation. If men had not yet grasped these principles in their full modern sense, and especially the essential interconnection between taxation and representation, they had at least made a start in that direction.

The role of Chapter 39 has been even more consequential in the evolution of constitutional liberty. This is true although it was probably intended merely as a written confirmation of the baronial right, recognized by feudal custom, not to be tried by inferiors, but only by men of baronial rank. The breadth of the language used has made it serve a far wider purpose. Coke, in his seventeenth-century commentary on Magna Charta, could read it as a guaranty of trial by jury to all men; as absolutely prohibiting arbitrary arrest; and as solemnly undertaking to dispense to all full, free, and speedy justice—equal to all. Even more suggestive for an American, in Coke's commentary, the crucial phrase at the end of the chapter, "by the law of the land," is read as equivalent to "due process of law" (a connotation that it had begun to acquire as early as the time of Edward III)—thus providing the link between the Great Charter and the most important clause of modern American Constitutions.

Of course, we read our own conceptions into the document sealed at Runnymede when we make of it an organic instrument designed, in Henry Hallam's[4] phrase, to "protect the personal liberty and property of all freemen by giving security from arbitrary imprisonment and arbitrary spoliation." Yet, intended so broadly or not by its framers, it can scarcely be doubted that the ultimate effect of Magna Charta, in [historian] Edward Creasy's words, "was to give and to guarantee full protection for person and property to every human being that breathes English air."

More important to the constitutional historian than the literal intent of the men of Runnymede is the meaning that future generations were able to read into their words. If, as [English legal historian F.W.] Maitland has strikingly put it, it was possible for later men to worship such words only because it was possible to misunderstand them, the significant thing, after all, is that the words were written in a way that could be "misunderstood" so as to serve the needs of later ages. Because of this, to quote Maitland again, the "document becomes and rightly becomes a sacred text, the nearest thing to a 'fundamental statute' that England has ever had." In age after age, men will turn to the Charter as a continuing source of inspiration and authority in their struggles to bridle the "Johns" of their day.

For the truly great thing about the Magna Charta has been what J.C. Holt[5] terms its adaptability—the ability to mean all things to all men—to project itself into the dreams and necessities of ages that the men of 1215 could, at best, not even dimly foresee. Thus it was that a document that may itself have been only a product of feudal class selfishness was able to serve as the basis for molding the foun-

4. constitutional historian 5. historian

dations of a Parliamentary monarchy in the next two centuries, as the vehicle to enable the Parliamentary leaders to resist the misdeeds of Stuart kings four centuries later, and even as the core of the rights of Englishmen asserted by American colonists against the England of the eighteenth century. "What Magna Carta has become," says Justice Frankfurter,[6] "is very different indeed from the immediate objects of the barons at Runnymede." Those who look at Magna Charta with only the pedantic rigor of the thirteenth-century specialist are bound to miss the mark so far as its ultimate significance in the history of freedom is concerned.

Indeed, the vital thing about the Great Charter is, not any specific provision contained in it, but its very coming into being—which alone has justified its continuing renown and significance. The mere existence of such a document, extorted from the king as it was, has been a standing condemnation of governmental absolutism. Instead, the Charter itself tells us that, in Winston Churchill's phrase, "here is a law which is above the King and which even he must not break. This reaffirmation of a supreme law and its expression in a general charter is the great work of Magna Carta; and this alone justifies the respect in which men have held it."

Magna Charta means that the king himself is and shall be bound by the law. This was the root principle laid down at Runnymede. With it, the bridling of power by law, which is the essential theme of English constitutional history, may be said to have begun its development. What follows is intended to ensure that such principle will survive and ultimately rise paramount as the *rule of law* that Anglo-Americans traditionally cherish as the central and most characteristic feature of their constitutional system.

6. U.S. Supreme Court justice Felix

The Travels of Marco Polo

James J. Walsh

James J. Walsh argues that historians often undervalue the explorers of the thirteenth century. Walsh claims these rugged adventurers not only mapped vast regions accurately but also chronicled many unknown customs, languages, and religions of unexplored countries. The author maintains that Marco Polo was undoubtedly the greatest of the century. At first his fantastic travels were seen as fiction, but later his contributions were verified. Indeed, Polo's travels opened up the East to Europe. Amazingly, Polo visited almost all the eastern lands, even some of the most remote.

Polo's observations detail many common practices adopted much later in Europe, such as the use of oil, coal, and asbestos. Polo's travels were straightforwardly compiled by a Pisan named Rusticiano, whose record of the great explorer inspired Christopher Columbus, more as a model of geographical inquiry than as a tale of adventure and exploration, and many of the great navigators who followed.

James J. Walsh was a writer, historian, and professor of biology and psychology at Cathedral College in New York. His works include *Modern Progress and History, The Popes and Science,* and *Old-Time Makers of Medicine.*

To most people it will come as a distinct surprise to learn that the travelers and explorers of the Thirteenth Century—merchants, ambassadors, and missionaries—succeeded in solving many of the

Excerpted from James J. Walsh, *The Thirteenth: Greatest of Centuries.* Copyright © 1907 James J. Walsh.

geographical problems that have been of deepest interest to the generations of the last half of the Nineteenth Century. The eastern part of Asia particularly was traveled over and very thoroughly described by them. Even the northern part of India, however, was not neglected in spite of the difficulties that were encountered, and Thibet was explored and Lhasa entered by travelers of the Thirteenth Century. Of China as much was written as had been learned by succeeding generations down practically to our own time. This may sound like a series of fairy-tales instead of serious science, but it is the travelers and explorers of the modern time who have thought it worth while to comment on the writings of these old-time wanderers of the Thirteenth Century, and who have pointed out the significance of their work. These men described not only the countries through which they passed, but also the characters of the people, their habits and customs, their forms of speech, with many marvelous hints as regards the relationship of the different languages, and even something about the religious practises of these countries and their attitude toward the great truths of Christianity when they were presented to them.

Marco Polo's Reputation

Undoubtedly one of the greatest travelers and explorers of all times was Marco Polo, whose book was for so long considered to be mainly made up of imaginary descriptions of things and places never seen, but which the development of modern geographical science by travels and expeditions has proved to be one of the most valuable contributions to this department of knowledge that has ever been made. It took many centuries for Marco Polo to come to his own in this respect but the Nineteenth and Twentieth centuries have almost more than made up for the neglect of their predecessors. Marco Polo suffered the same fate as did Herodotus[1] of whom Voltaire[2] sneered "father of history, say, rather, father of lies." So long as succeeding generations had no knowledge themselves of the things of which both these great writers had written, they were distrusted and even treated contemptuously. Just as soon, however, as definite knowledge began to come it was seen how wonderfully accurate both of them were in their descriptions of things they had actually seen, though they admitted certain over-wonderful stories on the authority of others. Herodotus has now come to be acknowledged as one of the greatest of historians. In his lives of celebrated travelers, James Augustus St. John states the change of mind with regard to Marco Polo rather forcibly:

"When the travels of Marco Polo first appeared, they were generally regarded as fiction; and as this absurd belief had so far gained

1. ancient Greek historian 2. eighteenth-century French writer

ground, that when he lay upon his death bed, his friends and nearest relatives, coming to take their eternal adieu, conjured him as he valued the salvation of his soul, to retract whatever he had advanced in his book, or at least many such passages as every person looked upon as untrue, but the traveler whose conscience was untouched upon that score, declared solemnly, in that awful moment, that far from being guilty of exaggeration, he had not described one-half of the wonderful things which he had beheld. Such was the reception which the discoveries of this extraordinary man experienced when first promulgated. By degrees, however, as enterprise lifted more and more the veil from Central and Eastern Asia the relations of our traveler rose in the estimation of geographers; and now that the world—though containing many unknown tracts—has been more successfully explored, we begin to perceive that Marco Polo, like Herodotus, was a man of the most rigid veracity, whose testimony presumptuous ignorance alone can call in question."

There is many a fable that clings around the name of Marco Polo, but this distinguished traveler needs no fictitious adornments of his tale to make him one of the greatest explorers of all time. It is sometimes said that he helped to introduce many important inventions into Europe and one even finds his name connected with the mariner's compass and with gunpowder. There are probably no good grounds for thinking that Europe owes any knowledge of either of these great inventions to the Venetian traveler. With regard to printing there is more doubt and Polo's passage with regard to movable blocks for printing paper money as used in China may have proved suggestive.

Marco Polo's Travels

There is no need, however, of surmises in order to increase his fame for the simple story of his travels is quite sufficient for his reputation for all time. As has been well said most of the modern travelers and explorers have only been developing what Polo indicated at least in outline, and they have been scarcely more than describing with more precision of detail what he first touched upon and brought to general notice. When it is remembered that he visited such cities in Eastern Turkestan as Kashgar, Yarkand, and Khotan, which have been the subject of much curiosity only satisfied in quite recent years, that he had visited Thibet, or at least had traveled along its frontier, that to him the medieval world owed some definite knowledge of the Christian kingdom of Abyssinia and all that it was to know of China for centuries almost, his merits will be readily appreciated. As a matter of fact there was scarcely an interesting country of the East of which Marco Polo did not have something to relate from his personal experiences. He told of Burmah, of Siam, of Cochin China, of Japan, of Java, of Sumatra, and of other islands of the great Archipelago, of Ceylon, and of India, and all of these not in the fabulous dreamland spirit of one who has not been in contact with the East but in very definite and precise fashion. Nor was this all. He had heard and could tell much, though his geographical lore was legendary and rather dim, of the Coast of Zanzibar, of the vast and distant Madagascar, and in the remotely opposite direction of Siberia, of the shores of the Arctic Ocean, and of the curious customs of the inhabitants of these distant countries.

Polo's Practical Observations

How wonderfully acute and yet how thoroughly practical some of Polo's observations were can be best appreciated by some quotations from his description of products and industries as he saw them on his travels. We are apt to think of the use of petroleum as dating from much later than the Thirteenth Century, but Marco Polo had not only seen it in the Near East on his travels, but evidently had learned much of the great rock-oil deposits at Baku which constitute the basis for the important Russian petroleum industry in modern times. He says:

"On the north (of Armenia) is found a fountain from which a liquor like oil flows, which, though unprofitable for the seasoning of meat, is good for burning and for anointing camels afflicted with the mange. This oil flows constantly and copiously, so that camels are laden with it."

He is quite as definite in the information acquired with regard to the use of coal. He knew and states very confidently that there were immense deposits of coal in China, deposits which are so extensive that distinguished geologists and mineralogists who have learned of them in modern times have predicted that eventually the world's great manufacturing industries would be transferred to China. We are apt to think that this mineral wealth is not exploited by the Chinese, yet even in Marco Polo's time, as one commentator has remarked, the rich and poor of that land had learned the value of the black stone.

"Through the whole Province of Cathay," says Polo, "certain black stones are dug from the mountains, which, put into the fire, burn like wood, and being kindled, preserve fire a long time, and if they be kindled in the evening they keep fire all the night."

Another important mineral product which even more than petroleum or coal is supposed to be essentially modern in its employment is asbestos. Polo had not only seen this but had realized exactly what it was, had found out its origin and had recognized its value. Curiously enough he attempts to explain the origin of a peculiar usage of the word salamander (the salamander having been supposed to be an animal which was not injured by fire) by reference to the incombustibility of asbestos. The whole passage as it appears in *The Romance of Travel and Exploration* deserves to be quoted. While discoursing about Dsungaria, Polo says:

"And you must know that in the mountain there is a substance from which Salamander is made. The real truth is that the Salamander is no beast as they allege in our part of the world, but is a substance found in the earth. Everybody can be aware that it can be no animal's nature to live in fire seeing that every animal is composed of all the four elements. Now I, Marco Polo, had a Turkish acquaintance who related that he had lived three years in that region on behalf of the Great Khan, in order to procure these salamanders for him. He said that the way they got them was by digging in that mountain till they found a certain vein. The substance of this vein was taken and crushed, and when so treated it divides, as it were, into fibres of wool, which they set forth to dry. When dry these fibres were pounded in a copper mortar and then washed so as to remove all the earth and to leave only the fibres, like fibres of wool. These were then spun and made into napkins." Needless to say this is an excellent description of asbestos.

It is not surprising, then, that the Twentieth Century so interested in travel and exploration should be ready to lay its tributes at the feet of Marco Polo, and that one of the important book announcements of recent years should be that of the publication of an annotated edition of Marco Polo from the hands of a modern explorer, who considered that there was no better way of putting definitely before the public in its true historical aspect the evolution of modern geographical knowledge with regard to Eastern countries.

The Record of Polo's Travels

It can scarcely fail to be surprising to the modern mind that Polo should practically have been forced into print. He had none of the itch of the modern traveler for publicity. The story of his travels he had often told and because of the wondrous tales he could unfold and the large numbers he found it frequently so necessary to use in order to give proper ideas of some of his wanderings, had acquired the nickname of Marco Millioni. He had never thought, however, of committing his story to writing or perhaps he feared the drudgery of such literary labor. After his return from his travels, however, he bravely accepted a patriot's duty of fighting for his native country on board one of her galleys and was captured by the Genoese in a famous sea-fight in the Adriatic in 1298. He was taken prisoner and remained in captivity in Genoa for nearly a year.

It was during this time that one Rusticiano, a writer by profession, was attracted to him and tempted him to tell him the complete story of his travels in order that they might be put into connected form.

Rusticiano was a Pisan who had been a compiler of French romances and accordingly Polo's story was first told in French prose. It is not surprising that Rusticiano should have chosen French since he naturally wished his story of Polo's travels to be read by as many people as possible and realized that it would be of quite as much interest to ordinary folk as to the literary circles of Europe. How interesting the story is only those who have read it even with the knowledge acquired by all the other explorers since his time, can properly appreciate. It lacks entirely the egotistic quality that usually characterizes an explorer's account of his travels, and, indeed, there can scarcely fail to be something of disappointment because of this fact. No doubt a touch more of personal adventure would have added to the interest of the book. It was not a characteristic of the Thirteenth Century, however, to insist on the merely personal and consequently the world has lost a treat it might otherwise have had. There is no question, however, of the greatness of Polo's work as a traveler, nor of the glory that was shed by it on the Thirteenth Century. Like nearly everything else that was done in this marvelous century he represents the acme of successful endeavor in his special line down even to our own time.

It has sometimes been said that Marco Polo's work greatly influenced [Christopher] Columbus and encouraged him in his attempt to seek India by sailing around the globe. Of this, however, there is considerable doubt. We have learned in recent times that a very definite tradition with regard to the possibility of finding land by sailing straight westward over the Atlantic existed long before Columbus' time. Polo's indirect influence on Columbus by his creation of an interest in geographical matters generally is much clearer. There can be no doubt of how much his work succeeded in drawing men's minds to geographical questions during the Fourteenth and Fifteenth centuries.

Francis of Assisi and the Founding of the Franciscan Order

R.H.C. Davis

R.H.C. Davis profiles the Italian friar Francis of Assisi, who in 1205 had a sudden conversion and renounced wordly matters and took a vow of poverty. Francis committed himself to traveling through the countryside preaching repentance and, when not on his journeys, living the life of a hermit. According to Davis, Francis's intent was to win souls through the power of love and the expression of humility and simplicity. People flocked to Francis and many sold their worldly goods and joined him. Although his ranks swelled, Francis rejected any elaborate organization, instead trusting individual inspiration.

Davis reports that the church leadership, at first approving, became uneasy with the growth of Francis's order. Pope Innocent III and his delegates imposed organization on the order and changed or modified many of its original tenets. According to Davis, Francis withdrew to live a more reclusive life and challenged his followers to observe their own consciences, even if it meant disobeying church superiors.

After his death in 1226, Francis was canonized, but later popes continued to restructure the order to bring it more under control. At one point, the church commissioned an official biography of St. Francis in which some of the saint's controversial ideas were softened. The church then reorganized the order and expanded it to address the growing needs of the poor.

R.H.C. Davis is a professor of medieval history at the University of Birmingham, England.

St. Francis (1182–1226) was born at Assisi, a hill-town in the vale of Spoleto, and he owed his name to the fact that his father, a merchant of the town, was away in France at the time of his birth. After a gay youth, in which he served in a war against Perugia and was on the point of becoming the squire of a local noble, he underwent one of those sudden conversions to Religion which were so typical of the Middle Ages. It was said that after a banquet, at which he was master of the revels, he and his companions went round the town singing. Gradually he dropped behind them, so that they shouted back to him to ask what he was thinking of. 'Was he thinking of getting married?' they asked. 'You have spoken the truth,' he replied, 'and you have never seen a nobler, wealthier or more beautiful bride than I intend to take.' He was referring to his Lady Poverty.

St. Francis's Conversion

He did not, however, enter Religion in the conventional way, for he remained a layman and did not join any Order. The story, as it was known to his closest companions, was simply that one day he went into the ruined church of St. Damian, outside the walls of the town, and prayed before the image of Christ crucified. The image spoke to him and said 'Francis, do you not see that my house is being destroyed? Go and repair it for me.' Francis obeyed. He rode into a neighbouring town, sold his possessions, and attempted to give the money thus acquired to the priest. The priest, however, refused to touch the money, and wisely, for Francis's father brought an action against his son for absconding with his property. Francis was summoned to appear before the civil authorities, but refused, claiming, as if he were a cleric or a monk, that he now owed obedience to God alone. He was therefore summoned before the bishop. This time he obeyed, and on the bishop's advice, he solemnly renounced his patrimony, in "The Legend of the Three Companions".

> Going into the bishop's chamber, he cast off all his garments, and laying the money on the clothes before the eyes of the bishop, his father and all who were present, he stepped naked before the door and said: 'Listen all of you, and understand. Up to now I have called Pietro Bernardone my father, but as I am now resolved to serve God, I give him back the money about which he was so perturbed, as well as the clothes I wore

which belong to him, and from now on I will say "Our Father which art in Heaven" instead of "my father Pietro Bernardone".'

From that time forward St. Francis owned no property. He had been converted to Religion and had renounced the world. But he was in an agony of doubt whether to be a hermit or a preacher. He tended lepers, retreated to the seclusion of *Rivo Torto* and *Carceri,* and eventually sought to end his dilemma by an appeal to authority. But the authority he sought was not that of the Church. As ever an individualist, he was insistent on seeking the authority of God in his own way. He asked two friends, Brother Silvester and St. Clare, to pray to God for a sign, and it was the revelation which they received from God which determined him to live a religious life not only on his own account but also for the purpose of winning souls for God.

Thenceforward he determined to preach as well as to pray, and from Portiuncula he travelled round the countryside, preaching repentance. He always went barefoot, and in the early days he took a broom with him so that he could sweep any of the churches that he found dirty. In the intervals between his journeys he would live the life of a hermit. After two years, that is to say in 1209, he was joined by his first two companions, Bernard of Quintavalle, formerly one of the richer men of Assisi, and Peter Cathanii, and together they determined to live according to the rule which Christ had given to the apostles, obeying his instructions literally, particularly in regard to the following three texts:

> If thou wilt be perfect, go and sell that thou hast and give to the poor. (Matthew xix. 21.)
> Take nothing for your journey, neither staves, nor scrip, neither bread, neither money; neither have two coats apiece. (Luke ix. 3.)
> If any man will come after me, let him deny himself, and take up his cross, and follow me. (Matthew xvi. 24.)

They renounced property in the most absolute fashion possible. They had no fixed habitation, and begged for food from door to door, finding the very act of begging an exercise in humility. . . .

The Appeal of St. Francis

The appeal that St. Francis made was such that men flocked to sell their goods and became his brethren or friars (*fratres*). By 1220 his followers were to be numbered in thousands, and no one could mistake the fact that here at last the Church had found its inspiration. It was also clear, however, that the Church would have to regularize and organize the new movement. The licence which could be given to one man who was a saint, or even to his more intimate associates, could not be given so freely to the commonalty of men. For St. Francis acted as the spirit moved him. We read how he said his prayers in the rain, discovered that there were devils in his pillow, took off his clothes before the brothers, cursed a cruel pig, cured the cattle at Fonte Colombo, and made Peter of Cathanii drag him through the streets; and in his case we are still left in no doubt of his sanctity—indeed, our certainty of it is increased. But however great might be the respect in which he himself was held, it was only natural to wonder whether it was right for his conduct to be copied by all and sundry. His followers were beginning to cover the earth, and the thought of them all acting as the spirit moved them must, to ordinary people, have been a little alarming. Was not some form of control desirable, or even imperative?

The difficulty was that St. Francis disliked the thought of any elaborate organization. In the early days he had watched over his converts himself, and had quite rightly insisted that the best way to train them was not to issue them with a set of rules and regulations but to inspire them with the love of God. But with the rapid expansion of the Order he could no longer supervise his friars individually, and some delegation of authority became imperative. In 1217, the year in which missions were first organized to countries outside Italy, he went so far as to designate territorial provinces and appoint 'ministers' to supervise them in his name; but he was still unwilling to frame any definite regulations for their guidance. He valued spontaneity for its own sake, and trusted that the inspiration of his own example would remain with the brethren even in his absence.

St. Francis's Relationship with the Church

The authorities of the Church, however, were understandably perturbed at the lack of consistent discipline. As one observer wrote in 1220:

> To us this religious order [religio] seems exposed to a great danger, for it accepts not only the perfect, but also the young and imperfect who ought to be trained and tested by a period of conventual discipline, and it sends them out, two by two, to all quarters of the globe.

It was true that in the early days St. Francis had never sent out any of his friars until they were fully prepared. But now the very success of the Order had increased its danger. Were all the thousands of converts convinced of their vocation? Had all the ministers of the Order caught the inspiration of their founder? And might not the friars, if inadequately trained, fall victim to the very heresies which they were supposed to counteract? Pope Honorius III decided that the danger was indeed great, and in 1220 he issued the bill Cum Secundum which imposed a novitiate of one year on all who wished to enter the Order.

This was the first direct intervention which the Papacy had made in the internal affairs of the Order. Its indirect influence, however, had been considerable for some time past, at least since 1216, when Pope Honorius III had appointed Cardinal Ugolino (subsequently famous as Pope Gregory IX) to be 'the father of the saint's family'. Ugolino was a remarkable man. He had a deep and intuitive sympathy for St. Francis and his ideals, and yet thought instinctively in terms of ecclesiastical organization. He had vision, and saw not only what St. Francis and his companions were, but also what they might become. He realized that their ideals were complementary to those of St. Dominic, and that, if combined, the followers of the two saints would form a spiritual army against the heretics of the time. But though St. Dominic was deeply affected by the Franciscan ideal, St. Francis himself would not unite with him, since he was not anxious to accept the Dominican emphasis on learning, and hated any suggestion that he or his brethren should be given positions of authority. . . .

None the less, the movement towards authority was irresistible. After the creation of provinces and the appointment of provincial ministers, the need for a definitive Rule was all the more pressing. There was, it is true, the primitive Rule (*Regula primitiva*) which St. Francis had written in 1210, and to which Innocent III had given his oral approval; but this Rule, designed only for the first eleven companions, consisted to a large extent of precepts from the Holy Gospel and lacked the precision and definition needed for the organization of a great religious Order. Cardinal Ugolino therefore persuaded St. Francis to write a new and fuller Rule, the *Regula Prima* of 1221, and then, when that proved unacceptable, to start again and write the *Regula Secunda* of 1223. Rules which did not meet with the approval of the ecclesiastical authorities were, like the *Regula Primitiva* and first draft of the *Regula Secunda*, conveniently lost or destroyed.

St. Francis's Withdrawal from His Order

It was not surprising therefore that St. Francis withdrew to an increasing extent from the activities of the Order which he had founded. In 1220 he resigned the position of Minister General, being succeeded first by Peter Cathanii, who died within six months, and then by Elias of Cortona, whose views were more or less in accord with those of Cardinal Ugolino. St. Francis withdrew to live a semi-eremitical life at such places as Portiuncula, La Verna, or Fonte Colombo, wooing his Lady Poverty, devoting himself to prayer, and defending by the example of his life the ideals for which he had originally stood and still did stand.

The development of the Order began to pass out of his control. Changes were made which could not have met with his approval, and the rule of poverty was gradually modified. In spite of his insistence that anyone who became his friar should first sell all that he had and give it to the poor, the *Regula Prima* added that this was 'if he wishes and can do so in a spiritual way and without impediment'. The brethren were allowed to possess servicebooks, and for clothing they were allowed not one tunic but two. Most important of all, however, was the weakening of the provision that the friars should have no papal privileges and no churches of their own. As early as 1222 Pope Honorius III gave them the privilege of saying Mass in times of interdict. 'We accord to you,' he wrote, 'permission to celebrate the Sacrament in time of interdict in your churches, *if you come to have any*'; and this, be it noted, was during St. Francis's lifetime.

That was the tragedy of the situation, and it was hardly surprising that during his last years St. Francis showed a very deep anxiety to prevent his Order from being corrupted by its own ministers. Most particularly was he determined to see that no Rule should be allowed to force the brethren out of the primitive way of life. Consequently, in spite of the extreme importance which he laid on obedience, he was always endeavouring to secure the right of the individual friar to disobey his superiors on a matter of conscience:

> If any of our ministers should give to any brother an order that is contrary to our life or his conscience [*animam suam*], that brother is not bound to obey him. For that in which a fault or sin is committed is not obedience.

Such a declaration was contrary to every previous religious Rule and to the whole spirit of the medieval Church. St. Benedict, for example, had firmly declared that a monk was to obey his superior, even when ordered to do an impossibility, and from the eleventh century onwards the Papacy had insisted, with ever-increasing force, that disobedience was as the sin of witchcraft. But St. Francis, foreshadowing in this respect one of the central features of Protestantism, was convinced that, important though obedience was, the conscience of the individual was more important still. In the *Regula Secunda*, Ugolino and [Minister General] Elias were able to modify many of the more uncompromising features which they had not been able to keep out of the former Rule; but in the matter of obedience St. Francis stood firm and had his way. Though the phrasing was altered in order to shift the emphasis, the essential provision remained:

> The brothers, who are subjects, must remember that on account of God they have renounced their wills. Whence I firmly order them to obey their ministers in all things which they promised God to observe *and which are not contrary to their conscience or our Rule.*

More direct was the appeal which St. Francis made in his Testament, the document which he dictated on his deathbed (1226). In it he stated quite simply how his conversion had been marked by the change in his attitude to lepers, whom he had previously shunned but subsequently tended. He declared his faith in the priests of the Roman Church—'even if they should persecute me'—and his belief in and devotion to the sacraments. He related how, having no one to show him how to govern the brethren, God had shown him what to do, revealing to him that they should live according to the rule of the Gospels, dividing their possessions among the poor, and being content with a single tunic, patched inside and out. He told how he and his companions had worked with their hands and begged for bread from door to door. He forbade his brethren to have any church or habitation built for them, and he forbade them to ask for letters of privilege from the Papal Curia. He declared his obedience to the Minister General and exhorted his brethren to obey their 'guardians' (*guardiani*). Finally, he explained that this was not 'another rule', but a 'reminder, admonition, and exhortation—[his] testament'. He commanded that it should be read alongside the Rule, with nothing added, nothing deleted, and nothing explained away :

> But as the Lord has given me [grace] to say and write the Rule and these words purely and simply, you are to understand them simply and purely, without glosses, and you are to observe them in blessed charity to the end.

St. Francis's Death

On 3 October 1226 St. Francis died in a little hut at his beloved Portiuncula. On the following day the Minister General, Brother Elias, announced to the world the miracle of the stigmata which had taken place some two years before. Barely two years later, on 16 July 1228, St. Francis was canonized by his old friend Ugolino, now Pope Gregory IX; and on the following day the foundation-stone was laid of the great basilica which was to be built in his honour at Assisi, as the *caput et mater* of the whole Order. In 1230 St. Francis's body was translated to the new basilica, so that the faithful might honour him more devoutly; and in the same year Pope Gregory IX declared authoritatively that the friars were not bound to observe the injunctions of the Testament, since St. Francis had had no right to lay commands on them without the consent of the Chapter General, and no power to commit his successors in any way. Now that he was officially raised to the company of the saints, it seemed as if the wishes of the *poverello* could at last be ignored. The final blow came in 1245, when Pope Innocent IV declared that the followers of St. Francis might enjoy the *use* of any property, such as houses, land, furniture, or books, so long as the legal ownership was vested in the Papacy.

Although the Order had thus been transformed, many of the more intimate friends of St. Francis—brothers Giles, Leo, Angelo, and Rufino for example—refused to be divorced from their Lady Poverty. They were known as 'observants' or 'spirituals' and fought a long, though losing, battle against the 'relaxing' or 'conventual' party. The ministers were normally against them, and so sometimes was the Rule (the *Regula Secunda*), but they appealed boldly to the authority of St. Francis's own life. They told and re-told the stories of his strict poverty—how he would not have more than one tunic, how he would not let a novice have a psalter, and how he insisted on abandoning a hut because, rough shelter though it was, it had been described as 'his'. The officials of the Order therefore realized that the only way of restoring unity was to have but a single authorized Life of the saint, which, while being truthful, would not insist too much on the points that were controversial. The early 'legends' (*i.e.* readings), such as those of the 'three companions', the writings of Brother Leo, and the two official Lives written in 1228 and 1244 by Thomas of Celano, were all, for one reason or another, considered unsuitable, and in 1260 St. Bonaventura, the Minister General, was commissioned to write a new one. It was a masterpiece of saintliness and tact, and in many ways it drew a picture of St. Francis which was accurate and true. But though it quoted some of St. Francis's own sayings about learning, it modified their force; though it recounted St. Francis's views on poverty, it somewhat softened the hardship of his early life; and it never mentioned the Testament at all. It was a Life written not so much for St. Francis as for the Franciscan Order, and in 1266 the Chapter General not only approved it, but decreed, though fortunately without success, that all previous 'legends' should be destroyed. Unity was to be purchased at the expense of a little tactful silence.

That is not to say, however, that the Order was not a wonderful achievement. Ugolino had diverted the Franciscan ideal into the main channels of ecclesiastical organization and had created a veritable army of missionaries where St. Francis had envisaged only a small band of ardent souls, loosely-knit in a form of personal union. He had seen that St. Francis could save the Church and he had thought it important to see that no modesty or idiosyncrasy prevented him from doing so. He revered his sanctity and sympathized with him as a man; but he was determined that he should fulfil what he considered to be the Lord's purpose.

The crying need of the time was for priests who would be brothers to the poor and help them, who would be at home in the squalor of the new industrial towns, and who would be accepted by the unprivileged classes as equals and friends; who would preach as St. Francis had preached, tend the sick as he had tended the lepers, and revive the Christian faith and Christian charity. Ugolino saw that the friars could supply the need. He recognized the genius of St. Francis and saw at once its full potentialities. But he realized also that what St. Francis could do spontaneously and by divine inspiration, could only be attempted by others after much training. He tried, as it were, to bring the saint to earth, and to show him what a wonderful contribution his followers could make to the life of the Church, if only he would let them be organized on a grand scale. He understood the necessity for rules and regulations, discipline and learning, and saw that, to be effective as missionaries, the friars would need not only to visit the poorer quarters of the towns but also to live in them, even at the cost of having houses. Given the means, he saw that they could reconvert the lost portions of Christendom.

The Vanity of Painted Women

Étienne de Bourbon

Étienne de Bourbon, a Dominican monk of the thirteenth century, compiled a collection of written sketches used to express moral viewpoints. In *Tractatus de diversis materiis praedicabilibus* he warned against the vain and lascivious nature of ladies when they paint their faces with makeup.

De Bourbon stated that women who alter their appearance with makeup insult God by suggesting that the way their creator made them needs improvement. Similarly, de Bourbon asserted that women's trains, the part of the gown that trails behind on the ground, are also sinful because they are purchased at high prices and therefore "rob Christ's poor." Moreover, the trains collect fleas, stir up dust, and avert the attention of men in church.

De Bourbon drew a parallel between the multi-faced devil and women who change their appearance by wearing head ornaments. Women, he claimed, vainly adorn themselves with superfluous decorations for sinful reasons. They do not do it for their husbands as women argue, rather, in the privacy of their bedrooms, women wear plain and simple things. It is only when they go out in public that women decorate themselves with expensive adornments so that men will admire them covetously, he concluded.

Against those women who, in spite of their age, paint and adorn themselves as if they were images so that they seem to be

Excerpted from Étienne de Bourbon, "Women's Ways," in *Dark and Middle Ages Reader*, edited by Harry E. Wedeck. Copyright © 1964 Harry E. Wedeck.

masked, like those jesters who wear painted masks that are called in French *artifices,* with which they make fun and delude men.

It is a great and singular glory for humans that they bear the image and the likeness of God, in which they have been created. But some women appear to inflict an injury on God and to declare, as it were, to their Creator: "You made me badly, I shall make a good job. You made me pale, I shall make myself red. You made me dark, I shall make myself white. You made me old, I shall make myself a young girl."

I have heard that a certain actor at the court of a noble, observing an old woman entering thus painted over, filled his mouth with water; and when she was among the women, the actor approached and suddenly, as tanners do who prepare skins, sprinkled the water in his mouth into her face. The water spread and made her visage look leprous.

Similarly, when a woman of the same type came to converse with a great and powerful noble, on seeing her appearance as he reclined on his cushion, he wanted to disconcert her. He made a little hole in the cushion and gradually, as it was pressed down, the feathers came out and he gently blew them into her face. They stuck to her painted and rouged cheeks. When she left the dark room, her face, covered with feathers, appeared to public view, to her own confusion. As she wanted to wipe them away and remove them by rubbing them off, they stuck all the more and the paint revealed her old age, making her more unsightly than ever, like a repaired image.

So with the trains that the ladies trail behind them, more than a cubit long. They commit a heinous sin, for they purchase them at a high price and rob Christ's poor. The trains collect fleas, sweep the ground, keep men praying in church from their orisons, stir up dust and darken the churches. They pollute and defile the altars and the sacred places as if with incense and dust; and on these trains they carry along the devil as though in a chariot. Master Jacob says that a holy man, seeing the devil laugh, adjured him to say why he was laughing. A certain lady, on her way to church, took along a companion in her train. When she had to cross over a muddy spot she raised her dress and the companion fell into the mud. Observing this defilement, the devil had been provoked to laughter.

They choose to resemble the devil more than God and the angels. Of Christ we read that he had one head, while the serpent, that is the devil, had seven. Likewise, sometimes one woman has many heads, that is many ornaments on her head. For she has one head for the night, another for the day, another for a festive day. According to the change of day and festival, she changes her head, that is the ornaments on her head. At home she has one head; out of doors, another; a different one among strangers. For her inner head she pays her husband; for when she is with him alone, she is satisfied to wear the worst ornament that she has, though she apologizes for her vain and unnecessary ornament when she is censured, saying that she adorns herself for her husband. I sometimes rebuked a certain woman for her vanity and the superfluous decorations on her head. She would reply that she did it for her husband, who had up till then bought her seven very expensive adornments for her head. She kept them in her chest, but put on none of them when she went into her husband's bedroom. She was content to have on her head a coarse-woven coif or a thread network cap, and laid aside all her other ornaments. But when she went to meetings or other places where other men congregated, then she put on other head adornments. Hence I charged her with adorning herself not for her own husband but for the covetous eyes of other libertines.

The Gothic Style

Robert C. Lamm, Neal M. Cross, and Rudy H. Turk

Robert C. Lamm, Neal M. Cross, and Rudy H. Turk write that after a devastating fire in 1194 the townspeople of Chartres, France rebuilt their cathedral in a style that epitomized late Gothic architecture. The Chartres's decorative sculpture was done in a more rounded, naturalistic style conveying a greater feeling for this world. Unlike the earlier Romanesque style, Christ is portrayed as benign rather than distant and harsh. Moreover, the fact that the church was dedicated to Our Lady (*Notre Dame*) rather than apostles or saints demonstrates a new emphasis on mercy, rather than justice. The authors argue further that the inclusion of classical thinkers among the religious sculpture indicates a new recognition of the secular world and an emerging wordly spirit. By the second half of the thirteenth century, the Gothic style was imitated throughout Europe. Although the style was adapted to fit varying tastes, it always expressed the creativity and intellectual boldness of the century.

Robert C. Lamm, Neal M. Cross, and Rudy H. Turk explain that Italian artists introduced a late Gothic style of painting. The Florentine Cimabue painted strong figures with soft lines and airy clothing. His work influenced the greatest painter of the medieval period, Giotto. The authors explain that Giotto revolutionized art by establishing the qualities of greater space, bulk, movement, and human expression.

Robert C. Lamm is a professor of Music History at Arizona State University, Tempe; Neal M. Cross is a writer and instructor of English; and Rudy H. Turk is a painter and professor of art history. He is also the director of the Arizona State University Art Museum.

After a disastrous fire in the village of Chartres in 1194, which left intact only the Early Gothic facade of the still unfinished cathedral, the rebuilding of Chartres Cathedral commenced immediately and moved rapidly, with the basic structure completed by 1220. The idea that Gothic cathedrals took decades or even centuries to build is erroneous and probably based on the fact that these buildings were never fully completed; there was always something to be added or elaborated.

Chartres Cathedral

The first masterpiece of the mature period, Chartres Cathedral has been called the Queen of Cathedrals, the epitome of Gothic architecture. Typically High Gothic but unique to Chartres, the south (right) tower begins with a square base that evolves smoothly into the octagonal shape of the fourth level. From here the graceful spire soars to a height of 344', the characteristic "finger pointing to God" of the Gothic age. The elaborate north tower, which was not completed until well into the Northern Renaissance, lacks the effortless verticality of the south tower. Verticality was a hallmark of Gothic; cities competed in unspoken contests to erect cathedrals with the highest vaults and the tallest towers. An inspiring House of God was also a symbol of civic achievement. With a facade 157' wide and measuring 427' in length, Chartres Cathedral is as prominent a landmark today as when it was built, thanks in part to modern zoning ordinances that control building heights throughout the village.

Incorporated into the facade when the cathedral was rebuilt, the Royal Portal (western doorways) of the earlier church emphasizes the Last Judgment theme of Romanesque[1] portals but with significant differences. Rather than the harsh Damnation of the Last Judgment, the theme is now the Second Coming with its promise of salvation. No longer is there the inventive freedom of the Romanesque; all is unified and controlled. The outer frame is provided by the twenty-four elders of the Apocalypse on the archivolts and the lower row of twelve Apostles. Surrounded by symbols of the four Evangelists, the now benign figure of Christ raises an arm in benediction in the manner of Caesar Augustus. Beneath the tympanum[2] are the jamb figures, a wholly new idea in architectural sculpture. Conceived and carved in the round, the figures were very likely fashioned after live models rather than copied from manuscripts, a further indication of the emerging this-worldly spirit of the age.

The Cathedral as Synthesis

The most significant manifestation of the new age was the dedication of the cathedrals themselves. Named after apostles and saints

1. architectural style that preceded the Gothic   2. semi-circular space above a doorway

Notre Dame in Paris was one of the many cathedrals dedicated to Mary. Its flying buttresses (exterior support arches) are a hallmark of the Gothic style.

in previous eras, the new churches were almost invariably dedicated to Our Lady (*Notre Dame*). Mary was Queen of Heaven, interceding for her faithful who, sinners all, wanted mercy, not justice. This was the Cult of the Virgin Mary, the spiritual counterpart of the vastly enhanced status of women. The masculine Romanesque was the age of feudalism and conflict; the more feminized Gothic was the Age of Chivalry, as derived from courts of love sponsored by powerful women like Eleanor of Aquitaine, Queen of France and then of England. With the development of cathedral schools such as those at Paris and Chartres, Mary was viewed much like Athena, as patroness of arts and science. The right doorway of the Chartres Royal Portal includes portraits of Aristotle, Cicero, Euclid, Ptolemy, Pythagoras and symbols of the Seven Liberal Arts. The Gothic cathedral represents the medieval synthesis of spiritual and secular life at its best.

Featuring a nave 53' in width, the most spacious of all Gothic naves, the interior of Notre Dame of Chartres is 130' in length and 122' high, the loftiest vault of its day. At the rounded end of the choir are the tall pointed arches of the arcade and the triforium gallery of the second level, culminating in the lofty and luminous stained glass windows. At the sides of the illustration can be seen two of the four enormous piers which frame the crossing and which are carved as clustered columns to minimize their bulk. Columns clustered around a central core have the same diameter as a solid pier, but their appearance gives the illusion of lightness and grace.

One of the chief glories of Gothic interiors is the kaleidoscopic color cascading from the mighty stained glass windows. Retaining most of its original windows, Chartres is a treasure house of the art, with clerestory windows 44' high, all in all some 20,000 square feet of medieval glass. Located at the south end of the transepts, the southern rose is like a gigantic multicolored jewel set above the five figurative lancet windows. Because it is a southern exposure window, the predominance of color leans towards the warm part of the spectrum from roses to oranges to reds. Its counterpart, the northern rose, transmits the cooler colors, especially many hues of blue. Contrary to what one might expect, direct sunlight on any of the southern windows upsets the chromatic balance of the interior. All of the windows were designed to function best under the even light of the generally grey skies of northern France, enabling the warm and cool colors to effect a balance of color tones. Surpassing anything up to that time, the craftsmanship and sheer beauty of Gothic stained glass remain incomparable.

As usually seen by tourists, a Gothic cathedral is an enormous empty building, very impressive but more like a museum than a church. Despite the awesome scale of the interior, the cathedral is not at all intimidating in the manner of, say, Egyptian temples. Rather, the church is built for people and when functioning as intended, the interior comes vibrantly alive as an inspirational setting for public worship. . . .

Amiens Cathedral

Designed originally by one of the first known masterbuilders, Robert de Luzarches, the Cathedral of Notre Dame of Amiens marks the culmination of the best ideas of the French Gothic style. Modeled after that of Notre Dame in Paris, the west front is not as controlled and majestic as its model. Its grandeur, however, is overwhelming. Looking like one gigantic and intricate work of sculpture, the facade is dominated by its incomparable portals. The imposing entrances thrusting outward from the facade proclaim the interior in unmistakable terms; the central portal announces the lofty nave and the two flanking doorways the side aisles. In other words, the inner structure is foretold by the exterior design.

Patterned after Chartres, the nave of Amiens is even more integrated, soaring in one breathtaking sweep to 144' above the pavement. Unfortunately minus its stained glass, the interior is still the culmination of the High Gothic style: lofty arcades with slender columns rising to the ribbed vaults. Once thought to have functioned as structural supports for the ceiling, the ribs are actually decorative extensions of columns carrying the design to the pinnacle of the ceiling, which with its groined vault is completely self-supporting. . . .

Gothic Cathedrals Outside of France

By the second half of the thirteenth century the Gothic style had been accepted throughout Europe, though Italy was less than enthusiastic. Regional variations gave each area its own brand of Gothic. Taking to Gothic as if they had invented it, the English built in the style from the twelfth to the nineteenth centuries. Drawing directly upon the Ile de France style, the English utilized clearly recognizable Gothic characteristics in a manner just as distinctly non-French. The clean lines of French verticality were abandoned at the outset in favor of a multiplicity of verticals topped by veritable forests of ribs that almost obscured the groined vaults, as evidenced in Canterbury Cathedral. The nave is not seen as a majestic succession of bays but rather as a steady procession of supports and arches. Because the ribs arch up from the triforium, the clerestory windows are not as prominent in the design as in the French style nor is the stained glass comparable in workmanship or design. A comparison of the interior of Canterbury with those of Chartres and Amiens reveals just how drastic the difference is, which the French are only too willing to point out. The English, on the other hand, view French interiors as cold and impersonal, while English Gothic is warmly intimate, hospitable, and comfortable. Different styles suit different people.

The Italians took up the Gothic style slowly and with many reservations; they were, after all, the ones who had labeled the new style as a barbaric creation of the Goths of the north. Distinctly unclassical, a Gothic cathedral is restless, unsettled, always incomplete, whereas a classical temple is at rest, serenely complete. Nevertheless, the Gothic spirit was on the move in Italy, becoming part of the classical and Romanesque traditions. For all its Gothic elements, the Cathedral of Siena has square doorways, triangular pediments, and a balanced design reminiscent of the classical and Romanesque traditions. There is a Gothic rose window minus stained glass plus Gothic towers, lacy blind arches, and the three portals. Most of the statuary has been liberated from its architectural bondage and the tympanums feature colorful mosaics. Faced with multicolored marble the facade is an ensemble of Gothic elements mixed with Tuscan Romanesque, all in all a notable example of Italian reaction to the Gothic spirit.

Whatever its regional variations, the Gothic cathedral epitomizes the explosive creativity and intellectual boldness of the Gothic age. Never completely finished, a process rather than an end product, it stood at the center of the storm of changes that would sweep away the medieval synthesis. It represents both the triumphant climax of the Age of Faith and the end of the Middle Ages.

Italian Painting

An integral part of Gothic architecture, stained glass windows and relief sculpture served the pictorial purposes once provided by mosaics,
murals, and frescoes. Virtually nonexistent in the Gothic north, large-
scale paintings were still done in Italy, which had maintained its contact with Byzantium.[1] It was Italian painters who synthesized Byzantine
and Gothic styles to create new procedures crucial to the future development of Western painting.

Renowned for his skill as a fresco and tempera painter, the Florentine Cimabue (chee-ma-BOO-uh; 1240?–1302) introduced features
that were incorporated into the developing Italian style. His *Madonna
Enthroned* illustrates the new characteristics of strong, forceful figures
in an atmosphere of complete serenity. The human scale of the lower
figures emphasizes the towering dignity of the Madonna as she holds
the mature-looking child. Distinguished from Byzantine icons by its
much greater size, the gable shape and solid throne are also Gothic in
origin as is the general verticality. The rigid, angular draperies and
rather flat body of the Madonna are from the Byzantine tradition, but
the softer lines of the angels' faces and their lightly hung draperies were
inspired by works from contemporary Constantinople.

Cimabue's naturalistic, monumentally scaled work had a profound
influence on his purported pupil Giotto (JOT-toe; ca. 1267–1337), the
acknowledged "father of Western painting." Giotto was a one-man revolution in art, who established the illusionary qualities of space, bulk,
movement, and human expression, all features of most pictorial art for
the next six centuries. . . .

To all of . . . Giotto's achievements he brought a profound sense
of humanity's awareness of human emotions and of their place in
the world. Difficult as it is to realize today, Giotto's contemporaries
saw these works as the ultimate reality, so "real" that you could walk
into them. We can give proper credit to this view by comparing
Giotto's work with that of his contemporaries and by remembering
also that reality, or the illusion of reality, changes from epoch to
epoch.

The International Style

From Siena came two artists whose work was unlike that of either
Cimabue or Giotto but who were instrumental in establishing the International Style, the first international movement in Western art.
Duccio (DOOT-cho; ca. 1255–1319) painted Byzantine-type faces
except for the eyes, but in a style comparable to northern Gothic
manuscripts and ivories. The most elegant painter of his time, his
Rucellai Madonna is highly decorative, with sinuous folds of back-

1. capital of the Byzantine Empire of eastern Europe

ground drapery and a remarkable delicacy of line for so large a work. Contrasting with the Byzantine-style flatness of the Madonna, the kneeling angels are portrayed much more in the round, combining the Hellenistic-Roman naturalistic tradition with that of French architectural sculpture. This one work is a virtual encyclopedia of the International Style synthesis of Mediterranean and northern cultures. . . .

Serving the pope's court in Avignon, Duccio's pupil Simone Martini (1284–1344) combined the grace of the Sienese school with the exquisite refinement of Late Gothic architecture. His *Annunciation* epitomizes the courtly style. Completely Gothic, the frame is replete with *crockets,* or ornamental leaves and flowers, and *finials,* or carved spires; signifying eternity, the gold-leaf background is Byzantine. Delineated in graceful curved lines, the Angel Gabriel kneels before the Virgin to proclaim "Hail Mary, full of grace. . . ." As the words travel literally from his lips she draws back in apprehension, her body arranged in an elaborate S-curve and covered by a rich blue robe. Between the two figures is an elegant vase containing white lilies symbolic of Mary's purity. As delicately executed as fine jewelry, the artistic conception is aristocratic and courtly, comparable to the polished sonnets of Petrarch,[2] who also served the papal court at Avignon.

With its combined Classical/Byzantine/Gothic attributes, the International Style was promulgated throughout the religious and secular courts of Europe. It found an enthusiastic response wherever wealthy clients prized grace, delicacy, and refinement in art, music, manners, and dress. Aesthetic pleasure was the goal, not spiritual enlightenment.

2. Italian poet, Francesco

The Fourth Crusade and the Sack of Constantinople

Terry Jones and Alan Ereira

In 1198 Lothario dei Conti de Segni was elected Pope Innocent III. He was a ruthless leader who wanted to subjugate both European monarchs and the Eastern Church seated in Constantinople. Once in power Innocent III taxed the clergy and altered canon law to make it easier to initiate a crusade to conquer the Holy Land from the Saracens, or Arabs, and recapture Jerusalem.

The crusaders and their allies, the Venetians, threatened Constantinople and the Byzantine emperor Alexius III, who had recently usurped the throne from Isaac Angelus and his son, the rightful heir, Prince Alexius, who had found sanctuary on one of the Venetian ships. Alexius III, seeing that the situation was hopeless, fled the city, and the crusaders pressured Byzantine officials to crown the young prince the new emperor, Alexius IV. Terry Jones and Alan Ereira write that the young emperor, his treasury empty, could not make the necessary payoffs to the crusaders for putting him on the throne so he traveled through his empire trying to persuade his subjects to pledge their submission to the pope in Rome and give Alexius money. Meanwhile, the crusaders, stuck in Constantinople while waiting for payment that would enable them to move on toward Jerusalem, grew restless and terrorized the citizens. In the turmoil, one of Alexius's trusted advisers, Murzuphlus, had the vulnerable ruler strangled and named himself emperor.

The authors argue that this coup incited the impatient crusaders to sack the city, plundering its wealth in a bloodthirsty rampage. The destruction of Constantinople finally subordinated the Eastern Church to the Western pope.

Terry Jones is an actor, director, and scriptwriter, and the author of *Chaucer's Knight: A Portrait of a Medieval Mercenary*. Alan Ereira is a social historian and a producer for the British Broadcasting Corporation. His writings include *The People's England* and *The Heart of the World*.

In 1198 Lothario dei Conti de Segni found himself, aged only thirty-seven, elected Pope in a world where no lay ruler could rival his power. The German Emperor had died leaving a child heir; France and England were locked in debilitating war. The young Lothario took the name of Innocent III and immediately put his own men in key positions in the Church and the administration of Rome. He had come to power from nowhere. He had been a mere deacon and so on his election as Pope he had first to be ordained as a priest.

Like Joseph Stalin, he took over power not because he was known for his politics but because he knew how to run the administration and watched all the details. And like Stalin, once he had arrived, he blossomed into a monster seeking unlimited power and ruthlessly destroying anyone who was not completely subservient. Unlike Stalin, the organization which he infused with his personality was already firmly established and would endure for centuries to come.

His ambition was total. He was the heir of the revolution begun by Gregory VII; he was determined that the Pope, representative of the supreme monarch in heaven, must be the supreme monarch on earth. That programme called for the submission of kings, the subjection of the Eastern Church to Rome, the elimination of all but his own interpretation of the Christian message and the reconquest of Jerusalem under his own command.

In 1199 he wrote to the Patriarch of Jerusalem for information which would help him direct the Crusade he planned. The Patriarch wrote back to say that no Crusade was necessary, thank you very much; in his view the Saracens[1] would happily withdraw from the Holy Land if they could be given guarantees of the security of their other possessions. The barons wanted to live in peace with al-Adil;[2]

---

1. nomadic Arabs of the deserts between Syria and Arabia 2. Arab sultan in Jerusalem

the last thing they wanted was another bunch of knights to come over, make a lot of trouble and then go away leaving them to live with the results. This was not the information Innocent wanted to hear. He ignored it.

Crusade Preparations

A priest by the name of Fulk, from near Paris, had been wandering about France preaching the need for a new Crusade. Fulk was no ragged itinerant like Peter the Hermit. He was respectable, well groomed and with great powers of oratory—a perfectly acceptable representative of papal intentions. Innocent III now gave Fulk's preaching full papal authority. In addition, he sent letters to the clergy and nobility throughout France and northern Italy urging them to take up the Cross. But he sent no letter to any king—not that he would have stopped them going, but why encourage them, since he himself was to be the ultimate commander?

There didn't seem to be quite the same enthusiasm for crusading as there had been in the time of Urban II, so Innocent resorted to un-precedented—even desperate—measures. For the first time ever he announced a tax upon the clergy themselves to pay for the Crusade. There was an outcry, of course. The Cistercians[3] were immediately up in arms and refused to pay. But the fact that the Pope was pre-pared to put other people's purses where his mouth was changed the whole basis of the Crusade. From now on it was less of a financial burden to go on Crusade; and would-be Crusade leaders who could get the tax assigned to them were even able to show a profit—espe-cially if they did not go after all.

Although a lawyer himself, the Pope also decided to throw Canon Law out of the window by announcing that men no longer needed their wives' consent to go on Crusade to the Holy Land. Innocent be-lieved firmly that the end justified the means. In the name of Divine Law and Christian morality, he would break any law that needed breaking—and any bones.

Attack on Constantinople

The Crusaders were overawed by the sight of 'that city which reigns supreme over all others'. Geoffrey de Villehardouin[4] reported that those who had never seen it before 'never imagined there could be so fine a place in all the world'. Alexius III,[5] the usurper, tried to buy them off with provisions and money, but the Crusaders refused to be diverted from their noble mission to restore the imperial throne to its rightful heir. They even sailed up close to the walls of Constantino-ple, showing off the young Prince on the deck and shouting out to

3. A monastic order 4. Crusade chronicler 5. Byzantine emperor

the Greeks: *'Here is your natural lord. . . . The man you now obey as your lord rules over you without just or fair claim to be your Emperor, in defiance of God and the right.'*

On the appointed day, the Franks and the main army attacked from the land, while the Venetians attacked from the sea. At this point the Doge[6] showed a remarkable degree of courage, according to Geoffrey de Villehardouin. The ancient blind man stood at the prow of his galley with the banner of Saint Mark and demanded that his men put himself and the banner on shore, whereupon his men leapt ashore and the siege began.

That night the usurper Alexius III analysed his position objectively. His people had little love for him. What remained of the imperial army consisted entirely of mercenaries and if things went against them, no soldier could be expected to risk his neck merely for a wage packet. And since the majority of Crusaders were Franks, the Frankish regiments in his pay could not be trusted either. Perhaps he could still count on the Varangian Guard, but even they were mainly Danish and English. The analysis complete, Alexius III took the wisest course of action—he did a bunk.

The Byzantine officials woke up next day to find themselves without an emperor. Their solution, however, was brilliant in its simplicity. They pulled the blinded ex-Emperor Isaac Angelus out of prison, set him back on the throne and announced to the Crusaders that the rightful ruler had been restored, according to their wishes, and there was thus no need for any more of their kind assistance. Would they therefore please stop attacking?

But the Crusaders were not to be cheated of their reward. At a private audience Geoffrey de Villehardouin explained to the reinstated Emperor the Crusaders' contract with his son:

> You know what service we have rendered your son, and you are aware that we have kept the terms of our agreement with him. We cannot, however, allow him to come here until he has given us a guarantee for the covenant he has made with us. He therefore, as your son, asks you to ratify this covenant in the same terms and the same manner as he has done himself.

Isaac Angelus grumbled that they were indeed hard conditions, but he signed the covenant, and the deal was celebrated with great jubilation and feasting. On 1 August 1203 the Prince was crowned Alexius IV alongside his father in the Church of Haghia Sophia.

The Overthrow of the New Emperor of Byzantium

The Crusaders now waited for their 200,000 marks and the submission of the Greek Empire to the Pope in Rome. While the blind fa-

---

6. Venetian leader Enrico Dundolo

ther shut himself away with his favourite astrologers, the young Alexius IV began to discover that it is one thing to make grand promises as a pretender to the throne, but another to carry them out as emperor. His attempt to enforce submission to Rome naturally roused tremendous resentment amongst both the clergy and the people. As for the money he had promised—it simply did not exist. Byzantium was broke.

Eventually he summoned the Doge and the barons to a meeting. There, in the time-honoured manner of debtors everywhere, he put a counter-proposal to his creditors. *'You are soon to leave,'* he said. *'I cannot hope to carry out all I have promised you in so short a time. The Greeks, I must tell you, hate me because of you. If you leave, I will lose my Empire and they will put me to death.'* He therefore begged them to stay until the following Easter, by which time he should have made his position more secure and, hopefully, raised the promised money.

The suggestion created uproar amongst the Crusaders. The idea of yet another delay seemed insupportable . . . and yet what else could they do? They had got themselves into a double-bind. Unable to go forward without more money, unwilling to delay another year. . . . In the end there was nothing to do but wait.

Alexius toured his Empire exacting submission (and, presumably, cash) from his not altogether willing subjects. In this enterprise he was supported by many of the crusading barons, and this further alienated his people.

Meanwhile the rest of the Crusaders strutted around Constantinople doing nothing to endear themselves to the Greek population. Drunken brawls were frequent, and during one a Frenchman set fire to the city. A terrible fire raged out of control for a week, after which no Latin dared to live in Constantinople. In January anti-Latin sentiment in the city broke out in a riot in which the wonderful statue of Athena, which Phidias the Athenian had made some 1500 years before at the request of Pericles, was utterly destroyed because it seemed to be beckoning to the invaders.

Finally the Doge insisted that matters be brought to a head. A delegation, including Geoffrey de Villehardouin, was given the extremely risky task of delivering an ultimatum to the now increasingly haughty young Emperor at a great assembly. *'The Greeks were much amazed and deeply shocked by this openly defiant message, and declared that no one had ever yet been so bold as to dare issue such a challenge to an Emperor of Constantinople in his own hall,'* Geoffrey reported. Angry voices filled the room. The Emperor scowled and the Franks beat a hasty retreat in fear of being torn limb from limb on the spot.

This was followed by a palace coup. A character by the name of Murzuphlus, who had been one of Alexius' most trusted advisers, now seized the young Emperor as he slept, threw him into prison, and had him strangled. Alexius's father, the blind old Emperor, died a few days later. Murzuphlus then had himself crowned Emperor to the popular acclaim of the Greek population. *'Have you ever heard of any people guilty of such atrocious treachery!'* exclaims Geoffrey de Villehardouin.

The Sack of Constantinople

This turn of events made it easy for the Venetians to persuade the Crusaders that there was now only one course of action open to them: they must put an end to the ancient Roman Empire. Their clergy offered moral justifications—the Greeks had committed a mortal sin in supporting the murder of their Emperor. And besides they were all schismatics who ought to be brought back into the fold of Rome. They even told the soldiers that all those who died in the enterprise would *'benefit from the indulgence granted by the Pope, as though you had completed the Crusade'*. In promising this, of course, the clerics were giving the death knell to the whole Crusade.

The Pope did not forbid the proposed attack; he simply said that Christians were only to be attacked if they were actively hindering the Holy War. Since it was common knowledge throughout the West that Byzantium had never done anything but actively hinder the Holy War, that seemed like a papal blessing.

In March the leaders of the Crusaders and the Venetians met to divide up the spoils to come. A quarter of everything was to go to whoever should be elected Emperor, after the conquest. The rest was to be divided fifty/fifty between the Crusaders and the Venetians.

Crusade to the Holy Land? What Crusade to the Holy Land?

On 6 April 1203 the Crusaders began the attack. On the 12th two of the Venetian ships, the *Pilgrim* and the *Paradise*, were blown by the wind so close to a tower that they were able to get a ladder fixed to it. Then the troops swarmed onto the tower, got ladders against other towers and within a short time had broken into the city. Murzuphlus fled with his wife and family, and by the next morning the Doge and the crusading barons were ensconced in the Great Palace.

The soldiers were then told they had three days to pillage the city. Every house was open to rape and murder. In Haghia Sophia, drunken soldiers tore down the silk hangings. The iconostasis, the screen across the church, was solid silver; they tore it to pieces. A prostitute sat on the Patriarch's throne and sang ribald songs. Nuns were ravished in their convents. Children and women were left to die in the streets. The bloodshed went on and on. Even the Saracens would have been more merciful, cried the historian Nicetas Choniates.

But the booty—ah! the booty! *'Geoffrey de Villehardouin here declares that, to his knowledge, so much booty had never been*

After the Crusaders invaded and sacked the city of Constantinople, they abandoned their quest to rescue the Holy Land, returning to their homelands laden with booty.

gained in any city since the creation of the world.' No one could calculate the treasures that were looted in those three days—gold and silver, table-services and precious stones, satin and silk and the finest furs. Confronted by so much wealth, after all their delays and hardships, the Crusaders went crazy. Nor were those in holy orders exempt from the hysteria.

Abbot Martin from Paris openly threatened to kill one elderly Greek priest from the Church of the Pantocrator unless he immediately revealed the whereabouts of the most precious relics of the saints. The old man opened up an iron chest and Abbot Martin greedily plunged in both his hands. Then he and his chaplain, *'briskly tucking up their skirts, filled the folds with holy sacrilege. . . . As he hurried to the ships, he was seen by those who knew him. They asked him joyfully whether he had carried anything off. He answered with a smiling face: "We have done well". To which they replied: "Thanks be to God".'* Some of the loot remains on display to this day in Venice, including the most famous piece—the sixth-century Quadriga—the four horses from the Hippodrome, which still adorn the church of San Marco.

The Crusaders celebrated Palm Sunday with hearts full of joy. Nobody mentioned anything more about their pious urge to rescue the Holy Land or about avenging *'the outrage suffered by Our Lord'.* Boniface now owned Macedonia. Baldwin, Count of Flanders and Hainault, was elected emperor and the Byzantine Empire was divided up between him, the Marquis [Boniface of Montferrat, a famous knight of the Fourth Crusade] and the Doge of Venice.

The Fourth Crusade had done nothing whatever to harm the Moslems. But it had completed another agenda that had been part of the crusading movement from the beginning. Urban had wanted the Eastern Church to be subordinated to the Western; now it was. Bohemond [the Norman leader of the First Crusade] had dreamed of a European conquest of Byzantium; now it was conquered.

The Destruction of Constantinople

Nicetas Choniates

Nicetas Choniates, a Greek historian, described the sack of Constantinople in 1204 by the Venetians and crusaders of the Fourth Crusade. The author was outraged by the conquering soldiers' behavior as they destroyed the relics of holy martyrs, stole precious reliquaries, and dismantled precious metals from the sacred altar of the great church, Hagia (Saint) Sophia. The looters loaded the booty on mules that polluted the sacred pavement of the church. A harlot insulted Christ by sitting in the patriarch's seat and singing an obscene song.

Shocked by the intensity of the barbarians' sinful zeal and fury, Choniates related that they spread distress to every corner of the city and inflicted unspeakable grief on all levels of society; they left no place and no person untouched by their barbarity.

How shall I begin to tell of the deeds wrought by these nefarious men! Alas, the images, which ought to have been adored, were trodden under foot! Alas, the relics of the holy martyrs were thrown into unclean places! Then was seen what one shudders to hear, namely, the divine body and blood of Christ was spilled upon the ground or thrown about. They snatched the precious reliquaries, thrust into their bosoms the ornaments which these contained, and used the broken remnants for pans and drinking cups,—precursors of Anti-christ, authors and heralds of his nefarious deeds which we momentarily expect. Manifestly, indeed, by that race then, just as formerly, Christ was robbed and insulted and His garments were divided by lot; only one thing was lacking, that His side, pierced by a spear, should pour rivers of divine blood on the ground.

Nor can the violation of the Great Church[1] be listened to with equanimity. For the sacred altar, formed of all kinds of precious materials and admired by the whole world, was broken into bits and distributed among the soldiers, as was all the other sacred wealth of so great and infinite splendor.

When the sacred vases and utensils of unsurpassable art and grace and rare material, and the fine silver, wrought with gold, which encircled the screen of the tribunal and the ambo, of admirable workmanship, and the door and many other ornaments, were to be borne away as booty, mules and saddled horses were led to the very sanctuary of the temple. Some of these which were unable to keep their footing on the splendid and slippery pavement, were stabbed when they fell, so that the sacred pavement was polluted with blood and filth.

Nay more, a certain harlot, a sharer in their guilt, a minister of the furies, a servant of the demons, a worker of incantations and poisonings, insulting Christ, sat in the patriarch's seat, singing an obscene song and dancing frequently. Nor, indeed, were these crimes committed and others left undone, on the ground that these were of lesser guilt, the others of greater. But with one consent all the most heinous sins and crimes were committed by all with equal zeal. Could those, who showed so great madness against God Himself, have spared the honorable matrons and maidens or the virgins consecrated to God?

Nothing was more difficult and laborious than to soften by prayers, to render benevolent, these wrathful barbarians, vomiting forth bile at every unpleasing word, so that nothing failed to inflame their fury. Whoever attempted it was derided as insane and a man of intemperate language. Often they drew their daggers against any one who opposed them at all or hindered their demands.

No one was without a share in the grief. In the alleys, in the streets, in the temples, complaints, weeping, lamentations, grief, the groaning of men, the shrieks of women, wounds, rape, captivity, the separation of those most closely united. Nobles wandered about ignominiously, those of venerable age in tears, the rich in poverty. Thus it was in the streets, on the corners, in the temple, in the dens, for no place remained unassailed or defended the suppliants. All places everywhere were filled full of all kinds of crime. Oh, immortal God, how great the afflictions of the men, how great the distress!

1. Hagia Sophia

The University System in Thirteenth-Century Europe

Jacques Le Goff

Jacques Le Goff, a French historian, argues that as medieval European universities became influential institutions, they clashed with other powerful organizations, both secular and ecclesiastical. At the outset of the thirteenth century teaching was an ecclesiastical function under the rule of the residing bishop, who served as the university chancellor's superior. But as the university's power increased, the chancellor's interests were increasingly aligned toward the university and away from the bishop.

To maintain their autonomy, the universities also had to fight against both the interests of powerful city leaders and royal authority. Le Goff explains that the most potent weapons of the universities were strikes and secession. One advantage that the universities did enjoy was the support of the papacy, which repeatedly gave them official statutes granting independence. Le Goff reminds the reader that this pontifical support had a motive, namely an attempt to control them by making them indebted to the pope.

According to Le Goff, scattered records concerning the age of students, degrees, and curricula were imprecise and inconsistent, but there

Excerpted from Jacques Le Goff, *Intellectuals in the Middle Ages.* English Translation © 1993 Basil Blackwell. Reprinted with permission from Blackwell Publishers.

were established economic standards. A degree in the arts took six years, generally earned between the ages of fourteen and twenty. Law, medicine, and theological degrees required additional years of study.

The thirteenth century was the age of the universities because it was the age of corporations. In any town where there was a profession bringing together a large number of members, they organized to defend their interests, and to establish a profitable monopoly. This was the institutional phase of medieval urban development which solidified acquired political freedoms into communes, and economic advantages into guilds. The word freedom here is ambiguous: was it independence or privilege? The same ambiguity will be seen again in the university corporation. Corporative organization then fixed what it had consolidated. As the consequence of and authorized by progress, that organization lost its verve and succumbed to decadence. Such was the case for the universities in the thirteenth century, in accord with the trends of the age. Demographic expansion was at its height, but was slowing down; and the population of western Christian Europe would soon stabilize. The great wave of land clearing which had provided the land needed to feed this human surplus, slowed down and stopped. A surge of construction raised a series of new churches for this larger Christian population, churches showing a new spirit, but the era of the great Gothic cathedrals ended in the previous century. The university's evolution followed the same curve: after the thirteenth century, Bologna, Paris, and Oxford were never to have as many masters and students, and the university method, scholasticism, would raise no more brilliant monuments than the *summae* of Albert the Great, Alexander of Hales, Roger Bacon, St Bonaventure, and St Thomas of Aquinas.

The intellectual who established his place in the town nonetheless proved incapable, faced with the choices available to him, of choosing solutions for the future. In a series of crises which one might attribute to growth, and which were the warnings of maturity, he was unable to opt for rejuvenation, and settled into social structures and intellectual habits in which he became bogged down.

The origins of university corporations are often as obscure as those of other professional bodies. They were organized slowly, by violent, successive conquests, by chance incidents which were only so many unexpected opportunities. Statutes often belatedly sanctioned these conquests. And we are not always sure that the statutes we possess were the first. There is nothing surprising in all this. In the towns where they were formed, the universities, through the number and quality of their members, manifested a strength which worried the other powers. It was only by fighting, sometimes against ecclesiastical powers, sometimes against lay powers, that they won their autonomy.

Universities Versus Ecclesiastical Powers

University academics were clerks. The bishop of the area claimed them as subjects. Teaching was an ecclesiastical function. The bishop, head of the schools, had for a long time delegated his powers in the matter to one of his officers who was generally called an *écolâtre* in the twelfth century, and who was soon after called a chancellor. The chancellor was reluctant to relinquish any control. When that control was no longer absolute, when abbeys acquired a strong scholastic position, they created other adversaries within the university corporation. Indeed, culture was a matter of faith; the bishop insisted on retaining control of it.

In 1213 in Paris the chancellor practically lost the privilege of conferring the *license,* that is, the authorization to teach. This right was bestowed upon the university masters. In 1219, when members of the mendicant orders were admitted into the university, the chancellor attempted to oppose that innovation. In the attempt he lost his last remaining prerogatives. In 1301 he even ceased to be the official head of the schools. At the time of the great strike of 1229–31 the university was withdrawn from the jurisdiction of the bishop.

At Oxford, the bishop of Lincoln, at a distance of 120 miles from the university, officially presided over it through his intermediary, his chancellor, whereas the abbot of the monastery of Oseney and the prior of St Frideswide held only honorific positions. But soon the chancellor was absorbed by the university, elected by it, and became its officer instead of working for the bishop. . . .

Universities Versus Secular Authority

University corporations also had to fight against lay powers and primarily against royal authority. Rulers sought to lay their hands on corporations which brought wealth and prestige to their kingdoms, and which formed breeding-grounds out of which their officers and functionaries would come. Rulers wanted to impose an authority upon those inhabitants of their states, i.e., the academics of the towns in their kingdoms, an authority which, with the progress of monarchical centralization in the thirteenth century, was being increasingly felt by their subjects.

In Paris the autonomy of the university was definitively achieved after the bloody events of 1229, which set students against the royal police. In one confrontation several students were killed by the royal soldiers. Most of the university went on strike and moved to Orleans. For two years there were almost no courses given in Paris. It was only in 1231 that St Louis[1] and Blanche of Castile[2] solemnly recognized the university's independence and renewed and extended the privileges that Philip Augustus[3] had granted it in 1200.

But there were also struggles against communal power. The bourgeoisie of the commune was irritated in seeing the university population escape from their jurisdiction; they were concerned about the racket, the plundering, the crimes of certain students, and ill tolerated the fact that masters and students limited their economic power by having rents taxed, by imposing a ceiling on the price of commodities, and by having justice respected in commercial transactions.

In Paris in 1229 the royal police had to brutally intervene following brawls between students and the townsmen. In Oxford in 1214 the university took the first steps toward independence following the arbitrary hanging of two students in 1209 by townsmen exasperated after the murder of a woman. And in Bologna the conflict between the university and the townsmen was all the more violent since the commune until 1278 had governed the city almost exclusively, under the distant rule of the emperor who, in 1158, in the person of Frederick Barbarossa, had accorded privileges to masters and students. The commune had imposed perpetual residence on professors, had turned them into functionaries, and had intervened in the conferring of degrees. The increasing authority of the archdeacon limited the commune's meddling in university affairs. A series of conflicts followed by strikes and the departure of academics seeking refuge in Vicenza, Arezzo, Padua, and Siena brought the commune to terms. The last confrontation took place in 1321. The university no longer had to put up with communal interventions.

How did university corporations emerge victorious from those battles? First, through their cohesion and determination, and also by threatening to use and by effectively using those fearful weapons, the strike and secession. Civil and ecclesiastical powers found too many advantages in the presence of academics—who represented an important economic clientele, a unique breeding-ground for counselors and functionaries, a bright source of prestige—to resist these tactics of defense.

Universities and the Papacy

But more important, the academics found an all-powerful ally in the papacy.

In 1194 in Paris, Celestine III granted the corporation its first privileges, and it was primarily Innocent III and Gregory IX who assured its autonomy. In 1215 the papal legate Cardinal Robert de Courçon, gave the university its first official statutes. In 1231 Gregory IX,

1. king of France 2. mother of Louis 3. king of France

who accused the bishop of Paris of negligence and forced the king of France and his mother to give in, granted new statutes to the university through the famous bull *Parens scientiarum,* which has been called the university's "Magna Carta." As of 1229 the pontiff had written to the bishop:

> Whereas a man learned in theology is like the morning sun which shines through the fog and must illuminate his homeland with the splendor of the saints and settle discord, you were not content simply to neglect this duty, but, according to the assertions of trustworthy souls, it is due to your machinations that the river of the teaching of *"belles-lettres"* which, after the grace of the Holy Spirit, waters and fertilizes the paradise of the universal Church, has left its bed, that is, the city of Paris, where it was vigorously flowing up to now. Subsequently, divided in several places, it has been reduced to nothing, like a river which has left its bed and is divided into several creeks, dries up.

In Oxford it was likewise a legate of Innocent III, Cardinal Nicholas of Tusculum who granted the beginnings of the university's independence. Against Henry III, Innocent IV placed it "under the protection of St Peter and the Pope," and ordered the bishops of London and Salisbury to protect it against royal schemes.

In Bologna Honorius III placed the archdeacon at the head of the university who defended it against the commune. The university was definitively emancipated when in 1278 the city of Bologna recognized the pope as its ruler.

This pontifical support was a fact of primary importance. The Holy See undoubtedly recognized the importance and value of intellectual activity, but its interventions were not disinterested. If it rescued academics from secular jurisdictions, it was to place them under those of the Church: thus, to obtain that decisive support, intellectuals found themselves forced to choose the path of ecclesiastical adherence, against the strong current which was pushing them toward secularity. If the pope released the academics from the local control of the Church—not entirely, however, for we will see the importance, throughout the century, of episcopal condemnations in the intellectual realm—it was to subject them to the Holy See, to integrate them into its politics, to impose its control and its ends upon them.

Thus the intellectuals became subject, like the new religious orders, to the apostolic see which showed them favor in order to domesticate them. We know how in the course of the thirteenth century pontifical protection turned the mendicant orders away from their original principles and goals. We especially know of the reservations and the painful retreat of St Francis of Assisi in the face of his order's deviation, an order which was henceforth engaged in temporal intrigues, in the forcible repression of heretics, in Roman politics.

It was also the end of independence for the intellectuals, the end of the disinterested spirit of study and teaching. Without going as far as the extreme case of the University of Toulouse, established in 1229 upon the express request of the popes to fight against the Albeginsian heresy,[4] all universities henceforth endured that unrequested legacy. They certainly gained independence with regard to local forces which were often relatively more tyrannical, they witnessed the widening, in accordance with the growing dimensions of all of Western Christianity, of their horizons and their influence, and they were subject to a power which on many occasions proved to be quite open-minded. But they paid dearly for these gains. Western intellectuals had, to a certain extent, but most definitely, become agents of the pope. . . .

The University Program of Study

Information concerning the age of students and the number of years they studied is unfortunately imprecise and often contradictory. It has varied depending upon time and place, and scattered allusions lead us to believe that practice was often quite far from theory.

First, at what age did one enter the university, and with what intellectual baggage? Surely at a very young age, but it is here that the problem is raised: were grammar schools indeed a part of the university system, was the teaching of writing, for example, provided before a student entered the university, or, as Istvan Hajnal[5] claims, was it one of the university's essential functions? One fact is certain: the Middle Ages did not make a clear distinction in the levels of instruction. Medieval universities were not uniquely establishments of higher learning. What we consider as primary or secondary instruction was offered in part at the universities, and was controlled by them. The system of "colleges" . . . confused the issue even more by dispensing instruction to its members beginning at the age of eight.

In general one can say that at the universities basic instruction—that of the "arts"—lasted six years and was offered between the ages of fourteen and twenty; this is what the Paris statutes of Robert de Courçon stipulated. He delineated two stages in university education: the baccalaureate after around two years, and the doctorate at the end of one's studies. Medicine and law were then undoubtedly taught between the ages of twenty and twenty-five years old. The first statutes of the faculty of medicine in Paris stipulated six years of studies to obtain the license or doctorate in medicine—once the master-of-arts had been obtained. Finally, theology was a long-term proposition. Robert de Courçon's statutes ordered eight years of study and a minimum age

4. a movement that incorporated an exotic theology and protested ecclesiastical wealth 5. historian

of thirty-five to obtain the doctorate. In fact, it seems that the theologian had to study for fifteen or sixteen years: he was a mere auditor for the first six years, and then had to complete the following training: four years of Bible explication, and two years of studying and commenting on Peter Lombard's[6] *Sentences.* . . .

University Exams

Finally, there were regulations for exams and for the earning of degrees. Again, each university had its own practices, and modified them over time. Here are two typical scholarly curricula: that of the Bolognese jurist and the Parisian "artist." The new Bolognese doctor earned his degree in two stages: the exam in the strict sense (the *examen* or *examen privatum*) and the public examination (the *conventus, conventus publicus*, or *doctoratus*), which was rather a ceremony of investiture.

Some time before the private examination, the candidate was presented by the *consiliarius* of his nation to the rector, to whom he swore that he had complied with all the statutory conditions, and that he was not seeking to corrupt his examiners. In the week preceding the exam, one of the masters presented him to the archdeacon, thus guaranteeing the student's ability to undergo the trial. The morning of the exam, after attending a Mass of the Holy Ghost, the candidate appeared before the college of doctors, one of whom assigned him two passages to comment on. He went home to prepare that commentary, which he presented the same evening in a public place (most often in the cathedral), before a jury of doctors, and in the presence of the archdeacon, who could take no active part in the exam. After the required exposition he responded to the questions of the doctors, who then exited and voted. The decision being taken by a majority vote, the archdeacon then announced the results.

Having passed the exam, the candidate became a licentiate, but was not given the title of doctor and could not truly teach authoritatively until after the public exam. Driven in pomp to the cathedral on the day of the public examination, the licentiate delivered a speech and read a thesis on a point of law which he then defended against the students who attacked him, thus assuming for the first time the role of master in a university disputation. The archdeacon then solemnly conferred upon him the license to teach, and he was given the *insignia* of his function: a chair, an open book, a golden ring, and the magisterial *biretta* or beret.

6. theologian and student of Peter Abelard

The Jews and the Western Church

Ora Limor

Ora Limor writes that at the outset of the thirteenth century a papal bull, or decree, safeguarded the Jews. Moreover, papal letters to the bishops declared that nonbelievers could not be forced to believe and that they should have the right to live among Christians. Nevertheless, within a few years Jews were subjected to increased discrimination and frequently attacked. Limor explains that the Fourth Lateran Council of 1215, summoned by Pope Innocent III, established policies that would affect Jews for generations, such as restricting the interest rates money-lending Jews could charge and barring them from all jobs in which Christians would be their subordinates. Jews also were required to sew an identification badge onto their clothing, intended to distance them from Christians, with whom they were not to mix. To make matters worse, Inquisition regulations of the thirteenth century marked Christians who accepted Judaism and Jews who converted to Christianity and then returned to Judaism as heretics and condemned them to burn at the stake. Additionally, sexual relations between Jews and Christians were considered heresy.

Limor argues that both Jews and Christians debated their respective positions, each convinced of their absolute truth. According to Limor, a dramatic change in the disputes occurred in the thirteenth century when the Franciscan and Dominican Christian orders claimed that the modern Jew was no longer the Jew of the Old Testament, but rather a Jew of the Talmud, a work believed to be heresy and blasphemous. Limor concludes that after the Fourth Lateran Council a new and damaging diabolical image emerged of the Jew who was seen as "other," accused of witchcraft and of using human blood for sorcery.

Ora Limor teaches medieval studies at the Open University of Israel.

Excerpted from Ora Limor, "A Rejected People," in *The Illustrated History of the Jewish People*, edited by Nicholas de Lange. Copyright © 1997 Ora Limor. Reprinted with permission from Harcourt, Inc.

Throughout the Middle Ages, the papacy maintained its traditional tolerant attitude toward the Jews as formulated by Augustine.[1] The practical aspects of this policy were stated in papal bulls and encyclicals addressed to secular rulers or to Catholic clergy, enjoining them to protect the Jews under their jurisdiction. The most famous of these documents is the bull *Sicut Iudeis,* issued in 1120. From the twelfth to the fifteenth centuries, twenty-three popes reissued the bull, and it was even included in the Canon Law under the title *Constitutio pro Iudeis.* It stresses that the fundamental rights of the Jews must be safeguarded:

> This is why, although they prefer to persist in their obstinacy rather than acknowledge the words of the prophets and the eternal secrets of their own scriptures, thus arriving at an understanding of Christianity and salvation, nevertheless, in view of the fact that they have begged for our protection and our aid and in accordance with the clemency which Christian piety imposes, we, following in the footsteps of our predecessors, . . .grant their petition and offer them the shield of our protection.

> We decree that no Christian shall use violence to force them into baptism while they are unwilling and refuse . . . for surely none can be believed to possess the true Christian faith if he is known to have come to Christian baptism unwillingly and even against his wishes.

> Moreover, without the judgment of the authority of the Land, no Christian shall presume to wound their persons, or kill them, or rob them of their money, or change the good customs which they have thus far enjoyed in their place of habitation. Furthermore, while they celebrate their festivals, no one shall disturb them in any way by means of sticks and stones. . . . We decree that no one shall dare to desecrate or reduce a Jewish cemetery.

The Church's policies regarding the Jews were based on the consistent notion that one could not force a nonbeliever to believe. The medieval papacy, in the edict just cited and elsewhere, recognized that the Jews, despite their lack of proper belief, were entitled as a fundamental right not only to live among Christians but also to receive special protection in view of their sensitive situation, and to maintain their own religious rites.

The frequent republication of the bull *Sicut Iudeis* in the twelfth and thirteenth centuries was probably due to requests from the Jews, who saw it as protecting them from attack and persecution. Almost all thirteenth-century popes reissued the bull soon after assuming office. Innocent III, pope from 1198, appended an introduction to the

1. Theologian of Christian antiquity, 354–430

famous decree, in which he offered a theological justification for protecting the Jews: "Although the Jewish distortion of the faith is deserving of thorough condemnation, nevertheless, because the truth of our own faith is proved through them, they must not be severely oppressed by the faithful. So the prophet says, 'Thou shalt not kill them, lest in time they forget Thy Law'; or, more clearly put: Thou shalt not destroy the Jews completely so that the Christians may not possibly forget Thy Law which, though they themselves fail to understand it, they display in their books for those who do understand."

When the accusation of ritual murder and ritual cannibalism (blood libel) began to spread through Europe, *Sicut Iudeis* became the basis for papal condemnations and warnings; the popes consistently opposed the blood libel and forbade their flock to repeat the accusations—admittedly without much success. The relative failure of such means invites broader assessment: it is doubtful whether this bull and other similar ones could actually protect the Jews. They attest not so much to the conditions in the cities where the Jews lived as to papal policies. They could not halt rioting or prevent expulsions or restore forcibly converted Jews to Judaism. Rather, they should be seen as a theoretical expression of ecclesiastical tolerance. As such, their importance is undeniable, but their practical influence was hardly decisive.

The Fourth Lateran Council

A major landmark in relations between the Church and the Jews was the Fourth Lateran Council, convened in 1215 at the Lateran Palace in Rome, summoned by Pope Innocent III to discuss urgent issues then troubling Christendom. The Jewish question and Christian-Jewish relations were not among the major points on the agenda, which was primarily concerned with the doctrine of transubstantiation,[2] the spread of the Albigensian heresy—the Albigenses, a dualistic sect, maintained that matter is evil and only the human spirit good, and rejected much Christian dogma—in the south of France and methods of combating it, new calls for a crusade and so on. The council was at pains to create greater unity and uniformity in the Christian world and to achieve a sharper definition of the limits of faith. The resolutions adopted included four regulations relating to Jews, which laid down a policy that would affect Jewish life in Europe for generations to come. They imposed restrictions on the interest rates that Jews could charge and forbade them to hold positions in which Christians would be subordinate to them. They also ruled that Jews who had converted willingly to Christianity could not return to Judaism, and, finally, endeavored to reduce contacts be-

2. the belief that the bread and wine of Catholic Communion actually become the body and blood of Christ

tween Jews and Christians by requiring Jews to wear special apparel. The requirement of special dress—the most known, and most pervasive, of the council's resolutions regarding the Jews—was to influence Jewish life right into the twentieth century: "(Canon 68) There are provinces in which a difference of costume distinguishes the Jews and the Saracens[3] from the Christians, but there are provinces in which the confusion has reached such proportions that no distinction whatsoever can be made. It has therefore occurred at times, by mistake, that Christians have mixed with Jewish or Saracen women, and Jews or Saracens with Christian women. So as to remove in the future any pretext of error or mistake in connection with this deplorable licentiousness and confusion, we have decreed that in the future [Jewish and Saracen] men and women shall be differentiated at all times and in all Christian lands from other people through their dress."

This provision was applied to different degrees in different countries and regions; its most familiar—and most long-lived—manifestation was the badge worn by Jews on their outer clothes whenever they left their homes. The modern observer cannot but recall the Nazis' regulation requiring Jews in the occupied countries to wear a yellow badge in the shape of a Shield of David, inscribed with the word *Jude.* However, though this modern badge was certainly a remote descendant of the medieval one, it was quite common in the Middle Ages to show various emblems on one's dress, and indeed the Jews were not the only group identified by a special device. Neither should it be forgotten that the Jews, for their part, were interested in maintaining their identity and avoiding Christian company. Of course, for Christians the wearing of a special badge marked one's membership in a certain knightly order or guild; it was voluntary and indicated the bearer's high station or exclusive status. The Jewish badge, by contrast, was compulsory and, though initially designed to set the Jews apart, in the final analysis it marked them as inferior. Little wonder, therefore, that the Jews made every effort to oppose the decree and, risking punishment, refrain from wearing the badge, but they were not always successful.

The Inquisition and the Jews

The Inquisition's attitude to the Jews is of particular interest. The Inquisition was established by the papacy in the thirteenth century in order to combat various heresies within Christendom, so that the Jews were not originally within its terms of reference. Nevertheless, relapsed converts to Christianity, even if converted under duress, were declared heretics and therefore subject to the jurisdiction of the

3. nomadic Arabs

Inquisition. Jews who aided them were also punished. Christian converts to Judaism, too, were considered heretics and accordingly condemned to burn at the stake—the specific punishment meted out to heretics from the thirteenth century on. Jewish communities that rendered them assistance were severely punished—they had to pay large sums of money, so that the communities were completely impoverished. Pope Clement IV, in a bull *Turbato corde* issued in 1267, ordered the Dominicans and Franciscans[4] to investigate reports that Jews were trying to convert Christians. Other popes repeated this order during the thirteenth century. Sexual relations between Jews and Christians were considered heresy, and those involved could expect to be burned at the stake.

Some of the inquisitors tried to extend the Church's jurisdiction in relation to the Jews. They argued that Jews who maligned Christianity should also be punished as heretics, and that the Church was entitled to interfere in Jewish matters when the Jews themselves violated their own law—that is, to define heresy in Jewish terms. Interference of this sort occurred in 1232, during the Maimonidean Controversy (disputes around philosophical and religious themes in Maimonides'[5] writings), and during the Disputation of Paris in 1240, where the Talmud was accused of heresy—meaning heresy against the Old Testament. In both cases the intervention resulted in the burning of Jewish books.

Generally, however, the old rule was observed: the Church did not intervene in the Jews' internal affairs as long as they presented no threat to Christianity. In Spain, too, the Inquisition was concerned mainly with *conversos*, that is, converts to Christianity, not with Jews, as we shall see later.

Jewish/Christian Disputations

Christianity and Judaism were both convinced of their absolute truth. Each of the two religions was certain that it, and it alone, held the key to the divine message, while the other was in grave error. The conflict assumed various forms and found expression in various literary genres, ranging from explicitly polemical tracts, listing arguments in favor of the writer's side and against his opponent, to exegetical works, mainly biblical commentaries, historiography and belles lettres. Artistic media were also brought into play [such as] the figure of Synagoga, a polemical Christian portrayal of Judaism. Synagoga was not always a dejected, defeated figure, as she is, for example, at Strasbourg Cathedral. She was sometimes shown with a serpent bound about her eyes, as though blinded by a satanic agency. Jews might also be represented by biblical "villains," of whom the

4. religious orders of friars 5. Jewish philosopher

most prominent is Cain, shown wearing a Jewish hat—a figure of evil second only to that of Judas Iscariot, the archetypal representative of the diabolical, treacherous Jew. Indeed, such artistic argumentation was accessible to a larger, more varied Christian audience than polemical literature, which was aimed primarily at the intellectual clergy. Jewish polemical works were largely a mirror image of the Christian works, both in the characteristics of the genre and its content.

Besides the polemic literature, there were also physical, face-to-face confrontations of Jews and Christians. The very nature of the considerable similarity in the two religions' conceptual worlds, as against the sharp disagreement over the interpretation of those concepts, coupled with the fact that Jews and Christians were constantly rubbing shoulders with one another, produced frequent exchanges on matters of faith. Of course, we have little information about such private arguments. Not so the great public disputations, which were carefully planned by the Christian side and possessed far-reaching propaganda significance. . . .

The Jewish-Christian dispute revolved around several areas of contention: the Deity (is God one or three? can God be divine and human at one and the same time?); religious law (should the precepts of Mosaic Law be observed as they stand, or were they abrogated by the coming of Jesus, or were they perhaps always intended merely allegorically?); the Messiah (had he already come, as the Christians claimed, or would he come only in the future, as the Jews believed?); the meaning of Jewish history—that is, why had the Jews languished in exile so many years (for their sin of deicide, said the Christians; for reasons known only to God, retorted the Jews). And there were other subjects too. The furor of the dispute did not lessen with the elapsing years. Scholars have repeatedly come back to the question of the degree to which the written polemical tracts reflect arguments that were actually presented at the face-to-face disputations. Many authorities hold that these tracts were written primarily for internal apologetical reasons; the Jews wrote them for their brethren, to provide them with ammunition for their own disputations, and the Christians wrote them for their co-religionists, to provide them with ammunition against the Jews. However, even if one allows the truth of this argument, it is clear that the great quantity of polemical works written during the Middle Ages and the early Modern Era, mainly on the Christian side, is indicative of the fact that the problem refused to go away.

The thirteenth century saw a change in the nature of the disputations. Up to that time the Christians had drawn their proofs for the truth of Christianity from the Old Testament; now, however, the Talmud provided the grounds for the attacks on Judaism and, consequently, for the substantiation of Christianity. This shift in itself implied another difference: as long as they were citing the Bible, the Christians were fighting the Jews, as it were, on familiar ground, for the Bible was available in a Latin translation, its content was known and there was a standard interpretation. When it came to the Talmud, however, the Christian world was dependent mainly on apostates (such as Petrus Alphonsi at the beginning of the twelfth century or Pablo Christiani in the mid-thirteenth century), who were well versed in Hebrew and familiar with the world of the Talmud and the Midrash. Even learned Christians, however knowledgeable in Hebrew and however capable of reading the Bible in the original tongue, could not approach the talmudic literature unaided. One might say that the entry of the Talmud into the arena of the interfaith dispute in the thirteenth century, through the activities of apostates, vigorously encouraged by the Franciscans and Dominicans, was responsible for a sharp change in Christian Europe's attitude to the Jews. Once they had "discovered" the Talmud, European Christians came to realize that the Jews were not what they had thought them to be. No biblical Jews were these, descendants of the Jews described in the Old Testament; they were talmudic Jews, their behavior dictated by laws and regulations set out in the Talmud—a work fraught, so Christians believed, with heresy and blasphemy. . . .

The Diabolical Image of Jews

Beginning in the eleventh and twelfth centuries, Christian Europe embarked on a process of exclusion, marginalization and, finally, persecution of heretics, Jews, lepers and other groups. The consolidation of Christian society and emergence of a well-defined European consciousness were accompanied by social classification and the use of similar rhetoric in relation to various groups of "others," who were seen as enemies, contaminating society itself. These groups were required to wear distinctive dress for the protection of the true believers. After the Fourth Lateran Council and the formulation of the doctrine of Transubstantiation, the heretics and, later, also the Jews were accused of desecrating the Host, as we will see. Moreover, both Jews and heretics were accused of witchcraft and of using human blood for sorcery. Gradually, there emerged a diabolical image of Judaism, which found expression in art, literature and popular belief.

The deterioration in the Jewish condition at this time was due to a combination of socioeconomic and ideological reasons. As cities developed, and with them the Christian merchant guilds, which were closed to any non-Christian, Jews were gradually forced out of local and international trade. They became mainly money-lenders, a profession off limits to Christians because of the Church's persistent objection to lending at interest. In so doing they played a vital—but detested—economic role and became a symbol of negative power, both economic and religious. The transition to a profit-based economy produced guilt feelings in Christians, because of the growing gap between religious imperatives and economic behavior. Christian guilt was projected onto the Jews, who now became the scapegoat of a changing, troubled society.

Rising tensions in the cities gave birth to two new religious orders, the Franciscans and the Dominicans, both founded at the beginning of the thirteenth century, who made it their business to purge Christianity of all heresies. As we have already seen, their struggle involved vigorous missionizing among the Jews, compulsory sermons in synagogues, enforced religious disputations and sometimes incitement for its own sake.

It was no accident that the friars associated Judaism with heresy. Since the earliest centuries of Christianity, despite the legal and theological differentiation between Jews and heretics, both ecclesiastical literature and popular perception not infrequently lumped the two groups together; Jews were suspected of cooperating with heretical sects and even inspiring them. Each party in the early Christological debates tended to accuse the other of Judaizing. Complaints of Jewish influence were leveled against later medieval heresies—the Passagii (a sect in twelfth-century Lombardy that wished to return to Old Testament religiosity), the Albigenses and the Waldenses (a Christian community created by Peter Valdes from Lyons in the twelfth century); such influence has never been verified. At any rate, the comparison of Jews and heretics in the mendicant preachers' sermons generally signaled a deterioration in the situation of the Jews and contributed to their diabolical image.

Decree of the Hanseatic League

The Hanseatic League

The Hanseatic League was a collection of German cities that banded together to promote and protect the flow of trade. The powerful alliance had its origins in a 1241 agreement between the German cities of Hamburg and Lübeck to work in unison to protect against robbers. In this agreement the two cities agreed to share expenses to stop crime and punish offenders in either place.

In later Hanseatic League decrees, 1260 to 1264, the participating cities extended their agreement to cover such inter-city problems as pirates at sea, kidnapping, marriage laws, war, and the mutual sentencing of robbers.

The advocate, council and commune of Lübeck. . . . We have made the following agreement with our dear friends, the citizens of Hamburg.

1. If robbers or other depredators attack citizens of either city anywhere from the mouth of the Trave river to Hamburg, or anywhere on the Elbe river, the two cities shall bear the expenses equally in destroying and extirpating them.

2. If anyone who lives outside the city, kills, wounds, beats, or mishandles, without cause, a citizen of either city, the two cities shall bear the expenses equally in punishing the offender. We furthermore agree to share the expenses equally in punishing those who injure their citizens in the neighborhood of their city and those who injure our citizens in the neighborhood of our city.

Excerpted from editors Oliver J. Thatcher and Edgar H. McNeal, *A Source Book for Medieval History.* Copyright © 1905 Charles Scribner's Sons.

3. If any of their citizens are injured near our city [Lübeck], they shall ask our officials to punish the offender, and if any of our citizens are injured near their city [Hamburg], they shall ask their officials to punish the offender. . . .

We wish to inform you of the action taken in support of all merchants who are governed by the law of Lübeck.

(1) Each city shall, to the best of her ability, keep the sea clear of pirates, so that merchants may freely carry on their business by sea. (2) Whoever is expelled from one city because of a crime shall not be received in another. (3) If a citizen is seized [by pirates, robbers, or bandits] he shall not be ransomed, but his sword-belt and knife shall be sent to him [as a threat to his captors]. (4) Any merchant ransoming him shall lose all his possessions in all the cities which have the law of Lübeck. (5) Whoever is proscribed in one city for robbery or theft shall be proscribed in all. (6) If a lord besieges a city, no one shall aid him in any way to the detriment of the besieged city, unless the besieger is his lord. (7) If there is a war in the country, no city shall on that account injure a citizen from the other cities, either in his person or goods, but shall give him protection. (8) If any man marries a woman in one city, and another woman from some other city comes and proves that he is her lawful husband, he shall be beheaded. (9) If a citizen gives his daughter or niece in marriage to a man [from another city], and another man comes and says that she is his lawful wife, but cannot prove it, he shall be beheaded.

This law shall be binding for a year, and after that the cities shall inform each by letter of what decisions they make.

Asia

The thirteenth century in Asia is defined by military conquest. More specifically, the thirteenth century witnessed the last major conflict of an age-old struggle between nomadic cultures and sedentary, agriculturally based civilizations. The Mongols, a nomadic people out of the eastern steppes of Central Asia (present-day Mongolia), won staggering victories over highly sophisticated farming and trading civilizations like China. The Mongol warriors' willingness to live sparsely off the land, survive extremes in weather, and fight from horseback gave these fierce fighters an edge as they made a supreme attempt at world domination.

In 1206, after years of inner turmoil and bloodshed, a military genius named Genghis Khan ruthlessly pulled together an intimidating Mongol fighting machine. Genghis was able to unify the warring Mongol tribes and impose strict laws, establish a culture based on obedience, and command the loyalty of his generals. In 1211 Genghis attacked China, toppling Peking in 1215. The Mongols believed that they were ordered by God to rule the earth at any cost; hence, almost any atrocity could be justified as service to a divine plan. The Mongol fighting forces were pitiless and their reputation terrorized the Asian world. After China, Genghis Khan attacked the Islamic states, scoring one victory after another, each characterized by looting, burning, and slaughter. When Genghis Khan died in 1227 he was, arguably, one of the most successful world conquerors in history.

After Genghis Khan's death his third son, Ogedei, was elected as the Great Khan. Ogedei continued his father's world campaign by pushing in three directions: farther into China, farther into the Middle East, and into Europe. The general of the European campaign, Batu, a grandson of Genghis Khan, attacked Russia in the winter of 1237, earning the only successful winter invasion in Russian history. The Mongol army moved through Kiev into Poland, Hungary, and the Balkans. Perhaps all of Europe would have fallen to the Mongols had not the death of Ogedei required Batu to return to Mongolia to safeguard his position during the transfer of power.

In China, Kublai Khan (grandson of Genghis) attacked and defeated the highly civilized Song dynasty of China. After fighting for twenty years in the rugged landscape of southern China, the victorious Kublai proclaimed his own dynasty in 1271, called the Yuan dynasty, and established his Mongol Yuan capital in Beijing. Although the Chinese were treated as an inferior caste and their land was expropriated, the government under Kublai was, in some aspects of society, actually less severe than before the takeover of the Mongols: Taxes were collected more equitably, punishments were meted out more impartially, and there was limited religious and intellectual freedom. In traditional Song culture, scholars held a place of honor and the illiterate Mongols, recognizing the value of the intellectuals, came to depend on them to do administrative tasks and serve as instructors in government-sponsored schools. The numerous Chinese literati were able to keep some of the arts flourishing by exercising intellectual influence. For example, Zhao Mengfu, a skilled poet, scholar, and painter, worked in Kublai's court as an artisan and a prominent adviser.

The Mongols also set their sights on Japan. At the outset of the thirteenth century Japan was plagued by a long and unproductive series of clan struggles. As a result, power shifted from an imperial family to the generals, called shoguns, and their warriors, called samurai. Despite Japan's militaristic society and despite a harsh peasant life, a small leisure class developed works of art in literature, pottery, painting, lacquer work, silk weaving, and flower arrangement. Merchants in the West treasured these works of art and traveled to Japan to trade with the once isolated civilization. In 1268 Kublai Khan and the Mongols attacked Japan with an armada of 450 ships. Luckily for the Japanese, a typhoon wreaked havoc on the Mongol fleet, forcing it to return to the mainland. The reprieve allowed the Japanese to refortify, stockpile weapons, and renew their border fighting forces. In 1281 a second and even larger Mongol amphibious fleet headed for Japan and once again it was hit by a typhoon, which the Japanese called kamikaze, or "divine wind." The Mongol quest for Japan failed.

Westerners knew very little of the East before the thirteenth century. But with the conquest of China and most of Asia, the Mongols opened up rugged but relatively safe trade routes for adventurous Europeans. One explorer, Marco Polo, described his travels in Asia and his service in the court of Kublai Khan in a book he titled *Description of the World*. In an attempt to assess the importance of Polo's travel reminiscences, the noted historian Daniel Boorstin argues that "his copious, vivid, and factual account of Eastern ways was the discovery of Asia."[1] Polo himself understood the potential value of his book when he wrote in its prologue, "Emperors and kings, dukes and marquises, counts, knights, and townsfolk, and all people who wish to know the various races of men and the peculiarities of the various regions of the world, take this book, take this book and have it read to you."[2]

1. Daniel J. Boorstin, *The Discoverers*. New York: Random House, 1983, p. 138 2. quoted in Boorstin, *The Discoverers*, p. 134

Mongol Expansion

Geoffrey Parker

Geoffrey Parker characterizes the Mongols as bellicose, skilled horse-archers who occupied the vast prairie grasslands of Asia called the steppe. Their great leader Genghis Khan solidified the numerous nomadic tribes of the steppe and ultimately proclaimed himself supreme ruler of the Mongol empire. In 1211 he attacked China and by 1215 he conquered Peking. Genghis Khan then turned to the Islamic states and led a successful three-year campaign in which the Mongols looted and burned settlements and slaughtered and enslaved the inhabitants. By the time Genghis Khan died in 1227 he was one of the great world conquerors, ruling an empire that stretched from the Pacific Ocean to the Caspian Sea.

Parker explains that after Genghis Khan's death, his third son, Ogedei, was elected the Great Khan. Ogedei pushed the ferocious Mongol armies in three directions: farther into China, into Persia, and into Europe. The general of the European campaign was Batu, a grandson of Genghis Khan. He attacked Russia in the winter of 1237, and, according to Parker, accomplished the only successful winter invasion in Russian history. Batu then moved into Poland and Hungary and swept along the Adriatic and into the Balkans. Europe was at his mercy, but when the Great Khan Ogedei died in 1241, Batu suddenly withdrew his forces to safeguard his own position during the transfer of power.

The other two campaigns, in China and the Islamic states, were likewise bloody and successful. Parker suggests that the Mongol conquest of Baghdad in 1258 struck a devastating blow to Arabic civilization. As in Europe, the seemingly unstoppable invasion force in the Arab states ended suddenly when the generals withdrew unexpectedly to attend to internal power struggles. Arab forces rose up and eventually defeated the remaining Mongols, while the Eurasian world was given more than twenty years of peace, providing them an opportunity to exchange goods and ideas between the Far East and the Far West. According to Parker, the Mongol influence was in decline by the end of the thirteenth century. The Mongols were illiterate and left an unsubstantial social and cultural legacy. As civilization moved forward, the once victorious Mongols were the last nomadic people to influence the civilized world.

Geoffrey Parker is a professor of military history at Yale University. He has written numerous books, including *The Spanish Armada, Europe in Crisis, 1598–1648*, and *The Thirty Years' War.*

Geographically, the vast continent of Asia falls broadly into four divisions: the northern forest, or *taiga;* the steppe, or prairie grassland; the desert; and the great river valleys of the south—the Yellow River and Yangtze, the Ganges and Indus, and the Euphrates and Tigris. The last zone provided the life-blood of the early civilizations of China, India and Mesopotamia; but the second, the steppe,was the home of the pastoral nomad. From northern China to Hungary, a distance of some 5,000 miles, pastoral nomads had lived on the steppe for centuries by raising animals, mainly horses and sheep, spending their lives wandering from place to place with their herds as they followed the pasture and the seasons.

Nomadic societies had always been both patriarchal and predatory—organized into clans which spent most of their time contesting the best grazing lands with their neighbours, or combining to plunder the fields and cities of the more sedentary people around them. So, by the very nature of his society, the nomad was compelled always to be ready for war. Since his livelihood—his herds of livestock—his home (a felt tent or *yurt*) and his family all had to move with him, there could be no walls for defence. Security depended on constant vigilance, readiness and, above all, mobility. Once the nomad had adopted the horse, the stirrup and the bow, he became a skilful horse-archer, the most formidable cavalryman in the world until modern times, with rider and horse both able to survive on the meagre resources of the wind-swept, thinly-populated steppe through even the most severe winter.

Life on the vast, open grasslands of Asia is hard and cruel. Summer lasts only three months, when from June to August the steppe blossoms into a carpet of grass and flowers. By September the cold is fierce. In October the plateaux are swept by blizzards; by November the rivers are frozen; and until the following March, snowfalls are frequent and the bare plain is swept by ferocious winds; and yet, from this harsh environment the Mongols staged their sudden, devastating and brief irruption into world history.

The Rule of Genghis Khan

Theirs was not the first empire of the steppe. In the seventh century AD, in the wake of the upheavals that destroyed the ancient world, a confederation of Turkish tribes had managed to dominate the grass-lands from the Great Wall of China to the Black Sea; but by 750 their rule had been undermined by feud and faction. For the next four centuries, no single tribe or confederation gained supremacy over the steppe. It was into this turbulent, unstable society that, about the year 1162, Temujin, the son of the chief of the Mangkhol tribe from which the Mongols take their name, was born.

At first the young man did not seem destined to be a world conqueror. After his father's murder by rivals, Temujin, his mother and six siblings were forced to fend for themselves in a country where those who could claim no tribal protection almost invariably perished. But the group somehow survived and, as Temujin grew to manhood, the renown of his exploits and achievements—which all displayed to a high degree the qualities required from a clan leader—began to attract followers. Gradually he established himself as a minor chief and, making the most of his descent from the legendary Khans of Mongolia as well as of his military prowess, he steadily extended his authority over more and more tribes, Turkish as well as Mongol. Eventually, in 1206, at a *kuriltai* (or full assembly) of the tribes, held in the heart of Mongolia on the banks of the river Onon, Temujin was proclaimed supreme ruler 'of all who dwell in tents of felt' and assumed the name Genghis Khan, 'prince of all that lies between the Oceans'. The palace of this great ruler might have been a tent; but from it, plans were laid to conquer the world.

Genghis looked first to the East. China was, at this time, divided between two hostile dynasties: the Chin, themselves formerly nomads from the steppes, in the north; and the highly civilized Sung in the south. In 1211, the Mongols attacked. After mounting a series of raids deep into the country south of the Great Wall, they decided that more was to be gained by conquest than by plunder. Three armies advanced into Chin territory and occupied large tracts of territory. But, at first, they found the defences of the Chin cities unassailable: the walls of Peking, for example, stretched for eighteen miles and were forty feet wide and forty feet high. Only when a corps of engineers, skilled in siegecraft, had been created from Chinese prisoners could Peking be blockaded and captured in 1215. It was the first of many populous capitals to feel the savage fury of fierce nomads who feared and hated a way of life they could not understand: its buildings were looted and burned; its inhabitants were enslaved or slaughtered.

After the fall of Peking, Genghis was compelled to lead his armies towards the west against the Islamic state of Khwarizm, which stretched from the Caspian Sea to the Pamir Mountains. Under its ambitious ruler, Mohammed Shah, Khwarizm had expanded considerably while the Mongols were tied down in China. Now, in 1218, Genghis demanded that Mohammed should acknowledge him as Great Khan and overlord; when he refused, and murdered the Mongol ambassadors, Genghis took the offensive and commenced a three-year campaign of sustained devastation during which most of the Khwarizmian towns were totally destroyed. At Bukhara, for example, which the Mongols reached in 1220, they first set the wooden buildings on fire and drove the inhabitants before them—as cover—in an all-out attack on the citadel. Fire-bombs and rocks were hurled in, and assaults of increasing ferocity were launched against the walls until, finally, the citadel was taken. The 30,000 defenders were slaughtered and their women and children taken as slaves, while all buildings were razed to the ground. Eventually, the Great Khan climbed into the pulpit of the city's mosque and delivered an admirably terse sermon to the surviving population: 'Oh people, know that you have committed great sins. . . . If you ask me what proof I have for these words, I say it is because I am the punishment of God. If you had not committed great sins, God would not have sent a punishment like me upon you!'

Genghis remained in the west until 1223, mopping up resistance. It was his last effective campaign. He invaded China again in 1226, but was already an old man and seriously ill: he died the next year . . . at Chen-jung, a little south of the Great Wall. On his death bed, the Khan told his courtiers, 'I die without regrets, but my spirit wishes to return to my native land'. After a brief period of mourning, his corpse was carried in state across the desolate steppes of Asia to his homeland in Mongolia, where he was buried on a mountain spur. But every living thing that crossed the procession's path was slain, with the words: 'Depart for the next world and there attend upon your dead lord'. The Mongol leader died as he had lived: amid desolation and massacre.

As a conqueror, Genghis ranks with Alexander the Great, Napoleon and Hitler. In twenty years he had extended his rule from the Pacific Ocean to the Caspian Sea—a remarkable achievement indeed. But how can it be explained? The question is easy to pose, but hard to answer, because there are so few surviving contemporary records. Before Genghis, the Mongols were a non-literate society, and only one chronicle written in their language is known to us: the anonymous *Secret History of the Mongols,* compiled in about 1240, which tells the story of Genghis. But even that source has only survived in a much later Chinese transcription and we depend, for most of our knowledge, upon the accounts written by scholars from nations conquered or attacked by the Mongols. Naturally, these were biased. For example, the detailed biography of Genghis, *The History of the World Conqueror* written in the 1250s by the Persian civil servant Juvaĭnĭ, is both illuminating and revealing; but it must be remembered that its author spent his entire life under Mongol rule. He could not afford to be too outspoken or critical. Nevertheless, Juvaĭnĭ does offer a plausible explanation for the Mongol's amazing military success. The first thing to remember, he wrote, was their sheer weight of numbers:

> The troops of the Great Khan were more numerous than ants or locusts, being in their multitude beyond estimation or computation. Detachment after detachment arrived, each like a billowing sea.

Nor was that all. Lightly equipped, fast moving, agile and efficient, the Mongols were able to cover over 100 miles a day. They were also masters of deception. Sometimes they stampeded riderless horses into the enemy to confuse them; sometimes they tied stuffed sacks to their horses to appear more numerous. They had also perfected techniques of feigned withdrawal, luring the enemy into ambush. But beyond these tactical devices, the Mongol rules of war were simple. Those who surrendered instantly became their slaves: those who did not were massacred.

Mongol Invasion of Europe

At a general assembly of Mongol leaders in 1229, the third son of Genghis, Ogedei, was elected Great Khan. He was not an outstanding soldier like his father, nor yet a gifted administrator: rather, he was chosen because his popularity and political skills made his authority acceptable to the numerous and powerful descendants of Genghis. Conquest was left to his generals, and during the reign of Ogedei the frontiers of the Mongol empire were significantly advanced in three directions: against the Chin empire in China, against the remnants of Khwarizmian power in Persia, and into Europe.

The Chin were finally overthrown by the Mongols in 1234 . . . and in the next year Ogedei planned an invasion of Europe, which was to be led by Batu, a grandson of Genghis, who became viceroy of the westernmost parts of the empire. Batu had at his disposal about 150,000 troops, at a time when no European power could muster much more than 20,000. Not surprisingly, there were frenzied attempts by rulers near the Mongol line of advance to find allies, but all of them proved vain. The Mongols' first European target was Russia and a campaign was launched over the winter of 1237–38, the frozen rivers serving as highways for the advancing cavalry. The unprepared and disunited principalities of southern Russia were unable to offer effective resistance. One by one they were destroyed, and all was laid waste. . . . Batu's achievement is all the more remarkable when we consider the fate of the winter campaigns against Russia directed by Napoleon or Hitler. His was, in fact, the only successful winter invasion of Russia in history.

The campaign was renewed in 1240 with the storming of the city of Kiev, which was rendered as desolate as Bukhara or Peking. Then followed a two-pronged assault against Poland and Hungary. The river Oder was passed at Ratibor and the Mongol army swept northwards up the river valley. Breslau was bypassed and on 9 April 1241 a combined German-Polish army was annihilated at Liegnitz. After the defeat of a second Christian army in Hungary at Mohi, a few days later, an eye witness reported: 'During a march of two days, you could see nothing along the roads but fallen warriors, their dead bodies lying about like stones in a quarry'. He might have added that the Mongols also used the severed heads of the vanquished to ornament beacons warning enemies of the fate that awaited them unless they surrendered. The invaders swept through Budapest and Gran, nearly reaching Vienna before swinging southwards along the Adriatic and into the Balkans.

However, in the winter of 1242–43, Batu unexpectedly led his troops back to the Volga. The Mongols had held Europe at their mercy: they seemed poised to conquer Europe as easily as they had subjugated Asia. Why, then, did they not press home their advantage? Most authorities agree that only the death of the Great Khan Ogedei, in December 1241, halted the Mongols' westward advance, for it unleashed disputes over the succession which persuaded Batu to return eastwards in order to safeguard his own position.

Mongol Capture of Baghdad

Eventually, Ogedei's ambitious nephew Möngke was elected Great Khan, and the Mongol chieftains decided to abandon the conquest of Europe in favour of simultaneous campaigns against the Sung empire in southern China and the Islamic states of the Near East 'as far as the borders of Egypt'. Möngke himself was to take charge of the Chinese war, while the campaign in the west was entrusted to his younger brother Hülegü. Both operations were planned with the usual Mongol thoroughness. On New Year's Day 1256, a powerful army made the passage of the river Oxus, heading for the Islamic heartland. The key to the campaign was the capture of Baghdad and the city fell early in 1258. The palace of the caliph, the Great Mosque, the tombs of the Abbasids and other public buildings were all burnt: much of the cultural accumulation of five centuries was destroyed, and a blow was struck at Arabic civilization from which it never recovered. Never had the fortunes of Islam stood at such a low level. It no longer had a recognized head or centre of unity; ferocious pagans were in occupation of its plundered metropolis; and no Muslim prince reigned east of the Tigris save by the Mongols'

permission and as their slave. Worse yet, Hülegü had been ordered
to subdue 'all the lands of the West', and it seemed that even the holy
cities of Mecca and Medina might not be safe from the sacrilegious
enemy.

But the situation was transformed once again by a distant and unexpected event. At his camp near Aleppo, early in 1260, Hülegü received
the news that his brother Möngke had died in China the previous Au-

Kublai Khan

gust. Just as Christian Europe
was saved by the death of
Ogedei in 1241, so the death
of Möngke saved Muslim
Asia. A succession dispute
broke out between the late
Khan's youngest brother,
Kublai, and a faction supporting one of his cousins.
Hülegü therefore withdrew
his army from Syria and set
out for the Mongol heartland,
leaving only a skeleton force
in the Near East. This soon
became known in Cairo and
the sultan of Egypt marched
to the defence of Islam. At
Ain Jalut, near the Sea of
Galilee, on 3 September
1260, the Mongols were de-
cisively defeated by the supe-
rior Egyptian army: the battle was a turning point in world history, for
the spell of Mongol invincibility was shattered and their westward advance was never seriously renewed.

Nevertheless, it is possible to exaggerate the importance of Ain
Jalut. Certainly it set a limit to Mongol influence in the west; but its
verdict was never subsequently challenged because the short-lived
unity of the Mongol empire really came to an end with the death of
Möngke. Kublai was eventually successful in the struggle for power
and was proclaimed the fifth (and last) Great Khan. But almost the
whole of his long life was spent in China; and, although never for-
getting that he was the grandson of the world-conqueror, his primary
objective became the restoration of the unity of the Chinese realm,
which had been shattered by the fall of the T'ang dynasty in AD 907.
In the 1270s, after more than a decade of conflict, he achieved this
aim by overthrowing the Sung empire south of the Yangtze. . . . But
outside China, Kublai exercized only a nominal suzerainty over the
other Mongol dynasties established to the west: the Il-Khans of Per-

sia, descended from Hülegü (who died in 1265); the Khans of the Golden Horde in Russia; and the rulers of the Mongol heartland.

Mongol Legacy

It is hard to reconcile the history of the civilized ruling élites of Kublai's China or Hülegü's Persia with the rapacious savages portrayed in western sources such as the 'Great Chronicle' of Matthew Paris, composed at St Albans in England in the 1240s and 1250s: 'Mongols are inhuman and beastly, rather monsters than men, thirsting for and drinking blood, tearing and devouring the flesh of dogs and men'. Yet this was not mere fantasy. The Arab historian Ibn al-Athir waited for many years before writing his history of Genghis Khan because (he told his readers) the events he had seen were too horrible to record. The Mongol conquest was, he protested, the greatest calamity that had ever befallen mankind. However, the Mongols did give the Eurasian world almost a century of peace, which permitted the exchange of goods and ideas between the far east and the far west on an unprecedented scale. The 'Silk Road' of ancient times was revived: silver and gold from Europe reached China; Chinese porcelain circulated in Europe. But the Mongols themselves had little positive to offer, and it is not easy to trace any substantial social and cultural legacy of their shattering intervention in world history. They entirely failed to match the achievements of the Arabs, who also began as illiterate nomads, but quickly absorbed the learning of their subject peoples and created an enduring civilization. Rather, the Mongol conquests can be seen as the end of an epoch. From the dawn of civilization, city-dwellers and the cultivators of the soil had been menaced by assaults from the fierce riders of the steppe. But during the life of the Mongol empire came the development of firearms: no longer would battles be decided solely by endurance, resourcefulness and speed. During the succeeding centuries Russia and China, the two nations which had suffered most from nomad aggression, steadily moved in to contain once and for all the recalcitrant herdsmen of the steppes. The Mongols were the last nomadic people to hold the civilized world to ransom.

Marco Polo Describes Kublai Khan

Marco Polo

From 1271 to 1288 the Italian adventurer Marco Polo served as an emissary for the great Mongol ruler Kublai Khan. In his work *The Travels of Marco Polo* the author explained that Khan had four wives, each with a court of 10,000 people. In addition to his wives he had many concubines who attended to Khan's needs. His legitimate wives had borne him twenty-two sons, seven of whom were kings of vast provinces.

For three months every year Kublai Khan lived at his great palace in Khan-balik, the capital of Cathay. Along a mile square perimeter wall were eight palaces, each housing different types of equipment and arms. Inside the outer perimeter was an inner wall that also had eight palaces, and within this second wall was the Great Khan's palace. The interior walls were covered in silver and gold, the ceiling was decorated with paintings, and the main reception area could seat more than 6,000 people. Khan's private rooms were at the back of the palace where he collected his goods, treasure, and concubines. Lush parks, a stocked artificial lake, and a plantation of the finest trees in the world surrounded the palace. Both the palace and its environment were designed to delight the senses, wrote Polo.

Kublai Khan, the Lord of Lords, is a man of medium height, well built but not fat, with well-formed limbs. He has a pink and white complexion like a rose, fine black eyes and a handsome nose. He has four legitimate wives. His eldest son is heir apparent to the empire. The wives are all called empresses, and each one has her own court with no less than 300 beautiful girls in attendance, as well as many eunuchs and other men and women. Each court consists of about 10,000 people. When the Great Khan wishes to sleep with one of his wives, he either goes to her room or summons her to his.

Besides his wives he has many young concubines who come from a Tartar city called Kungurat where the people are very beautiful and fair-skinned. About once every two years the Great Khan sends ambassadors to Kungurat to select the most beautiful girls and bring them to the court. Here they are looked after by ladies of the court who observe them at night in their rooms and check that their breath is sweet, that they are virgins and perfect in every way. If they are beautiful, good and healthy they are sent to attend on the Great Khan. For three days and three nights, six of these girls wait on the Khan in his room and his bed, doing whatever he requires. At the end of this time the six girls are replaced by another six, and so on in rotation.

Khan's Children

The Great Khan's four wives have borne him twenty-two sons. The eldest was called Genghis after the illustrious Genghis Khan and he was to inherit his father's empire. But he died, leaving a son called Temur who, being the son of the Khan's eldest son, will succeed his grandfather. Temur is wise and courageous and has already proved himself in battle.

The Great Khan's concubines have given him a further twenty-five sons, all good and brave soldiers. Every one of these is a powerful lord.

Of his twenty-two legitimate sons, seven are kings of vast provinces which they rule wisely and well. This is not surprising, for their father is wise and gifted, the best ruler the Tartars have ever had.

Let us now turn to the court and how the Great Khan lives.

Khan's Palace

For three months every year Kublai Khan lives in the capital of Cathay, at Khan-balik, where he has a great palace. It is surrounded by a square wall, each side of which is a mile long. The wall is very thick and ten paces high, painted white and crenellated. At each of the four corners of the square there is a splendid and beautiful palace where the Great Khan's arms are stored. Half-way along each side of the square there is another similar palace, making eight in all. Every palace houses different equipment. For example, in one there is harness for the horses; in another there are bows, ropes, arrows, quivers and all the implements for archery; in a third there are breastplates and armour made of boiled leather; and so it goes on.

There are five gates in the south side of the wall. The central one is only opened for the Great Khan himself. Two small gates on either side of the main gate and two large ones near the corners of the wall are for citizens and other people.

Inside this wall is another one, slightly longer than it is wide. It has eight palaces like those in the outer wall, and, like the outer wall, it has five gates in the south side. There is one door in each of the other three sides of both walls.

Within the second wall is the Great Khan's palace—the biggest palace ever to be seen. It abuts onto the northern wall, but to the south is a wide open space where barons and soldiers parade. It is built on only one floor, with a very high roof, and is raised at least ten spans from the ground, surrounded by a marble wall two paces wide within which are the foundations of the palace. The protruding edge of the wall provides a terrace on which people can walk round the palace. The outside edge of the wall supports a very fine loggia on columns. On each side of the palace a large marble staircase leads up to the top of the wall, forming entrances to the palace.

The walls inside are covered with silver and gold and there are paintings of horsemen, dragons and every kind of bird and animal. The vaulted ceiling is also entirely covered with paintings and gold ornamentation. The main reception room can seat more than 6,000 people. There is an overwhelming number of rooms; no architect in the world could have designed the palace better. The roof is beautifully painted in many colours—vermilion, green, blue, yellow and so forth—so that it shines like a jewel and can be seen from afar. This roof is solidly built to withstand the passage of time.

In the rear of the palace are large halls and rooms containing the Great Khan's private possessions—his personal treasure, gold and silver, precious stones and pearls, silver and gold vases. His concubines live in this part of the palace and his private apartments are also here.

Between the inner and outer walls are parks planted with beautiful trees, where white harts, musk deer, squirrels and many other animals live. The paths which cross the fields are paved and raised at least two cubits so that they are never muddy and puddles cannot form, the water draining off into the fields where the grass grows thick and green.

Between the two walls on the north-west side there is a deep, wide and very well-built artificial lake which is fed by a small river.

Kublai Khan has stocked the lake with many kinds of fish. Iron grills at the river's entrance to the lake and at its outlet prevent the fish from swimming away. Between the walls to the north the Great Khan has had a hillock made from the soil excavated from the lake. It is a good 100 paces high, a mile in circumference, and covered in evergreen trees. If the Great Khan learns of a beautiful tree, he has it dug up, its roots still in earth, and carried to the hill by an elephant. He will have trees of any size transplanted and has a plantation of the finest trees in the world. The whole hillock is covered with a precious bright-green powder, so that not only the trees, but everything which meets the eye is green; hence its name, the 'Green Mount'. And at the top of the Green Mount is a green palace. The hillock, the trees and the palace are so beautiful that they delight all who see them. Indeed, Kublai Khan had them put there for this reason.

The Chinese Literati Under Mongol Rule

Patricia Buckley Ebrey

Patricia Buckley Ebrey writes that through the course of four centuries China was conquered by three Asian tribal peoples: the Khitans' Liao dynasty, 907–1125; the Juchens'Chin dynasty, 1125–1234; and the Mongol Yuan dynasty, 1276–1368. Kublai Khan, the grandson of the great Genghis Khan, led the conquest of China and its ruling Sung dynasty, and established the Yuan dynasty with Peking as his capital.

The Mongols did not disrupt some aspects of Chinese cultural life but Chinese land was expropriated, taxation was high, and native Chinese were treated as an inferior caste. To preserve the privileges of the conqueror, all three alien rulers classified and categorized the Chinese by occupation and ethnicity. Chinese scholars, who held a place of honor during the Sung dynasty, were used by the illiterate Mongols to do administrative paperwork and serve as instructors at government-sponsored academies. The ranks of displaced Chinese literati were able to keep some of the arts flourishing, particularly drama. One of the most notable names of the literati is Zhao Mengfu, who as a member of the conquered Sung imperial clan was skilled in poetry, painting, and calligraphy. Eventually, he worked with Kublai's court as a scholar, painter, art collector, and adviser. His second wife, Guan Daosheng, is recognized as the first woman in China to attain fame as a painter.

Patricia Buckley Ebrey is a professor of East Asian studies at the University of Illinois at Urbana-Champaign. She has written extensively about Asia in her books *The Inner Quarters: Marriage and the Lives of Chinese Women in the Sung Period* and *Chinese Civilization: A Sourcebook.*

Editor's note: There is no clear way to translate some sounds of Chinese into English. The People's Republic of China has an official translation system known as pinyin. Another translation system called Wade-Giles and traditional, Anglicized pronunciations add to the confusion for readers. Patricia Buckley Ebrey uses the pinyin system while the editors use conventional spellings where possible: Khubilai=Kublai, Song=Sung, Chinygis=Genghis, and Jurchen=Juchen.

It was not until Chinggis's grandson Khubilai (r. 1260–94) came to power that the conquest of the Song[1] began in earnest. Before succeeding to the title of great khan, Khubilai had ruled a prefecture in Hebei as an appanage and thus knew something of Chinese ways. He had Chinese as well as Uighur and Central Asian advisors, and even knew a little spoken Chinese. In 1264 he transferred the capital from Karakorum in Mongolia to Beijing, known then as Dadu, and in 1271 he adopted a Chinese name for his dynasty, Yuan, and instituted Chinese court rituals.

China south of the Yangzi had never been captured by non-Chinese from the steppe, in large part because the rivers, canals, and streams of the region posed an effective barrier to cavalry forces. But on the advice of a surrendered Song commander, the Mongols began the construction of a river fleet. In 1268 they set siege to Xiangyang, a city on the Han river in Hubei recognized by both sides as the key to control of the Yangzi valley. Both sides were equally determined to win, and the siege lasted five years. Thousands of boats and tens of thousands of troops were involved on both sides. The Mongols employed Chinese, Korean, Jurchen, Uighur, and Persian experts in naval and siege warfare. Muslim engineers designed artillery that sent a barrage of rocks weighing up to a hundred pounds each. The Chinese started with substantial food stores, but had to run the blockade to get in supplies of salt and other essentials, leading to many naval engagements on the river.

The Song did not lack officials and generals devoted to the cause of stemming the Mongol onslaught, but co-ordination of their efforts was poor. The emperor at this time was a child, and the highest officials got caught up in opposing each other's plans. In 1275, after the Mongol armies crossed the Yangzi, Empress Dowager Xie is-

1. ruling Chinese dynasty, A.D. 907–1276

sued an appeal to the populace to rise up and fight the barbarians, and within a couple of months 200,000 soldiers had been recruited. But even this force could not counter the Mongols' scare tactics; during their advance towards Hangzhou they ordered the total slaughter of the population of the major city of Changzhou. Empress Dowager Xie surrendered in hopes of sparing the people of the capital of a similar fate. Three years later, in 1279, the Mongols were able to defeat the last of the loyalists in a naval battle off the coast of Guangdong during which the last of the Song princes drowned.

By the time the Mongols had conquered the Song, there was no longer a pan-Asian Mongol empire. Much of Asia was in the hands of Mongol successor states, but these were generally hostile to each other. Khubilai was often at war with the Khanate of Central Asia, then held by his cousin Khaidu, and he had little contact with the Khanate of the Golden Horde in south Russia. In these other areas the Mongols tended to merge with the Turkish nomads already there and, like them, to convert to Islam. Thus, from Khubilai's time on China proper was united with Mongolia, Manchuria, and Tibet, but not with Persia, Iraq, or Russia.

Like the Khitans, the Mongols resisted assimilation. Although the Mongol rulers developed a taste for the material fruits of Chinese civilization, they purposely avoided many Chinese social and political practices. The rulers conducted their business in the Mongol language and spent their summers in Mongolia. Khubilai discouraged Mongols from marrying Chinese and took only Mongol women into the palace. Some Mongol princes preferred to live in tents erected in the palace grounds rather than in the grand palaces constructed at Beijing. Mongols continued to choose their rulers through competition, often bloody. As recorded in the Chinese history of the Yuan dynasty, succession after Khubilai is a sordid tale of assassinations, *coups d'etat,* enthronements of youthful incompetents, fratricide, and domination by nobles.

Cultural Life Under Alien Rule

Under these alien rulers, the Chinese were not forced to adopt the customs of their conquerors. Chinese cultural life continued, much as it had under the Northern Dynasties, with members of the Chinese elite continuing to read and write books and ordinary Chinese continuing to worship gods of their choice in their own ways. To Song literati, the culture of the Chinese living under the Liao, Jin, or early Yuan[2] was rather provincial, but that did not make it non-Chinese.

Still, it would be difficult to argue that ordinary Chinese fared as well under these alien rulers as under earlier native dynasties. Large

2. Liao dynasty, 907–1125; Jin or Chin dynasty, 1125–1234; Yuan dynasty, 1276–1368

numbers had their lands expropriated or were forced into serfdom or slavery, sometimes transported far from home. Taxation, especially under the Mongols, was often ruinous. The economy of north China seems to have taken a downward turn that took centuries to reverse. Added to this was the indignity of being treated as a legally inferior caste. The Venetian merchant Marco Polo, who spent twenty years in Mongol-ruled China (1275–95), found ethnic animosity intense. 'All the Cathaians detested the rule of the great khan because he set over them Tartars [i.e. Mongols], or still more frequently Saracens [i.e. Muslims], whom they could not endure, for they treated them just like slaves.'

Classification of Society

Since all three sets of conquerors were interested in maximizing their revenues, they did not purposely damage the economy. All three encouraged trade beyond their borders, the Jin managing extensive officially sanctioned trade with the Southern Song, and the Mongols encouraging trade throughout Eurasia. The Jurchen allowed the circulation of Khitan and Song money and issued their own currency, including paper money, which, however, suffered from serious inflation after 1190. The Mongols similarly tried to maintain the existing paper currency system and even allowed conversion of Song paper money into Yuan currency. They were no more expert than the Jurchen in its management, however, and inflation became ruinous by the fourteenth century. The Mongols, of course, fostered north-south trade within China by reunifying the country. Added to this, they rebuilt the northern section of the Grand Canal, inoperative since Northern Song times, and extended it to the capital they had built at Beijing.

None of the three conquest dynasties aimed at as open or mobile a society as the Song, preferring to place people in hereditary occupational and ethnic categories. Ethnic divisions were codified to preserve the conquerors' privileges. At times the rulers' greatest concern was to prevent their own people from being assimilated into Chinese culture, at other times, to prevent Chinese from learning their language and adopting their identity. Intermarriage was usually discouraged but certainly occurred. Chinese were sometimes encouraged to learn the conqueror's language (as it demonstrated the conqueror's dominance), and sometimes discouraged (as it might undermine their privileges). During the Yuan period, the ethnic hierarchy was particularly complex, with the Mongols the most privileged, then allies of the Mongols from areas outside China (Uighurs, Turks, Tibetans, Tanguts, Persians, Central Asians, called collectively *semu*), then former subjects of the Jin (Chinese and sinified Khitans and Jurchens, called Hanren), with the bottom occupied by former subjects of Song (called 'southerners'). This system of classification affected methods of taxation, judicial process, and appointment to office. Chinese in north China, for instance, were taxed by household in ways that reflected Jin practice, whereas Chinese in south China were taxed by land owned, following Song precedents. Each ethnic group was judged and sentenced according to its own legal traditions, so that, for instance, the Chinese, but no other ethnic groups, were tattooed if convicted of theft.

Other ethnic distinctions were clearly based on the fear that the Chinese were the most likely of all the Mongols' subjects to rebel. Chinese, for instance, were forbidden to congregate in public or to own weapons. Khubilai even prohibited Chinese from dealing in bamboo since it could be used for the manufacture of bows and arrows. Chinese were subject to severe penalties if they fought back when attacked by a Mongol; by contrast, Mongols who murdered Chinese could get off by paying a fine. Probably because Chinese so outnumbered them, the Mongols were particularly vigilant in their efforts to keep the Chinese from trying to pass as Mongols and prohibited the taking of Mongol names.

Hereditary rank and station were a normal part of the social structure of these nomadic peoples, so they fostered it to make society more stable, but for China it was a regressive step. The Mongols went the furthest in this regard, registering the population into hereditary statuses by occupation, such as ordinary farmers, scholars, physicians, astrologers, soldiers, military agricultural workers, artisans, salt producers, and miners. Specialized occupational groups were required to provide unpaid services needed by the state according to rotational quotas and to earn their living during the rest of the year. The rigidity of the system led to widespread absconding by families unable to provide the required services.

Chinese Adaptation to Alien Rule

The Chinese may not have welcomed alien rule but at all social levels they found ways to adapt creatively to their new situations. The Khitan, Jurchen, and Mongol rulers all needed men capable of handling the paperwork that made centralized bureaucratic government possible, and for this purpose functionaries, whom the Chinese literati dismissed as 'clerks', could be just as useful as men who had studied the classics. But scholars also found employment, if somewhat more slowly, and at lower levels than they would have liked. During the Yuan period, Chinese scholars in the north took to serving the Mongols more readily than those in the south. They were already accustomed to rule by non-Han conquerors, and saw that Mongol rule would be more palatable if Chinese scholars were the administrators. Moreover, they anticipated that the Mongols would gradually become more sinified as the Jurchens had, and could view themselves as shielding Chinese society from the most brutal effects of Mongol rule. Scholars like Xu Heng devoted their lives to teaching the Mongol rulers Chinese principles of the moral basis of politics. In the south, where the literati had identified so strongly with resistance to the Mongols, accommodation was slower. Still, as southern Chinese literati came to realize that Mongol dominance was not to be an ephemeral event, more and more accepted posts where they could put their learning to use, particularly by serving as instructors at government-sponsored academies. . . .

Chinese Drama in the Yuan Dynasty

Those southern literati who could not or would not work for the Mongols often supported themselves as doctors, fortune-tellers, Daoist priests, teachers of children, or playwrights. This abundant supply of talented and educated men seems to have proved beneficial to the literary art of drama, which flourished in this period. The presence of an alien elite controlling the government did not diminish the prestige of the literati within Chinese society, and they continued to be accepted by ordinary Chinese as the natural leaders of local society, active in local defence and kinship organization. Educated men could also concentrate on their cultural responsibilities, looking on themselves as trustees of the Confucian tradition. In Yuan times, in particular, academies flourished as alternative centres of cultural life, beyond the scope of state domination. These were places where scholars could attempt to assert the importance of civil as opposed to military values, and to sustain confidence in their own moral and intellectual autonomy. . . .

The Career of Zhao Mengfu

The decision to take up service under the Mongols was not an easy one for subjects of the Song. The conflicting pressures they experienced can be illustrated by the career of Zhao Mengfu (1254–1322), a member of the Song imperial clan (an eleventh-generation descendant of the founding emperor). Too young to have served in office under the Song, he had, however, enrolled in the Imperial Academy in Hangzhou. For ten years after the fall of Hangzhou, Zhao kept to himself and his circle of talented friends interested in poetry, paintings, and calligraphy, known as the 'Eight Talents' of Wuxing. Several of them had lost their property in the wars and relied on patrons, donations, or teaching to subsist. They saw painting in archaic styles as a way to express longing for the past and disapproval of the present.

In 1286, in an attempt to win over the southern literati, Khubilai sent a southerner in his employ to recruit eminent scholars in the south. Zhao was among some two dozen who agreed to travel north. After his decision became known, there were friends who refused to speak to him and members of the Song imperial clan who no longer recognized him as a relative.

Zhao quickly gained favour with Khubilai, which enabled him to speak up for Confucian values at court. He made bold proposals on currency reform, did all he could to help bring about the downfall of the notoriously corrupt Tibetan chief minister, Sangha, and argued that literati should be exempt from corporal punishment. By 1316 he had risen to the high post of president of the Hanlin Academy.

For men like Zhao, getting to see north China—to them the 'central plains', the heartland of Chinese culture—compensated a little for the humiliation of serving conquerors. During his first decade in office Zhao travelled over much of north China on various official business and gathered a large collection of paintings by Tang and Northern Song masters, paintings no one in the south had ever had a chance to see. This experience made it possible for him to break with Southern Song painting styles and gain fresh inspiration from earlier masterpieces. When he returned to Hangzhou to visit his old friends, he described for them what he had seen in the north and even painted a picture of one man's ancestral home in Shandong for him.

On a side note, Zhao's second wife, Guan Daosheng, was the first woman in China to attain fame as a painter. She was noted for her paintings of bamboo, orchids, plum blossoms, and Buddhist figures. In the epitaph Zhao Mengfu wrote for her, he reported that the Mongol emperor once asked for a piece of her calligraphy.

The Advice of Yeh-lü Ch'u-ts'ai

Sung Lien

In the dynastic history *Yüan shi*, roll 146, historian Sung Lien wrote about a non-Mongol named Yeh-lü Ch'u-ts'ai who advised the Great Kahn Ogodei, leader of the Mongol conquerors of China. Sung Lien reported that Yeh-lü Ch'u-ts'ai skillfully used reason to persuade the Mongol ruler to see things from a different perspective. When the city of Kaifeng was captured, Yeh-lü Ch'u-ts'ai convinced the Great Khan Ogodei to spare the people so there would be workers to farm and artisans to provide goods. Because of Yeh-lü Ch'u-ts'ai the Mongol leader also relaxed the enforcement of his policy to kill the families of anyone who sheltered an army deserter.

Yeh-lü Ch'u-ts'ai disagreed with the Mongol generals about employing Chinese and Muslims in distant wars. He convinced the Great Khan that the long journey, the unfamiliar climates, and a susceptibility to disease would weaken the army. Because of his reasoning, the Great Khan dropped the idea. He even convinced the Great Khan to limit his drinking by showing him a ladle eroded by strong wine. Once when Great Khan Ogodei was seriously ill, Yeh-lü Ch'u-ts'ai argued that heaven would show mercy if the ruler ordered a general clemency for prisoners. The Great Khan agreed and he recovered the next day. Using his logic and persuasion skills, Yeh-lü Ch'u-ts'ai worked from the inside to lessen the harsh treatment of the Chinese by playing to Mongol self-interest.

Excerpted from Sung Lien, "Yeh-lü Ch'u-ts'ai," in *The Civilization of China,* translated and edited by Dun J. Li. Copyright © 1975 Dun J. Li. Reprinted with permission from Scribner, a division of Simon & Schuster.

According to Mongol law, any city that chose to resist by force after the Mongols had demanded its surrender would be put to the sword once the city was captured. When Kaifeng was about to be captured, General Su-pu-t'ai proposed the extermination of all of its residents in view of its resistance that had caused the loss of many Mongol lives. Having heard about the general's proposal, Yeh-lü Ch'u-ts'ai immediately went to the Great Khan to protest. "Our officers and men have fought for more than a generation," he said. "Their hope is that in victory they will acquire land for themselves. What is the use of land when nobody is there to work on it?" Facing contradictory advice, the Great Khan could not make a decision for the moment. "In this city there are numerous skillful artisans," Ch'u-ts'ai spoke again. "If we kill all the people in the city, we will lose these artisans too." The Great Khan agreed to this reasoning and issued an order to spare the lives of the city residents. At the time when Kaifeng fell to the Mongols, it had a population of 1,470,000, composed largely of refugees.

The Mongols captured a large number of people after their conquest of the areas south of the Yellow River. Most of the captured (70 to 80 percent) chose to flee and head for home once they were conscripted into the Mongol army. According to the Mongol law, anyone who opened his door to a deserter or provided him with financial assistance subjected not only himself but also his relatives, friends, neighbors, and fellow villagers to capital punishment. As this law was strictly enforced, thousands of deserters died of starvation on the road since no one dared offer them any assistance. Deploring this miserable state of affairs, Yeh-lü Ch'u-ts'ai reported to the Great Khan as follows: "Once a territory is conquered, all the people in it are Your Majesty's subjects. It is not a wise policy to force them out of their homes. It is not right, either, to kill one hundred persons on account of one deserter." Despite Ch'u-ts'ai's protest, Ogodei did not change the law governing deserters. Nevertheless he secretly ordered his commanders to relax its enforcement.

During an imperial conference held in the year of Yi-wei [1235] some Mongol generals recommended the employment of Chinese for the conquest of the Western Regions and the employment of Muslims for the conquest of South China. This strategy, said the generals, would enable the Mongols to control both groups easily. Yeh-lü Ch'u-ts'ai disagreed. "An enormous distance exists between China and the Western Regions," he explained. "The employment of Chinese in the Western Regions or the employment of Muslims in China would mean long travels for both; they and their horses would be totally exhausted even before the engagement of battle. Furthermore, the Chinese are not used to the climate of the Western Regions; nor are the Muslims used to the climate of China. Both groups would suffer diseases of epidemic proportions that could not but weaken the army itself." The Great Khan agreed to this reasoning, and the suggestion of using Chinese against the Muslims and vice versa was then dropped. . . .

The Great Khan loved to drink and intoxicated himself daily with some of his closest advisers, despite repeated remonstrations from Yeh-lü Ch'u-ts'ai. One day Ch'u-ts'ai brought him a ladle of wine and showed him the erosion in the ladle. "If wine can erode a ladle made of iron," said he, "imagine what it can do to Your Majesty's stomach." After Ch'u-ts'ai left, the Great Khan said to his drinking companions, "You all love me, but none loves me more than my Long Beard." He ordered gold and silk to be awarded to Ch'u-ts'ai and instructed his drinking companions to limit their daily presentation to him to three goblets only. . . .

On the third day of the second month, in the year of Hsin-ch'u [1241], Great Khan Ogodei was seriously ill, as the attending physician reported that the patient's pulse had been too weak to be discernible. Not knowing what to do, the empress summoned Yeh-lü Ch'u-ts'ai to her presence to seek advice. "There are many innocent men in jail," said Ch'u-ts'ai. "A little mercy on our part may inspire Heaven to show mercy on us. I am recommending a general clemency." The empress wanted to issue an order of general clemency right away, but Ch'u-ts'ai objected, on the grounds that only the Great Khan could issue such an order. A little while later the Great Khan awakened, and the empress and Ch'u-ts'ai went into his room to request an order of general clemency. The Khan, having already lost his speech, nodded his head. On that night, while the order of general clemency was read aloud and thus officially became the law, the Great Khan's pulse became stronger and stronger until it was as normal as that of a healthy man. He completely recovered on the next day.

Nine months later the Great Khan, as was his wont, was planning a hunting trip. Yeh-lü Ch'u-ts'ai, having consulted his books, declared that the trip was inauspicious. The Khan's other advisers said, "How could the Great Khan amuse himself without the chase?" On the fifth day of the eleventh month [8 December 1241] Great Khan Ogodei died in a hunting lodge.

Islamic Envoy to Genghis Khan in Peking

Juzjani

In 1215 the sultan of Khorazmia, a territory south of the Aral Sea in western Asia, sent a large embassy headed by Baha ad-Din to Peking to make trade arrangements with the Mongol conqueror of China, Genghis Khan. The thirteenth-century historian Juzjani included in his chronicles an eyewitness account by Baha ad-Din in which the envoy leader recorded shocking evidence of Mongol violence. Baha ad-Din documented seeing a large white hill composed of human bones, earth greasy with human fat, and a site where 60,000 women and girls threw themselves to their death in order to avoid capture by the Mongols.

When the envoy met Genghis Khan, the Mongol leader proclaimed himself the sovereign of the sunrise and the sultan the sovereign of the sunset. He requested that the two monarchs support a peace treaty to sustain free trade.

When we arrived within the boundaries of China, and near to Peking, the seat of government of the Golden Emperor, from a considerable distance a high white mound appeared in sight, so distant that between us and that high place was a distance of two or three stages (24–36 miles), or more than that. We, who were the persons sent by Sultan Muhammad's government, supposed that white eminence was perhaps a hill of snow, and we made inquiries of the guides and the people of that part respecting it, and they replied:

'The whole of it is the bones of men slain.'

When we had proceeded onwards another stage, the ground became so greasy and dark from human fat, that it was necessary for us to advance another three stages on that same road, until we came to dry ground again. Through the infections arising from the ground, some of the party became ill and some perished.

On reaching the gate of the city of Peking, we perceived, in a place under a bastion of the citadel, an immense quantity of human bones collected. Inquiry was made, and the people replied, that, on the day the city was captured, 60,000 young girls, virgins, threw themselves from the bastion of the fortress and destroyed themselves, in order that they might not fall captives into the hands of the Mongol forces, and that all these were their bones.

When we reached the presence of Genghis Khan, they brought in bound, where we were, the son of the Golden Emperor, and the minister (Yeh-lu) and uncle of his father. Then, turning his face towards them, Genghis Khan said:

'Behold, my affairs and my sovereignty have attained to such a pitch of grandeur, that the monarch of the empire of the setting sun has sent ambassadors unto me.'

At the time of our return, Genghis Khan sent a great number of rarities and offerings with us for presentation to Sultan Muhammad, and said:

'I am the sovereign of the sunrise, and thou the sovereign of the sunset. Let there be between us a firm treaty of friendship, amity, and peace, and let the traders and caravans on both sides come and go, and let the precious products and ordinary commodities which may be in my territories be conveyed by them into thine, and those of thine, in the same manner, let them bring into mine.'

In short, when he sent us away, he requested that envoys on both sides, and merchants, and caravans, should constantly come and go, and bring and take away with them choice descriptions of arms, cloths and stuffs, and other articles of value and elegance of both empires, and that between the two monarchs a permanent treaty should be maintained.

Japan in the Thirteenth Century

J.M. Roberts

J.M. Roberts explains that the sea has not only fed the island country
of Japan but also protected it from foreign invasion. Roberts writes that
although Japan's philosophy, writing, and government were greatly influenced by China, the roots of Japanese civilization are at home. Japanese society was organized under an emperor, seen as a descendant of a
sun goddess, who ruled over clans that often warred with one another.
Roberts writes that in 1185 a clan war brought general Minamoto Yoritomo of the Minamoto clan to power, ushering in the Kamakura age,
named after the district where the Minamoto people were centered.

Roberts reports that during the Kamakura age the imperial influence
dwindled and power passed to shoguns, clan commanders-in-chief. This
decentralization of power generated frequent civil war. As a result, the
society as a whole became more militaristic, spawning the creation of
a class of warriors called samurai. Although peasant life remained harsh,
a small, ruling leisure class developed exquisite Japanese literature, pottery, painting, lacquer work, silk weaving, flower arranging, and gar-
dening. These works of art were considered treasures by Westerners
exposed to them via European traders who penetrated the once-isolated
civilization during the Renaissance.

J.M. Roberts was the warden of Merton College, Oxford University.
He has written extensively and is the general editor of *The Short History of the Modern World* and *The New Oxford History of England.*

Because Japan is an island country, the sea has protected her—she has never been successfully invaded—and has helped to feed her people. Only recently has fishing ceased to provide the bulk of the protein consumed by Japanese. For a long time Japan was able to take from outside what she wanted while keeping out what she did not, because of the sea, which made the Japanese sailors too, though for a long time this showed in successful piracy and fishing (like the sea-faring of English westcountrymen) rather than in distant enterprises.

Korea is the Asian mainland nearest to Japan, and the Japanese have always been very sensitive about that country. At one time, in the eighth century AD, Japan's rulers held territory there and for much of the twentieth century they dominated it. But China was for much longer the nominal overlord of Korea and China was always the foreign power whose behaviour mattered to Japan more than any other. From very ancient times she influenced Japan deeply. Though their languages are different, both the Japanese and Chinese peoples are Mongoloid. . . . In pre-historic times bronze technology seems to have passed from China to Japan. Then, after the Han[1] collapse, when the Japanese began to show much more interest in Korea, contacts with the great mainland civilization multiplied rapidly. The title of 'emperor' given to Japan's ruler, together with Confucianism, Buddhism and a knowledge of iron-working, all passed from China to Japan. Chinese potters came to Japan at an early date, setting up kilns there and inter-marrying with the natives, and from this sprang much of Japan's later artistic achievement. Chinese script was adapted for writing the Japanese language, and government began to show traces of Chinese influence too. In the sixth and seventh centuries, when Chinese influence was at its height, reforming Japanese statesmen made great efforts to set up a centralized government with a civil service on Chinese lines, based on merit, not birth, and an emperor who was a real ruler and not just the head of the most respected clan.

All this may make it appear that Japan borrowed from abroad all that made her a civilized nation. Given the impressiveness of T'ang China[2] and the frequent evidence of Buddhist influence on Japanese art, it would be easy to understand if this were true, but it is in fact not so. The roots of Japanese civilization and government lay at home.

Ascendancy of the Minamoto Clan

The first Japanese chronicles (compiled in the eighth century) explain how the land and people of Japan were made by the gods, but the earliest firm chronology comes from Chinese and Korean sources three

1. ruling dynasties from 206 B.C. to A.D. 220 2. ruling dynasty from A.D. 618 to 907

centuries earlier. It shows that at the beginning of the fifth century government was already centred on an emperor. He was supposed to be a descendant of the sun goddess and exercised a general headship over the Japanese national family from his ancestral domains in what was later the province of Yamato. That national family was organized in clans, the main units of Japanese as of earlier Chinese society. From time to time one clan rose to greater power than the others, usually by influencing or even controlling the emperors. But the imperial family itself went on in an unbroken line (though sometimes helped out by adoption); the present emperor still traces his succession directly back to the first, a remarkable claim to continuity.

Between 500 and 1500 there were two important periods when individual clans dominated Japan. In the eighth century the Fujiwara came to the top. For the next two or three centuries they effectively controlled the emperors through marriage alliances and the relationships that followed. During the Fujiwara era the imperial capital was at Heian, the modern Kyoto. The emperor lived there, carrying out his heavy ceremonial and religious duties. But the power of the Fujiwara ebbed. There was fighting between the clans, and a ruthless and able general, Minamoto Yoritomo, took power in 1185; this was the beginning of the ascendancy of the Minamoto (usually described as the Kamakura era, from the district where the main Minamoto lands were to be found). The Minamoto themselves gave way in the fourteenth century, and after that Japan dissolved into violent and bloody civil wars until the sixteenth century.

The Rise of the Shogun

At first sight this does not look very interesting. It seems to be on about the same level as the struggles of barons and great families in medieval Europe. In fact it was an important age, in which Japan developed on very individual lines. To begin with, in spite of some attempts to create a strong civil service recruited by merit at the beginning of Fujiwara times, imperial power dwindled away. Power remained in the hands of the nobles. In the end this was to make it very difficult for other interests to be taken into account, and Japanese society tended to freeze into immobility. Offices became hereditary, and rights to levy imperial taxes were granted to those enjoying Fujiwara favour. This eclipse of the emperors was completed in the 'Kamakura' period (1185–1333) when effective government passed to the Minamoto 'shogun', or commander-in-chief, who ruled in the emperor's name but in fact independently and in the interest of his own clan, whose lands were not in the area of Heian but of Kamakura. Yet there was a steady progress from the erosion of the power of the emperor, to the erosion of any idea of central authority at all. It was very unlike China, and the consequence, often, and repeatedly, was anarchy and even civil war between magnates.

All this would have been very dangerous (and might not have happened) without the protection of the sea. But for most of this era the Japanese had only had one 'national' military problem, the containment of the Ainu barbarians, and Japanese society was not developed enough in other ways to make people demand a more centralized government. Most Japanese seem to have been content to accept the authority of clan and family and the national cult, Shinto.

Another important trend in these centuries was towards a much more military society in which the martial virtues of loyalty, endurance and bravery came to be held in great esteem. In part this was because the lesser nobles and country squires became more independent as the Fujiwara era drew to a close. The civil wars, in which warriors bound themselves to serve lords as retainers, greatly strengthened this. In a much exaggerated form it was not unlike what was going on at about the same time in Europe within the way of ordering society which has been called 'feudal'. In Japan, there gradually emerged as the most respected class below the great nobility the 'samurai', whose knightly ideals have ever since been an inspiration to Japanese patriots—and have also often helped to make Japanese society very violent.

Japanese admiration for the warrior went with a developing sense of Japanese superiority and military invincibility which owed much to the successful resistance to two attempted Mongol invasions, the first in 1274, the second in 1281. There were huge undertakings by well-equipped expeditions (among other things the Mongols made use of Chinese technology and used catapults to throw bombs which burst in the air). The second was effectively destroyed by a storm which wrecked the Mongol fleet—the kamikaze, or 'divine wind', which was seen as a heavenly intervention on behalf of Japan.

Against this background the lot of the ordinary Japanese peasant changed only for the worse. For a long time the economy did not much thrive; farming remained what it had always been technically and there was no town growth like that in China. Japan managed slowly to grow more food but largely through the gradual increase in the size of estates and therefore of farmed area rather than through technical advance. The peasant paid heavy taxes, usually to his lord, to whom the right of levying them had been granted by the shogunate, and raised the rice crop which provided most of Japan's food. In the fifteenth century things rapidly worsened. There were plagues and famine, peasants formed leagues to protect themselves, with unemployed warriors as their leaders, and risings followed.

Development of the Arts

On this poverty there nonetheless rested a brilliant civilization. Under the Fujiwara its brilliance was restricted to the imperial court circle, but later it came to be shared by the whole ruling class. Japan gradually shook off Chinese cultural influences or remoulded them to its own needs. The first Japanese literature and the No drama—a unique combination of poetry, mime and music carried out in elaborate costumes and masks—made their appearance. Interestingly some of the most famous Japanese books were by ladies of the Heian court; it seems to have been felt that, as they were probably not up to anything very serious, women could properly write in Japanese although men should still use Chinese for the serious works of art or learning they produced (much as educated Europeans long went on using Latin as the language of scholarship).

Some of the most beautiful works of art which have ever been made came from this culture. Japanese artists have always emphasized scale, simplicity, and perfect craftsmanship and have shown it in pottery, painting, lacquerwork, and silk-weaving as well as in arts which are much more especially Japanese, such as flower-arrangement, landscape-gardening, or the production of beautiful swords by armourers. Great artists enjoyed widespread fame and admiration. All the arts came to high perfection, too, during the most anarchic period of Japan's history, despite the social and economic damage caused by civil strife.

Some of the beautiful things made by the Japanese eventually began to find their way to markets abroad. In the fifteenth century China was an important customer and Buddhist monks played an important part in her trade with Japan. Inevitably, interest was awoken, and sooner or later people would want to know more about the remote island empire from which such treasures came. Among the curious would be Europeans, the first among whom to arrive were the Portuguese, probably in 1543. Others soon followed. Japan's internal conditions at that time put no obstacle in their way. Nagasaki, a little village, was opened in 1570 to the Portuguese by one magnate who was already converted to Christianity. Besides their faith, though, the intruders had also brought firearms, whose first impact on Japanese society was to inflame still more its appetite for internal strife. The eagerness with which Japanese adopted the new weapons seems in retrospect a portent of what was to come, the most considered and well-motivated of all processes of deliberate modernization by a non-European people, albeit one that lay two and a half centuries ahead.

The Mongol Invasions of Japan

Jerrold M. Packard

Beginning in 1234, aggressive Mongol tribes under Genghis Khan and his grandson Kublai Khan invaded and established Mongol rule over China. By 1268 the Kublai turned his attention to Japan and sent an envoy to the Japanese regents demanding that they surrender. After several rejections, the outraged Kublai attacked with an armada of 450 ships. Fortunately for the Japanese a typhoon weakened the Mongol forces and they returned to the mainland. In the following article, Jerrold M. Packard explains that the reprieve allowed the Japanese to fortify the shoreline, stockpile weapons, and bolster their fighting force.

In 1281 Kublai sent a second envoy to the Japanese imperial court demanding surrender. The Japanese response was to sever the heads of the envoy and stick them on stakes. According to Packard, the outraged Mongols launched the largest amphibious force in history until D day in World War II. Over one hundred thousand men on three-thousand five hundred vessels attacked the Japanese for over seven weeks. The Japanese monarch, sensing defeat, prayed for divine assistance, which seemingly appeared in the form of a "divine wind," another typhoon that devastated the Mongol fleet and opened the way for a Japanese victory. Although it managed to turn back the Mongols, the ruling Hojo government was severely weakened by the war. Packard argues that the court retreated into a self-absorbed, frivolous courtly existence oblivious to growing national dissent.

Jerrold M. Packard is a historian whose works include *The Queen and Her Court* and *Peter's Kingdom.*

Excerpted from Jerrold M. Packard, *Sons of Heaven: A Portrait of Japanese Monarchy.* Copyright © 1987 Jerrold M. Packard. Reprinted with permission from Frederick Hill Associates.

In the early part of the thirteenth century, the Mongolian tribes of central Asia had been united into a nation under the brutal but effective leadership of a chief, or *khan,* called Genghis. This astonishingly aggressive potentate decided early in his terror-filled career to expand his insignificant desert state as rapidly and as widely as possible, the results being that within a few years he amassed an empire stretching from eastern Europe—bands of his warriors reached as far as the Tigris and Euphrates rivers in what had once been the heart of the Babylonian empire—to eastern Asia, sowing little culture but inflicting massive destruction throughout the entirety of his new dominions. The predatory Mongol first smashed through China's Great Wall to overthrow the Chin empire in the north in 1234, but it was his grandson Kublai rather than Genghis who brought the Mongols to the zenith of their glory by establishing rule over China under the name by which the clan was known to history, the Yuan dynasty. Immediately on subjugating the continent to its Pacific edge, Kublai turned his attention to the great archipelago lying so tantalizingly close to its shores.

The First Mongol Attack on Japan

It was a Korean named Cho who suggested to the Great Kublai that he now demand Japan's vassalage. The khan's first thought was to attempt to subjugate the offshore prey by the relatively peaceful means of turning Japan into a vassal state, and then to bleed by taxation the country's treasure to finance his own Yuan court. The island empire would be left to govern itself under local overlords, a privilege by no means universal to the many less fortunate territories the khan had already brought under the Mongol boot. Japan, however, didn't appreciate this subtle distinction, and had no intention of acquiescing to the khan's view of the inevitable.

The first Mongol overture to Japan came in 1268, via the kingdom of Koryo, one of its vassal states on the Korean peninsula. The invitation to the "King of Japan"—snidely characterized in the smaller print at the bottom of the khan's petition as a "ruler of a small country"—sought "friendly intercourse" with China, but threatened war against the "king's" subjects if he didn't accede. After consulting with the court in Kyoto, which had been quite prepared to negotiate with the khan's fiercesome-looking envoys and would probably have submitted to the foreign demands, the Hojo[1] government (by now the shogun was of course powerless, the shogunal regent the real power) rejected the thinly disguised threat. The envoys were sent back without an answer or even an acknowledgment that they and their invitation had been received, a diplomatic

---

1. the ruling clan

snub that added a dangerous insult to the injury of a negative reply to Kublai.

After floating additional entreaties to the defiant Japanese, the outraged Kublai finally ordered his military to subdue these cheeky Japanese nonentities. Sensing such a reaction, the Hojo leadership began preparing for the inevitable. Reasoning that the mainlanders' attack would arrive at the southernmost island of Kyushu, nearest the China coast and a convenient jumping-off place for a further killing blow on the main island of Honshu, the Hojo regent urgently initiated a massive buildup of defense fortifications in the southern sector. Not only did he instruct the samurai of the area to keep themselves especially vigilant, but the regent also sent spies to Korea, the probable embarcation site of any Mongol invasion fleet. Having eschewed the usual luxurious trappings of rule that still characterized the free-spending ways of the Kyoto court, the Kamakura bakufu[2] was, fortunately for Japan, in a financial position to put its emergency plans into action.

The inevitable came six years later. Kublai had indeed used Korea as his staging site, ordering one of its captive regional kings to build a thousand junks and amass forty thousand troops for his invasion. In November 1274, an armada of 450 of these ships carrying the mixed Mongol and Korean troops, one of the most fear-inspiring invasion forces that had ever been assembled, landed at Hakozaki Bay on the north coast of Kyushu—directly in the maw of the defenses that the Hojo bakufu had wisely prepared. Nonetheless, the terrifying techniques used by the troops of the Mongol khan—especially the catapults flinging horrifying bombs—caused the Japanese defenders, armed only with their swords and bows and arrows, to wisely withdraw to a fortified line of defense.

Nature, in the form of a typhoon, came to the aid of the Japanese. Afraid of being caught on the high seas it raised in their own escape route, the Mongols withdrew all the way back to Korea. The exhausted defenders were, fortunately unbeknown to the attackers, on the verge of defeat. For the time being, the Japanese were given a truly miraculous respite.

Taking full advantage of the situation, the Kamakura government again ordered massive new defense preparations, the central feature of which was a stone wall running all the way around the shoreline of Hakozaki Bay, where it was reckoned that a second invasion force would try to overcome already probed and weakened Japanese defenses; the works were built by and at the expense of the landowners who dominated the area. A new fleet of small ships was rapidly constructed, a manpower draft put into effect, and stores of weapons

2. shogunal leadership in Kamakura

stockpiled. Even the court made its own small but undoubtedly appreciated contribution: temporary abstinence from certain minor luxuries, the funds thus "saved" diverted to the military buildup. In truth, the nation had rarely shown such unity and never was it more needed than in the face of the great trial that was to come. Much to everyone's surprise, even the local pirates, the buccaneers who normally terrorized the Inland Sea, threw their support to the government, the defense of the greater economic interests evidently taking precedence over their normal felonious activities.

The Second Mongol Invasion

Shortly, the Great Khan sent another, even more demanding mission to the "King of Japan." This time the ultimatum borne by the five emissaries bid the sovereign to come directly to the khan's court in Peking, there to do obeisance and ask forgiveness for the trouble that had already been suffered by the patient but by now long-tormented Mongol state. Overcome by fear on hearing the new demand, the imperial court in Kyoto awaited word from Kamakura, which to its credit resolutely rejected the ultimatum. Looking for a way to convince the khan that they didn't wish even to have the matter *raised* again, the shogunal regent ordered that the heads of the members of the Mongol diplomatic party be severed from their shoulders and stuck on pillories outside the city. Kublai was understandably annoyed when told of this supreme impertinence. The man whose warriors had ravaged territory stretching from Hungary in the west to the China Sea in the east soon initiated the process he *knew* would finally subdue the intolerably insolent islanders.

This time the Japanese respite lasted just five years, until 1281. The largest amphibious invasion force ever to be assembled until D-Day in World War II—100,000 men borne by 3,500 vessels—sailed as had its predecessor up the Inland Sea into the waiting Japanese defenses, a fortuitous strategem from the Japanese viewpoint. The Mongols tried desperately to outflank the wall around the bay, the intense samurai courageously thwarting them with a contemptuousness for death that would mark their fighting spirit down to the twentieth century. Neither side could gain the upper hand. The fighting raged for seven weeks, from June into the typhoon season of August. In Kyoto, the emperor attempted intercession with his divine ancestors by writing imploring letters in his own hand, missives that begged divine assistance to throw off the hideous and subhuman invaders. The monarch was assisted with his priestly chores by a large number of monks who didn't hesitate to assert that they had seen portentous signs of heaven's assistance while praying with their usual fervid intensity, for which work the emperor generously gave out handsome emoluments. In sad contrast, the legions of gallant soldiers even then risking and gladly giving their lives in the name of their sovereign did so without any matching prospects of such fiscal compensation.

The elements of nature again proved the Mongol undoing when divine assistance arrived in the form of yet another "divine wind" whose churning dark clouds descended over the ungainly Mongol invasion craft. Over the next two days the tempest blew the Mongol flotilla into little more than kindling, destroying along with it the smaller Japanese ships that had been struggling against them with some small success. The Mongols caught on the shore were, along with those forced to shore from their sinking ships, quickly slaughtered by the superior Japanese land troops. Some three thousand prisoners were executed by the Japanese, while a spared trio was put on a boat to take their admonitory tale back to Peking. The continental threat was repelled (Kublai's death twenty years later permanently ended the Mongol danger to Japan), Japan was safe from foreign military invasion for another seven centuries, and the Hojo regency shone at its brightest. But the Kamakura government would bask in this peak of its ascendancy for only a short time more before it, too, started a slide that would end in ignominious destruction.

Effects of the Mongol Invasions

Wary of a repeat of the khan's adventurism, Kamakura's tent government rationalized the necessity to continue the extraordinary defense measures that had represented so large and burdensome a part of the nation's spending during the years of the Mongol threat. But contrary to the Kamakura victories against the Taira and against the court in the Shokyu incident,[3] this victory brought with it no new fresh supply of booty—either land or treasure—with which to reward a triumphant army. As happens when a hard-used military force goes unrewarded, resentment quickly dissipates whatever euphoria accompanied success. What should have been a threshold of glorious consequences for the bakufu turned into the precursor of an irremediable weakening of its grip over the nation.

After the Mongol danger was repulsed, and while a new drama of the seemingly unstoppable crumbling of the Hojo government and birth of its successor regime unfolded in Kamakura, the imperial court in Kyoto continued its placid play-acting, the monarch carrying out his sacerdotal functions meant to invoke the protection of the gods on Japan. The energy once derived from active participation in national affairs had been all but entirely drained from the imperial establishment, its now-reduced entourage carrying on only by the momentum gained in thirteen centuries of existence. Still, no gov-

3. two civil disturbances

ernment and no dictator envisioned the monarchy's actual extinction.

Pastimes both exquisite and ephemeral occupied these still self-infatuated and peacockish courtiers, men and women who played at titillating games and gigglingly crafted precious bits of poetry, worrying themselves sick over some minute question of sumptuary consequentiality—whether an official's skirt was a mite too long for his rank or its fabric slightly too rich for his station, whether his eyebrows were shaved cleanly or his cheeks rouged just so. The preparation of the courtier's queue, long and bound in handmade paper, might consume the better part of a day, leaving almost no time to do justice to an unfinished billet-doux destined for some exquisite lady made achingly desirable by her delightfully blackened teeth. While his less fortunate countrymen were still existing on the millet that had become the culinary mainstay of all classes below the ruling one, those in Kyoto's court stratum enjoyed dainty dishes based on Chinese models, exotic concoctions all but unknown to the masses. Bereft of the tools to regain power, let alone the spirit, the monarchy as an institution of political consequence just about gave up.

Islamic States

PREFACE

The thirteenth century was a time of great transformation and decline for the world of Islam. When the century opened, Islamic influence was widespread across Asia, the Mediterranean, and into Europe; at the close of the century, the golden age of Islam was over.

Muhammad, who was born around A.D. 570 and died in 632, built the foundations of Islam, establishing one of the religion's missions to bring the faith to the rest of humankind, both with the word and with might. The caliph, a leader who was considered by his followers as the deputy of God Himself and a successor of Muhammad, commanded both religious and political authority in the Islamic world. Muslims, loyal adherents of Muhammad and Islam, spread the message throughout Arabia and beyond. Indeed, at its height the Islamic empire spread from the Atlantic Ocean to India and China and from southern Europe to North Africa. As the thirteenth century began, the Islamic world was ruled by a dynasty that took power in 750 called the Abbasids, regimes that descended from Muhammad's uncle, Abbas. Much of the success of the Abbasids came from their willingness to organize a multicultural empire where many diverse peoples could be assimilated with common rituals and language.

Arabic-Islamic lands were under continued threat from three powerful sources: the Turks, the crusaders from Europe, and in the middle of the thirteenth century the Mongols. For centuries, displaced Turkish groups from Central Asia moved throughout the Islamic states. Most converted to Islam willingly. One group, the Mamluk Turks, began as military slaves, but during the second half of the thirteenth century they took control in Egypt and in Baghdad, providing a relatively stable society based on vigorous trade with Europe.

Beginning in 1096 and continuing throughout the Middle Ages, European Christians organized military campaigns, called the Crusades, to attack and obliterate the Turks and Muslims. The church sponsored the Crusades with the intention of bolstering its power and prestige while at the same time uniting the people behind a common, holy cause. While many crusaders spoke of the Crusades as a mission to take back the Holy Land, the Muslims saw the campaigns as unconscionable invasions. The Crusades continued into the thirteenth century, when in 1249 the king of France, Louis IX, launched a crusade against the Arabs of Egypt. But by 1250 a combination of Muslims and Mamluk Turks defeated the French, called the Franj in colloquial Arabic.

In the Islamic west the Mongols, headed by Hülegü, a grandson of the great Mongol leader Genghis Khan, threatened the stability of the entire Arab world. Hülegü's armies brutally sacked Baghdad, the Abbasid center of power, and killed the caliph, thereby devastating the entire Islamic empire. From Baghdad the Mongols pushed their way across Islamic lands to Cairo, Egypt. There, in 1260, after Hülegü returned to his homeland to guard his political interests, the Mamluk Turks who controlled Cairo attacked the remaining Mongol army. The surprise attack near the city of Ayn Jalut defeated the weakened Mongols and subsequently liberated the Muslims from the scourge of the Mongols. This marked the official beginning of the Mamluk period of sovereignty.

In North Africa, Islamic rule spread across the vast territory of the Maghrib, lands west of Libya and Egypt. The Muslims absorbed the conquered indigenous people, the Berbers, into a prosperous Islamic civilization that was united through religion, language, and worldview. Although persistent small wars flared between urban rulers, a relatively long period of peace, voluminous trade, and vast irrigation systems helped the North African peoples to prosper. Merchants from Europe and non-Islamic parts of the world traded in African markets for gold, ivory, and slaves. In turn, Islamic traders not only spread trade and goods across parts of Africa, but they also spread Islamic beliefs and customs.

Throughout the thirteenth century, Arabic-Islamic goods and art objects were highly prized by the European middle class. Characterized by its diverse and aesthetically pleasing style, Islamic art had widespread appeal. Moreover, Muslim artists created their art inexpensively, making it affordable to more than just the economically elite. Prized works included beautiful objects such as textiles, pottery, bronzes, and fine utensils that helped infuse pleasure into the daily routines of life. Arab artists generally expressed ideas without using realistic representation; rather their work forgoes concrete details and focuses on symbols and abstractions.

For the Arabic-Islamic civilization, the thirteenth century was a crucial turning point. The Abbasid regimes, which ruled from 750 to 1258, make up the classical period of the Arab Empire and its golden age. With the destruction of Baghdad in 1258 this comes to a crashing halt. During the Mamluk period that follows (1258–1517) non-Arabs who were not interested in advancing Arabic culture or advocating Islamic traditions governed the Arabs of the Middle East. Correspondingly, prosperity declined and world influence was diminished.

Islam in North Africa

E. Jefferson Murphy

E. Jefferson Murphy argues that although Christian historians have portrayed Islam as fanatical, in reality much of Islamic history reveals a great capacity for tolerance and accommodation. Islamic rule spread across the vast territory of the Maghrib, North African lands west of Libya and Egypt. The Arabs embraced key ideas from many different conquered cultures and wove them into an Islamic civilization united through religion, language, and philosophy.

Murphy writes that Islamic civilization in North Africa emerged from a long and hard process of conquest and acculturation. The advancing Arab armies met fierce resistance from indigenous people called Berbers. Eventually, however, through intermarriage and the successful blending of cultures the North Africans became Arabized. Although persistent small wars flared between urban rulers, a relatively long period of peace, abundant trade, and vast irrigation systems helped the North African peoples to prosper.

Murphy recounts the rise to power of Ibn Yasin, a religious leader, and his followers, called Almoravids. The Almoravids conquered and united North Africa in the eleventh century and initiated a renaissance of Islam. By the end of the twelfth century the Almoravids were swept from power by a rival group called the Almohads. According to Murphy, North Africa disintegrated into a group of petty states. In the thirteenth century Christian forces expelled the Muslims who had settled in Spain and Portugal, and they, in turn, invaded parts of North Africa. Nevertheless, life in North Africa from the thirteenth century to the sixteenth century remained relatively prosperous, fueled by active trading between cities and with Europe. Murphy concludes, however, that although life in medieval North Africa was stable it was not progressive.

E. Jefferson Murphy is a historian and anthropologist who has studied in all the major regions of Africa. He is the author of *Understanding Africa.*

Christian historians have traditionally portrayed Islam as a fanatical faith, spread by cruel and intolerant zealots. This view, largely developed as a result of the Crusades, grossly misrepresents both the Muslim faith and its early Arab disseminators. Although there were zealots who showed intolerance and persecuted infidels, much of Islam's history reveals a great capacity for tolerance and accommodation. More often than not, the Arabs were hailed as deliverers by the persecuted peoples of the Byzantine and Persian worlds. Arab conquerers, though eager to win converts for Islam, rarely forbade Christianity or persecuted Christians. Arabs and converts to Islam were accorded tax and land preferences under the Muslim administrative code, but Arab land reforms and religious tolerance more than compensated for these privileges in the eyes of the oppressed and persecuted peoples of the conquered territories.

The Arabs were early to recognize the importance of local cooperation, for there were relatively few Arabs among the vast populations of the empire. Converts were given status equivalent to that of pure Arabs, and formed the nucleus of a new elite that cemented and perpetuated Arab conquests. In the empire, zealous converts and the descendants of Arab-local marriages outnumbered those of pure Arab origin. This helped maintain the atmosphere of tolerance that followed initial conquest.

In the first centuries of the empire thousands of Arabs—soldiers, officers, holy men, and administrators—left Arabia to settle into key positions in the conquered lands. Yet many Arabs, especially those of the nomadic and seminomadic desert tribes, preferred to remain in their ancestral lands, and many of the Arab soldiers who settled in North Africa soon left the unfamiliar pursuits of urban life to settle in more remote areas where they could follow a more congenial way of life.

Islamic civilization was united through the religion, language, and the philosophy that the Arab conquerers spread. But Islam was merely a foundation, a common thread, upon which a hybrid civilization was built. The Arabs blended their language, religion, and sense of historic mission with the accomplishments of other civilizations. From Persia, Greece, Turkey, Mesopotamia, Egypt, and North Africa flowed ideas that gradually became integral components of Islamic civilization, including Greek science and philosophy, Persian poetry and literature, and naval and commercial ideas from Syria, North Africa, and Greece. Even elements of art and science from China and India were incorporated into the new culture. Within a few centuries, a new civilization had spread throughout the lands south of the Mediterranean, over the entire Near East and Arabia itself, into Turkey and Persia, and even into India. It produced great mathematicians, poets, physicians, architects, military strategists, historians, geographers, and philosophers.

Arab Conquest of North Africa

North Africa eventually became a major segment of Islamic civilization and for brief periods was its leading part, but the process of conquest and acculturation was long and difficult. For several decades, the desert, inhabited by warlike Berbers,[1] slowed the Arab westward advance. The Arabs had insufficient naval strength for major amphibious operations and their generals questioned the prudence of marching overland from Cyrenaica to face hostile Berbers who used horses and camels in much the same fashion as the Arabs, knew the desert intimately, and had built a reputation as skilled and courageous warriors during Byzantine days.

Finally, in 670, an Arab army set out from Cyrenaica across hundreds of miles of desert and invaded Tripolitania and Tunisia. In both countries most of the Romanized cities and the farmlands immediately adjacent to them were quickly captured, but raiding Berber cavalry from the hills, too elusive for even the swift Arab cavalry, restricted the Arabs to the cities. Evidently the urban peoples, whom the Arabs called Roums because of their Roman ways, hardly resisted Arab entry so thankful were they to see the last of Byzantine rule.

Under the Arab general Uqba ibn Nafi a powerful task force of troops, too strong for any Berber or Byzantine army, pushed the initial wave of Arab conquest of the Maghrib[2] to the Atlantic shores of Morocco. Building several powerful garrisons, including the great town of Kairouan near the present city of Tunis, Uqba simply bypassed those few cities still in Byzantine hands, but even these fell to him in short order. When he reached the Atlantic, Uqba is said to have cried out to his troops that only the boundless sea prevented him from conquering more lands for Allah's glory. But as Uqba and his many successors were to learn, the conquest of the Maghrib was far from complete. For more than a century Berber cavalry continued to descend onto the Arab-held plains, destroying farms and towns and then quickly retreating into the wild mountains and the trackless desert. Previously formed alliances allowed Berber war

1. indigenous population of North Africa 2. northwestern Africa

chiefs rapidly to assemble large forces for raids or for defensive purposes.

In the cities and plains, however, Arab rule was more easily established. Arabic gradually replaced Latin; Islam inexorably won converts at the expense of Christianity; and the ruling class of Arab governors and administrators was soon augmented by the large number of local people who accepted Islam. Through intermarriage, the thinly spread Arab population further blended with the North Africans. Under the leadership of the new class of Arabized North Africans, the cities and towns began to prosper. As great ideas and talented men from the conquered dominions were infused into Arabic civilization it became a thing almost apart from the Arabs. Neither the Arabs nor leaders from the dominions were powerful enough to exercise strong central control over the empire's vast territory, except for brief periods. Yet, for many centuries, the vigor of Islam and the Arab language provided a bond stronger than most central governments could have offered.

Weak central controls and the basically egalitarian qualities of Islam and the Arabic system proved deeply attractive to the Berbers and their cosmopolitan relatives in North Africa. Berber tribes that had stubbornly fought off the Arab armies gradually accepted Islam. The unifying bonds of Islamic civilization reached wider in North Africa than did the political control of the rulers in the cities. Although it took several centuries, North Africa slowly developed a sense of Islamic destiny, and even the fierce Berbers of the desert helped fight holy wars to spread Islamic civilization. Armies of Arabs and Berbers crossed the straits of Gibraltar from Morocco and conquered Spain and Portugal. The Moors, who for so long formed a part of the history of those countries, were Berbers from Morocco and other North African lands.

Within two centuries of the initial Arab invasion, North Africa had grown into one of the most powerful centers of the Arab Empire. At times, caliphs and governors based in Tunisia controlled all of North Africa, Spain, Portugal, Sicily and other islands in the western Mediterranean. For many centuries, North Africa was virtually independent of the Baghdad-based Arab Empire in the east, paying only the barest of lip service to the caliphs, who were recognized as Muhammad's spiritual successors. Great cities developed in Morocco, Algeria, and Tunisia—Fez, Marrakesh, Kairouan, Tunis, Sfax, Sousse, Mahdia—replete with ornate mosques, universities, vast palaces, libraries, and swimming baths.

Flourishing Islamic Cities in North Africa

Life in North Africa's great cities and towns reached a peak of affluence around the eleventh century. Vast irrigation systems brought the fertile lands of the plains to high productivity, and long periods of peace protected the daily lives of the farmers. The worship of Allah and the administration of Islamic law helped give the lives of ordinary men new meaning and tranquillity. Into the bustling ports flowed luxury goods from the Mediterranean world, and out of them poured the grains, wines, ivory, fruits, olives, and gold of Africa. In the cities, arts and fine crafts were encouraged. North African leatherwork, jewelry, knives, swords, daggers, and glass found ready markets in the Islamic world as well as in Europe and in Black Africa.

Yet even in the best of times, North Africa was not totally tranquil. The Berbers of the Sahara, increasingly Muslim in religion and conscious of their ties with the Islamic world, had become more dependent upon the urban centers for trade, but wars broke out when the more ambitious city rulers attempted to extend their control into the desert and the mountains. The Berbers came to play an ever more active role in North African political affairs, allying themselves with one urban ruler to bring down another who threatened Berber interests. By the tenth century, Berber leaders began to initiate wars of their own, aiming to seize control of urban governments, and in the eleventh century, a Berber religious leader, Ibn Yasin, led a victorious campaign that brought great changes to Black Africa as well as to North Africa. . . .

Rise of the Almoravids

Ibn Yasin, a holy man who had recently returned from his pilgrimage to Mecca, attempted to instill in the Berber Sanhaja nation a new sense of holy purpose and morality. At first rebuffed, Yasin established a mystic retreat on an island in the mouth of the Senegal River far below the Sahara. There he spent several years in ascetic worship and contemplation, joined by a constantly growing band of disciples, at first curious about the reputed holiness of Yasin, then fired by his call for creation of a new polity in which all men worshiped Allah with zeal and piety.

In 1042, Yasin and his followers, now numbering about a thousand, left their island monastery and embarked on a campaign to force the impious and heretical Berbers of the western Sahara to return to pure Islam. Now called Almoravids, from the Arabic for al-Murabitun, or people of the "ribat" (monastery), Yasin's followers met with success. Within a year or two, Yasin commanded an army of more than thirty thousand zealous troops, drawn largely from a confederation of Sanhaja Berber tribesmen in what is now Mauritania and southern Morocco.

One wing of Yasin's troops swept north into the Atlas Mountains of Morocco, another moved south into the great Soninke Empire of

Ghana. Before the close of the eleventh century, the Almoravid campaign had established both a renaissance of Islam and firm political control over an empire that stretched from northern Spain to modern Senegal and across the Mediterranean coast of North Africa through all of Algeria and Tunisia.

For several generations, this territory was maintained under successive Almoravid emirs. But the fanatic zeal and religious purity that had carried them into power was soon dissipated by the soft life in the cities from which they ruled. In the twelfth century, the Almohads, a movement springing from the Zenata Berbers of Morocco, swept the weakened Almoravids from power, but after less than a century, Almohad rule collapsed, and North Africa disintegrated into a group of emirates and petty states. . . .

Breakdown of North African Unity

The crumbling of the great North African political system was accompanied by a loss of Muslim possessions in Europe. The Normans, under King Roger I, had captured Sicily in the eleventh century, and the Spaniards and Portuguese drove the Muslims from their Iberian territory, except Granada, in the thirteenth century. By the fourteenth century all the lands in the central and western Mediterranean, both in Africa and in Europe, were divided into small kingdoms, principalities, and city-states, each with its own pretensions to power.

In North Africa the post-Almohad centers of power roughly coincided with the modern states of that region. One sultan claimed the cities and valleys on Morocco's Atlantic and Mediterranean coasts, another claimed the Tunisian plain. The caliphate held Egypt, and Libya was divided into Tripolitania and Cyrenaica. Algeria was divided into small units, composed of individual towns and adjacent farmlands. Strong Berber chiefs prevented the coastal sultans from effectively controlling the mountains and steppes. In Tunisia, long the most racially mixed region of North Africa, the rulers and leading men retained little of the Berber heritage. Even when Berber chiefs assumed control, founding new dynasties, they gradually became acculturated. In Morocco, traditionally more isolated, Berber ties remained stronger, as they did in Algeria. In both these countries large Berber populations maintained their traditional ways of life in the mountains.

For centuries North Africa continued in this way, the peak of civilization having passed by about the twelfth century. Spain and Portugal, having grown in power since the expulsion of most Muslims in the thirteenth century, frequently invaded Morocco. On several occasions, European forces from Italy and France invaded Tunisia and Algeria, remaining for short periods before being ejected by resurgent North African rulers. Much of North Africa came under the control of the Ottoman Empire in the sixteenth century, but Ottoman rule brought few changes of significance.

Thirteenth-Century Life in North Africa

Despite decline of the political bonds of the earlier Arab empire and Islamic civilization, life in North Africa between the thirteenth and nineteenth centuries remained generally prosperous. The major cities continued to trade with each other, with the Berbers of the interior, and with the growing economic centers in Europe, especially Venice and Genoa. North African wool was added to the olives, dates, wines, grains, and leather goods exported to the Mediterranean world. Near the important cities, the farms on the plains and valleys continued to prosper. But the irrigation systems of Carthaginian, Roman, and Arab times fell into disuse in the more remote regions. Few great new mosques, palaces, gardens, engineering works, and public buildings were built after the thirteenth century, but many of those built in former years continued to be used and were kept in good condition. Emirs, sultans, merchants, and government officials maintained an opulent existence, affluent from rarely failing tax revenues, customs duties, trade profits, and booty from privateering which they controlled. A tradition of education persisted and was even enriched for a time when the expelled scholars and nobles of Spain settled in Tunis and other North African cities in the thirteenth century.

The North African cities of the medieval period were cosmopolitan. In each could be found communities of Jews, which swelled after thirteenth century persecutions in Spain, Portugal, and Italy. Islamic scholars commonly traveled from one part of the Islamic world to another, spending months or years in cities as judges, religious philosophers, administrators, and teachers of the children of the wealthy. Some Europeans trickled in as representatives of the great commercial houses of Europe. Other Europeans were captured in wars and privateering ventures and became slaves of the sultans, often serving as officers and soldiers in the palace guard. Slaves from Black Africa, usually purchased from Berber caravaneers who brought them from Mali, Songhai, and Kanem-Bornu south of the Sahara, were also brought into the region.

The North Africans themselves were either wealthy nobles or commoners. Although a North African middle class of artisans, clerks, petty officials, traders, small landowners, and craftsmen remained in existence, some of the positions normally held by them were filled by European and Black African slaves and mercenaries. The average North African was a peasant farmer living just outside a city. Occasionally he owned a small plot of land, but often he tilled the soil on the estates of large landowners. He practiced his traditional way of life—Arabized, he still retained traces of the Berber heritage—and remained as aloof as possible from city affairs. In the cities, the commoners engaged in the myriad tasks necessary for maintenance of urban life: brickmasonry, carpentry, garbage collecting, petty trading, tailoring, shoe repairing, stevedoring, barbering, food vending, and laboring.

During the medieval centuries, the quality of North African government varied. Some sultans effected lighter tax burdens, more equitable laws, and better economic conditions; others were harsh, ineffective, or unjust. Decades of peace alternated with years or decades of war, either with foreign powers, Berber war chiefs of the interior, or neighboring North African states. Throughout the long medieval period, even after Ottoman rule was imposed, no reigns restored North Africa to the greatness of earlier days. Yet there were no reigns of incompetence and despotism long or harsh enough to destroy the fundamentals of civilized life. Sometimes troubled, sometimes tranquil, neither relapsing into barbarism nor moving forward into new greatness, North Africa maintained itself at roughly the same level until conquest by Europe imposed a new form of colonial rule in the nineteenth century.

The Mamluks in Egypt

Bernard G. Weiss and Arnold H. Green

Bernard G. Weiss and Arnold H. Green write that the Mongol conquest of Baghdad in the middle of the thirteenth century paved the way for Egypt and its new military regime, the Mamluks, to become the leading Arab power. By 1258 the Mongols, headed by Genghis Khan's grandson, Hülagü, conquered and plundered Baghdad and its surrounding areas. The victorious Mongols remained pagan and ravaged important structures and records of the centuries-old Islamic caliphate. When Hülagü returned to Mongolia in 1260 to protect his political position, the Mamluks from Egypt gathered their forces and attacked and defeated the weakened Mongol army at Ayn Jalut. This surprising victory made the Mamluks the most powerful Arab force in the area.

The authors report that prior to Ayn Jalut, the Mamluks, a Turkish military corps collectively called the Bahris, had distinguished themselves by defeating the Christian armies of Louis IX. After a bloody chain of political murders, an officer in the Bahris military named Baybars became sultan, officially marking the beginning of the Mamluk era.

Weiss and Green recount that in the Mamluk system the powerful ruling military, whose ranks were supplied mostly by captured Turks from the Asian steppe, remained separate and aloof from the indigenous population. Nevertheless, throughout the second half of the thirteenth century, the Bahris Mamluk military system provided the security and peace for a productive period of economic activity. Under Bahris rule public health improved, a stable monetary system was solidified, and vigorous trade with Europe was maintained.

According to Weiss and Green, during the Bahris Mamluk period the culture was rich in biographical and historical writing. Although it did not produce a body of "higher literature," it did generate much popular literature, including the famous *The Thousand and One Nights*. In Mamluk Egypt and Syria, Arabic remained the sole literary language.

Bernard G. Weiss and Arnold H. Green are professors of history at the American University in Cairo.

D uring the middle part of the thirteenth century, three developments of major importance for the future of the Arab lands took place: (1) the conquest of Iran and Iraq by a new nomadic people, the Mongols, (2) the emergence in Egypt of a new military regime, that of the Mamlūks, which was soon to extend its rule over Syria as well, and (3) the break-up of the former Muwahhid empire into three separate Maghrabī states, the Marīnid, Zayyānid, and Hafsid states.

The emergence of the Mamlūk regime was to make Egypt the primary political and cultural center of the eastern Arab lands. The Mongol conquest of Iraq placed that land for the time being within the orbit of Iranian civilization. The sack of Baghdad and the devastation of the countryside reduced Iraq to a place of secondary importance within the Islamic world. No longer a center of power in its own right, Iraq now lay on the periphery of an essentially Iranian world. This eclipse of Iraq enhanced the importance of Egypt. Egypt was now clearly the leading power within the Arab lands.

Hostility between the Mamlūk and Mongol states created a barrier between the Arabic-speaking lands under Mamlūk rule and the predominantly Persian-speaking Mongol dominions. As a result of this hostility, the greater part of the eastern Arab lands (Syria and Egypt) became even more separated from Iran than before. This separation, together with the virtual completion around the same time of the arabization of the Maghib[1] as a result of the westward migrations of bedouin[2] over the previous two centuries (leaving Berber-speaking enclaves only in certain areas), enables us from this point onward to make the Arab lands as presently constituted the object of our study. Arab history has become the history of the Arab lands. One important qualification must be made, however. Iraq remained for some time within the orbit of Iranian affairs owing to its proximity to Mongol-dominated Iran and to the inability of the Mamlūks to incorporate it into their empire. In any case, the decrease of Iraq's population together with economic stagnation under the Mongols undermined Iraq's importance as compared with other lands. . . .

---

1. northwestern Africa 2. nomadic desert Arabs

Mongol Expansion

The most dramatic event in the political history of the Islamic East in the thirteenth century was the Mongol conquest of large parts of the Islamic lands east of Syria. Some historians treat this event as a great watershed in Islamic history dividing the "classical" (or early medieval) from the "medieval" (or late medieval) period. With the coming of the Mongols, nomadism was once again in the ascendancy. Also, as was the case with earlier nomadic movements (Arab, Berber, Turkish), the Mongol movement produced a great empire.

The Mongols resembled the Turks in many respects. They came from the same type of homeland, the Steppe, and possessed similar traditions, values, and qualities of mind. However, they were ethnically distinct from the Turks and spoke a language basically unrelated to Turkish. Moreover, whereas the Seljuk Turks had been Islamized prior to their great conquests the Mongols entered the Islamic world for the most part as pagans, although some of their tribes had been converted to Christianity.

The expansion of the Mongols began around the beginning of the thirteenth century, after an energetic leader known as Genghis (more correctly Chingiz) Khan succeeded in placing himself at the head of a confederation of Mongol tribes. Proceeding from their Mongolian homeland, the Mongol armies first advanced southward subduing North China and then westward toward the Islamic lands. In 1220 the Mongols overran Transoxiana and then crossed the Oxus River in Khorasan, where they had no difficulty overcoming the Muslim resistance. From there they proceeded across northern Iran and up through the Caucasus into southern Russia, where they conducted

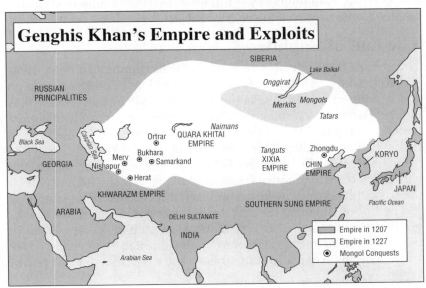

Genghis Khan's Empire and Exploits

numerous raids before turning back eastward. By the time of Genghis Khan's death in 1227, the Mongols were masters of a vast empire encompassing virtually the whole of the Central Asian Steppe as well as parts of China and Iran.

As the Mongol forces advanced, they absorbed many Turkish peoples whom they encountered in the way. As a result of this fusion of Turks and Mongols, the army led by Genghis Khan eventually took on a mixed Turkish-Mongol character (Mongolized Turks were known as "Tatars"). The leadership, however, remained firmly in the hands of the Mongol nobility headed by Genghis Khan. This predominance of the Mongol element explains why historians customarily describe the movement as a whole as Mongol.

The death of Genghis Khan created a momentary lull, during which the Mongol empire was divided between the sons of the deceased leader in accordance with the latter's plan. In 1236 Mongol armies were in motion again, the main direction of their movement being toward eastern Europe. Although the Mongols did not create a permanent foothold in Europe, they did establish a state in the area of the Volga River north of the Caspian Sea. The principal leader in these activities was Batu, a grandson of Genghis Khan who had acquired the inheritance originally assigned to his father after the latter's premature death. The armies which fought under Batu's command were called collectively the Golden Horde, and the state which arose out of their conquests north of the Caspian become known by this name. The capital of the Golden Horde was Serai, a new city erected on the banks of the lower Volga. When Batu died in 1256, he was succeeded after a brief interval by his brother Berke (1257–1267), who converted to Islam. This conversion, which set an example for the Mongol chieftains to follow, made the Golden Horde the first Muslim Mongol state.

The Fall of Baghdad

The year of Batu's death also marked the beginning of a new offensive against the central lands of Islam. The leader of this campaign was another grandson of Genghis Khan named Hulagu. After crossing the Oxus River, Hulagu's forces occupied northern Iran almost without resistance. By 1258 the Mongols (with many Turks in their ranks) had crossed the Zagros mountains into Iraq and had reached the gates of Baghdad. The city fell immediately into their hands and was given over to plunder for several days, in the course of which the Abbasid caliph[3] was killed and the caliphate itself abolished.

The fall of Baghdad created a shock wave that was felt throughout the Islamic East. The very name Mongol had spelled terror in the minds of the masses for more than a quarter of a century, ever since Genghis Khan's first incursions into Transoxiana and north-

3. ruling dynasty in Baghdad

ern Iran. The atrocities committed on occasion by the Mongols against vanquished populations had evoked widespread fear. The great Muslim cities of Transoxiana, for example, had been ruthlessly sacked and a large part of the population slaughtered. A similar fate had now befallen Baghdad, a city rich in past glories.

But the scandal of Baghdad's fall was due not only to the ruthlessness of the Mongols but also to their paganism. Unlike Berke of the Golden Horde, Hulagu and his followers made no pretense of being Muslims. Instead, they deliberately favored the non-Muslim population and themselves clung fast to their ancestral traditions. The Christians enjoyed an especially favored status owing partly to the fact that Hulagu's principal wife professed Christianity. The Sunnī[4] population, by contrast, found themselves out of favor. The Shī'īs,[5] on the other hand, were given a freer hand. In short, the central and eastern lands of Islam and seat of the time-honored caliphate had been ravaged and subdued by a professed enemy of Islam.

After capturing Baghdad, the Mongols proceeded westward toward the Mediterranean, taking by storm the great cities of Syria, Damascus and Aleppo. The Mongol advance seemed unstoppable, and the remaining lands of Islam seemed open to attack. However, at this juncture Hulagu was required to return to Mongolia to deal with an internal political crisis which had erupted among the Mongols. In his absence, the Mongol army, under the command of a deputy of Hulagu, reached the limit of its expansion. In a battle fought near the Palestinian village of 'Ayn Ja-lūt in 1260, the Mongol army suffered defeat at the hands of a new power which had recently emerged in Egypt, the Mamlūks. Thus, the unstoppable Mongol tide was finally stopped, and Egypt and the Islamic lands to the West were saved from the Mongol onslaught.

The victorious Mamlūks followed up their success at 'Ayn Ja-lūt by expelling the Mongols from the captured cities of Syria, in which endeavor they enjoyed the cooperation of these cities' inhabitants who were emboldened by the 'Ayn Ja-lūt victory to rise up against their Mongol occupiers. In due time most of Syria became Mamlūk territory, and the Mongols were obliged to settle for their gains in Iraq and the eastern lands.

The new Mongol state maintained its principal capital at Tabrīz, a city located near the northern border of modern Iran within a territory known as Azarbayjan (now divided between Iran and the U.S.S.R.). In the east, Khorasan (which the Mongols had controlled since the time of Genghis Khan) became a second important center of Mongol power and influence. After Hulagu's death in 1263, the rule over this predominantly Iranian empire passed on to his son

4. one branch of Islam; followers of Mu'awiya 5. branch of Islam, followers of 'Ali

Abaqa and remained within the line of his descendents for three-quarters of a century. These descendants bore the title of Il-Khan.

Under the sixth Il-Khanid ruler, Ghazan, a fundamental change in the religious policy of the state took place. Ghazan, a convert to Islam, restored Sunni Islam to its former pre-eminence and encouraged the mass conversion of the Mongols to Islam. In this way, the stigma of paganism was removed from the Il-Khanid state, and a more harmonious relationship between ruler and ruled was achieved. However, the Il-Khanid state continued to suffer from internal disorders. On the whole, the Il-Khanids ruled badly, and their lands, including Iraq, underwent serious economic decline.

Rise of the Mamlūk Regime

The rise to power of the Mamlūk regime in Egypt was the result of a chain of events set in motion by the death of the Ayyūbid sultan al-Malik al-Sālih in 1249. Al-Malik al-Sālih had created a corps of Turkish Mamlūk soldiers, the largest ever in Egypt's history up to his time, and had made this corps the mainstay of his army. These Mamlūks were stationed in barracks on an island in the Nile near Cairo and accordingly became known collectively as the Bahrīs (from Bahr, the common Arabic term in Egypt for the Nile). The Bahrīs had demonstrated their military prowess by inflicting a defeat on the Crusader army of Louis IX, which had invaded Egypt just before al-Malik al-Sālih's death. When the son of al-Malik al-Sālih, who had been engaged in duties in Mesopotamia, appeared in Cairo after his father's death to claim the throne, he brought with him Mamlūks of his own, whom he proceeded to appoint to high offices. This precipitated an immediate crisis. The Bahrīs interpreted the would-be sultan's action as an attempt to reduce their power. In 1250 a group of them murdered the new aspirant to the throne and rallied behind al-Malik al-Sālih's widow, Shajar al-Durr. The latter in turn appointed as co-ruler a Turkish general named Aybeg, whom she soon married and allowed to assume the title of sultan. This arrangement lasted only until 1257, when both Aybeg and Shajar al-Durr met their deaths as a result of palace intrigues. After a two-year inter-regnum, during which Aybeg's son was accepted as nominal ruler in order to allow time for the real struggle for power to take place, a former general under Aybeg named Qutuz ascended the throne. However, a year later Qutuz was assassinated by his own officers in order to clear the way for one of them to take his place. This new sultan was Baybars, a prominent officer of the Bahri corps. He was to rule as the undisputed master for the following seventeen years (1260–1277). Although later Egyptian historians were to count him as the fourth Mamlūk sultan, Baybars may be considered as the real founder of the new Mamlūk order. His reign, much more than the brief reigns of his ineffective predecessors, marks the real beginning of the Mamlūk era, a period which was to cover two and a half centuries of Egypt's and Syria's history.

A story was told concerning Baybars' rise to power which reveals the conception of rule that was to characterize the Mamlūk system of politics. It was said that after Baybars and his party had killed Qutuz they promptly reported this deed to a Mamlūk officer named Aqtay. "Which of you killed him?" asked Aqtay. "I did," replied Baybars. "Then sit on the throne in his place," said Aqtay. Whereupon all the Mamlūks promptly offered their allegiance to Baybars as the new sultan. The principle underlying this story, namely that the rule belongs to the most powerful, the one powerful enough to seize the throne and eliminate all rivals, was to become a cornerstone of the Mamlūk system. It reflected the circumstances that had given rise to the Mamlūk take-over and the cancellation of Ayyūbid legitimacy. In particular, it determined Baybars' own rise to power. It also was to determine the sequence of events after Baybars' death. . . .

Although the method of succession was a variable of Mamlūk politics, certain basic features of the Mamlūk system remained constant throughout the two and a half centuries of Mamlūk rule. The most striking of these features was the essentially alien character of the military class. The Mamlūk system seems to have been deliberately designed to keep the military aloof from the indigenous population. Persons born within Mamlūk territories, including sons of Mamlūk soldiers and officers, were barred from serving in the regular armed forces. Only an auxiliary and inferior force called the *halqa* was open to natives, and service in the *halqa* offered little opportunity for personal advancement.

The ranks of the regular forces were supplied exclusively from slave markets. The Mamlūk state kept up a lively slave trade, one of the principal suppliers being the Golden Horde Mongols, who obtained Turkish slaves directly from the Steppe. The first Mamlūks are thought to have purchased as many as 800 slaves a year, although the later Mamlūks bought much fewer. By means of these purchases, the mamlūk or slave character of the military was perpetuated from generation to generation. To be part of the Mamlūk military class was, by definition, to have a slave origin. The slaves were obtained as youth, immediately Islamized, and then put through a long and arduous training program. Once the training was completed, they were formally manumitted and admitted to the ranks of the adult soldiery. However, even as adults they continued to maintain steadfast loyalty to their original masters.

The rationale of this system appears obvious. Only youths fresh from the Steppe, so it was believed, possessed the toughness and spiritedness required for excellence in the military arts. Only they, by virtue of their slave origins, could be counted upon to be absolutely loyal to their superiors and unreservedly devoted to the military way of life. The native population, softened by the sedentary way of life, was believed to be incapable of cultivating the qualities and physical skills required of the true warrior.

The sons of the Mamlūks, being excluded from the nonhereditary ruling caste to which their fathers belonged, were obliged to enter civilian careers, unless they chose to serve in the socially inferior *halqa* corps. The principal civilian careers open to them were in religion and in the civil administration. In these fields, they worked together with, and soon became absorbed into, the indigenous population. . . .

Stability Under Bahrī Mamlūk Rule

These developments notwithstanding, the first century of Mamlūk rule (1250–1350), during which the Bahrīs were in power, proved to be a surprisingly prosperous period economically speaking. The following five factors may be mentioned to account for this prosperity: (1) the effectiveness of the Mamlūk government under the Bahrīs, (2) the improvement of public health, (3) the influx of economically productive populations from the eastern lands, (4) the stability of the monetary system, and (5) continuing trade with Europe.

The government of the Bahrī Mamlūks afforded peace and security within the Mamlūk territories at a time when turmoil prevailed in many other areas. This peace and security were naturally conducive to economic activity. Furthermore, the Mamlūk state itself, continuing in the tradition of its predecessors, encouraged and to a large extent sponsored international trade, granting residential privileges to foreign merchants and maintaining careful control over vital sea routes, especially the all-important Red Sea route.

Judging from the absence of evidence to the contrary in our sources, public health during the first century of Bahrī rule seems to have been good. The chronicles of the period mention very few epidemics or severe famines. The infrequency of such misfortunes increased longevity and reduced infant mortality, resulting in a growth of population and, consequently, of the labor force. Growth of population was also stimulated by the influx of large numbers of people from the land to the East, especially Iraq, as a result of the Mongol atrocities. Among these immigrants were many 'ulama', merchants, artisans, bureaucrats and soldiers, including even some Mongols, all of whom were capable of being absorbed in a productive manner into the economy of the Mamlūk empire.

The stability of the Mamlūk monetary system under the Bahrīs was due to the existence of a continuing supply of precious metals (gold and silver), making it possible to mint both dīnārs and dirhems of high quality. Gold was particularly abundant, being imported, as before, from West Africa. Close relations with West Africa were maintained. The geographer Ibn Battūta, who travelled to West Africa, mentions in one of his writings that Egyptians lived there, and both he and the historian Ibn Khaldūn testify to extensive commercial contacts between the two areas. Silver came to Egypt, as before, from Europe and Central Asia; while the supply of silver was not as steady as that of gold, it was sufficient to meet the needs of the Egyptian mints.

The trade with Europe provided a vital market for the products of Egyptian agriculture and industry as well as an important source of precious metals in the form of gold and silver coins. The transit trade, too, which entailed the transport to Europe of luxury goods from India and the Far East, brought enormous profits to the Mamlūk empire. European merchants continued to maintain hostels and consulates in Alexandria and to carry on business in Egyptian markets. Syria, on the other hand, attracted rather few European merchants in the Mamlūk period. This was partly due to the growth of rival trading centers in Cyprus and Little Armenia, both of which were Christian lands, and to the increased use of trade routes connecting these centers with the eastern lands.

The fall of Acre to the Mamlūks in 1291 had an adverse effect on trade with Europe. The Pope, hoping to weaken the Mamlūk economy as well as the Mamlūk army, attempted to place an embargo on trade between Europe and the Mamlūk empire. This effort succeeded to some extent in restricting the flow of war materials to Egypt, but it did not put an end to the trade with the Mamlūks, as the Pope had hoped. In fact, so strong was the demand for eastern goods and the desire for profit that the Pope himself was constrained to issue permits for this lucrative trade. Thus, in spite of the papal campaign against the Mamlūks, trade between Europe and Egypt continued after 1291, even if on a restricted basis. . . .

Cultural Life

The Mamlūk period is particularly rich in biographical and historical writing, traditions carried forward from earlier times. The greatest biographer of the period was Ibn Khāllikān (d. 1282) and the great historian al-Maqrīzī (d. 1441). Ibn Khāllikān's *Obituaries of Eminent Men* contains biographical notes on 865 of the most distinguished Muslims in history and has become an essential tool of Islamic studies. A British scholar, H. A. Nicholson, called it "the best general biography ever written" (*Literary History of the Arabs*, p. 452). To al-Maqrīzī we owe important works on the topography of Egypt, the history of the Fātimids, the history of the Ayyūbids and Mamlūks (to 1440), and a biography of famous Egyptians.

In literature proper, the Mamlūk period is famous not so much for its "higher literature" as for developments which took place in the domain of popular literature. It was in the Mamlūk period that the popular romantic legends centering around the figures of ʿAntar and Baybars took their present form. It was also in the same period that the famous collection of stories called *The Thousand and One Nights* entered the final stage of compilation. The earlier history of this collection is poorly known. The Shāhrazād story, which serves as the framework of the collection, has been traced to India, but the stories themselves are of diverse origin. Before these stories were assembled as written literature, they were transmitted by storytellers throughout the world of Islam. Egypt had an especially large share of storytellers, and old stories were often cast in the familiar setting of Egypt itself. For example, the *fāris* who appears often in the *Nights* portrays the Mamlūk warrior, rather than the soldier of the Abbasid period within which the stories are often nominally set. Also, the customs and manners displayed in the *Nights* often reflect Mamlūk Egypt. Being designed for popular consumption, these stories were of course originally told in the vernacular language and had to be, in assuming a literary character, adjusted at least superficially to the standards of classical Arabic.

In poetry the only figure of the Mamlūk period worth mentioning is al-Busīrī (d. 1296), a poet of Berber extraction who composed what is perhaps the most popular of all Arabic poems, an Ode to the Prophet entitled *The Mantle*. In some areas where this poem became known it was invested with miraculous powers and its verses were recited as charms. Numerous commentaries were written on it.

Before leaving aside the subject of cultural life under the Mamlūks, one final point should be noted. Whereas in the other Islamic lands (except the Maghrib) the Persian language flourished as a medium of artistic expression and was coming to exercise a great influence on the development of other Islamic literatures, in Mamlūk Syria and Egypt Arabic remained the sole literary language. Thus, while Islamic civilization was developing along new lines elsewhere, in the Mamlūk lands it continued to develop in its original Arabic form. The Mamlūk empire was a haven not only for Sunnī orthodoxy but also for Arab culture.

Islamic Art

Oleg Grabar

Oleg Grabar explains that representational images have historically played a limited role in Arab-Muslim art for reasons that are unclear. Although Muslim doctrine forbade the *worship* of images, there was no apparent prohibition of the making of images themselves. Grabar identifies three notable exceptions to this absence of representation of living forms: The first is princely art, which contained beautiful representations of worldly fun and pleasure. The second exception appeared in the twelfth and thirteenth centuries with a remarkable explosion of representational images, especially miniatures, on ceramics, glassware, and metalwork. According to Grabar this evolved with increased contact with Europe and Asia and a corresponding expression of vitality and worldliness. The third exception is a limited amount of folk art imbued with ancient cultlike or magical images.

The Arab-Muslim production of nonrepresentational art found a high level of expression in writing and calligraphy. Grabar argues that calligraphic arts represent the Muslim idea that all creations stem from the will of God, evoked by the Word. Arab artists also expressed ideas without representation through the arabesque. Grabar writes that the arabesque has two main features: the dematerialization of the world and the reliance on abstract forms rather than concrete details. The arabesque allowed Muslim artists to express a rich world of forms and to seek meanings that went well beyond decoration.

During the Middle Ages, Islamic art was highly prized. Grabar argues that Islamic artists were able to create decorative and inexpensive artwork accessible to many levels of society. This included beautiful utilitarian objects such as textiles, pottery, bronzes, and fine utensils that added pleasure to the daily routines of life. Grabar concludes that the greatest distinction of Islamic art is the diverse and aesthetically pleasing ways it satisfied individual needs and desires.

Excerpted from Oleg Grabar, "Architecture and Art," in *The Genius of Arab Civilization*, edited by John R. Hayes. Copyright © 1975, 1978, 1983 Mobil Oil Corporation. Reprinted with permission from The MIT Press.

Oleg Grabar is a professor of Islamic art at Harvard University in Cambridge, Massachusetts. He is the author of several books, including *Islamic Architecture and Its Decoration*, *The Formation of Islamic Art*, and *The Alhambra*.

R eflection on works of Islamic art other than buildings generally produces two immediate impressions: the virtual absence of representations of living forms and the predominance of useful and frequently luxurious objects—textiles, ceramics, glass, and metalwork. Both impressions are correct, but if they are not studied carefully they may also be misleading.

Representation of Living Forms

Neither the Qur'an[1] nor very early Muslim practice in Arabia itself indicates the existence of a Muslim doctrine on representation of living forms. It seems that the question never really arose, for images rarely appeared in Arabia. There were a few idols, rejected by Islam as idols but not as representations, and a few imported luxury objects decorated with representations, which never seemed to have disturbed anyone. In other words, although Islam asserted with full force that only God is the Creator and only He is to be worshipped, neither one of these basic tenets was associated with the matter of representation of living forms.

Attitudes changed considerably, however, when the Muslim conquest brought the Arabs into immediate contact with the Mediterranean and Iranian worlds. These cultures had unusually rich histories of painting and sculpture representing virtually every imaginable subject in dozens of different styles. Moreover, the seventh century was a unique period in the history of the arts. More than in any other recorded period of history, images and representations played an essential part in the affairs of church and state. Icons abounded. People at almost all levels, from pious folk to sophisticated intellectuals, were accustomed to equating art subjects with art objects in terms of both value and effectiveness. The state, for its part, had developed an extremely complex iconography of power, whereby a sophisticated system of signs could serve an immense number of internal and external purposes.

The Absence of Representational Images

The Arabs were clearly fascinated and tempted by this world of virtually operational representations. As Muslims they rejected the wor-

1. the Koran, the Islamic book of scripture

ship of images, and as still unsophisticated egalitarians they regarded elaborate ceremonies and official symbols as vain and pompous nonsense. The extent of the temptation is revealed most clearly in the Umayyad[2] private retreats, where a wealth of images of all sorts illustrates, among many other themes, the power of the new princes. In a celebrated fresco in the Jordanian bath at Qusayr Amrah, for example, six kings of the earth are shown greeting or saluting an Arab colleague. Although many comparable later examples have disappeared, literary evidence suggests that the Umayyad examples were not unique.

At the same time, the more common Muslim attitude toward the artistic practices they encountered was to reject the use of images as symbols of the faith and of the state. In part this rejection was based directly on Islamic theology, insofar as the absolute power of God and the sin of idolatry make the utilization of representations untenable. But there are reasons to believe that theological justification followed, rather than preceded, rejection. Social attitudes and political needs may, in fact, have been far more important. The egalitarian moralism of Arab Islam inspired a mistrust of any intermediary between man and God or, for that matter, between man and secular authority. There was no clergy, and at least initially and in theory caliphs were chosen by the whole community. From a political point of view there were obvious risks involved in adopting the ways of the predominant Christian system. Imitation would have cost the new culture its integrity as a new and better way, an exemplary path for others to follow.

Muslim iconoclasm, therefore, may be properly regarded as the result of concrete historical circumstances and not as a theological doctrine, as in the Old Testament. Its survival for so many centuries and its predominant importance in the Arab world, rather than in either Iran or Turkey, are no doubt attributable to a deeply established sentiment in the mentality of the Arab world. It is not a reflection of any traditional Semitic attitude. Although the matter still requires much investigation, this continuous iconoclastic tendency may be the product of a constant interplay between traditionally image-free nomadic worlds and urban, bourgeois morality.

Periods of Representational Art

Be this as it may, representations of living forms played a much more limited role in Arab-Islamic art than in most other artistic traditions. Three exceptions occur, however.

In the art of princes, a much more international taste dominated, and foreign influences were more constant. As a result, lifelike rep-

2. an Arab clan

resentations were employed—for example, in Spanish ivories with beautiful carvings of a princely life, in the woodwork in Egypt, and in numerous fragments of wall paintings in the palaces of Samarra. Unfortunately, little remains of this great art of princes, so admired by foreign visitors. Its characteristics are more easily detected through its impact elsewhere—for example, in the sculptures of the Armenian church at Akhtamar. A central feature of this princely art of images is its emphasis on royal pastime as the main expression of power. Hunting, feasting, listening to music, and watching dancers or acrobats are the most common themes of the princely tradition. Presumably, representations of this world of pleasure and fun served to remind the viewer of the difference between the ruler and the ruled.

The second exception is more difficult to explain. In the twelfth and thirteenth centuries, almost all techniques suddenly become animated with images. Ceramics, glassware, and metalwork, produced for very broad segments of society, are covered with all sorts of images, ranging from astronomy to a princely cycle applicable to the urban bourgeoisie as well. Even animated sculpture appears in a number of official architectural monuments, such as the citadel of Aleppo, a caravanserai[3] in Sinjar in Iraq, and a gate in Baghdad. But the most remarkable example of this explosion of images occurs in the creation of an Arab art of book illustration. Scientific manuals, such as the herbals of Dioscorides and of pseudo-Galen, and literary works, such as the *Kitab al-Aghani,* the ancient stories of *Kalila and Dimna,* and *Maqamat* by al-Hariri, the best example of the newer genre of picaresque adventures—all these books are illustrated with miniatures. Almost always directly connected with some textual reference, these illustrations display a striking wealth of practical observations on the life of the times. Then, in the fourteenth century, almost as abruptly as it began, this fascination with representations disappears. Why did it develop? And why at this particular time? The most plausible explanation, although not entirely satisfactory, is that the twelfth and thirteenth centuries were periods of unusually broad contacts between all parts of Europe and Asia. Everywhere, from England to China, exciting innovations appeared simultaneously at all levels of society and in all realms. It was a time of new conquests for Islam, in Anatolia and in India. The victory over the Crusaders was a major achievement. And many Arab Christians converted to Islam. In ways that are still quite unclear, the growth of images in the twelfth and thirteenth centuries seems to have been one of several ways in which the Arab world expressed the excitement and vitality of the times, a vitality soon to be sapped by the Mongol invasions.

3. an Arabian inn

The third exception, which occurred in folk art and folk traditions, is of lesser importance. Like any other rich culture, the Arab-Islamic world possessed a substratum of popular cults and beliefs imbued with ancient magic or pseudomagic images. Some of these appear occasionally on ceramics and may have affected certain stylistic tendencies in Egypt and Iraq.

Interesting though they are, these exceptions should not mask the fact that images are absent in most Arab-Islamic art and that representations are never used in any art form related to the Faith. This does not mean, however, that the Arab-Islamic world did not develop means to express itself visually. Its major contribution to world art lies precisely in its success in finding other ways to express its ideas.

Writing as Art

The most important is writing. At the simplest level is calligraphy, the art of beautiful writing, with all sorts of temporal and regional differentiation in style. Calligraphic art is best known and has been best preserved in manuscripts of the Qur'an dating from the eighth or ninth century or later, but almost every Arabic manuscript exhibits a preoccupation with aesthetic values in the writing of script. In addition, a wide variety of illumination techniques were introduced to enhance the beauty of a book. The names of great calligraphers have been preserved, even though their actual works have not often been identified. Calligraphers did not always give as much care to writing on objects as they gave to writing in books. On objects they often replaced meaningful phrases with imitations of letters. Yet their writing on objects shows more personality than their writing in books. On objects the calligraphy functions almost like a signature.

The artistic function of writing was not limited to the aesthetic qualities of the script, however. Especially on objects and in architecture, the choice of texts served an iconographic function as well. Specific passages were selected in order to communicate the kind of information that images and representations provide in other artistic traditions. Thus, on many ceramics and bronzes proverbs or expressions of good wishes indicate the social purpose of the objects involved. In other instances, mostly in architecture, the choice of passages from the Qur'an has a precise purpose, and in still other examples signatures and dates have led to any number of social and economic observations.

Beyond its iconographic and literal significance, calligraphy serves a third, more aesthetic purpose in Arab-Islamic art. When the decorators of the Alhambra[4] covered its walls with endless repetitions of formulas such as "There is no victor but God" and when ar-

4. royal architectural monument

tisans inscribed objects with the simple phrase "Blessing from God" (often reduced to "Blessing" alone), it was not mere ritualistic redundancy. Their objective was to evoke the key Muslim idea that all creations and all acts occur only by the will of God. The means by which this evocation occurs is the Word, whose presence must be the constant accompaniment of man's life.

The Arabesque

The other means whereby Arab-Islamic art was able to express ideas visually without resorting to representations is a stylistic tendency that, for lack of a better term, we may call "the arabesque." The arabesque consists of two main and interdependent features. One is the dematerialization of the natural world. Few designs in Islamic art ever strive for accurate reproductions of visible elements, even when their ultimate sources are in nature. Persons or animals are rarely depicted with the volume and spatial qualities that are theirs in reality or in the classical tradition. In general, the artist chooses a few characteristic details and reproduces them in flat, two-dimensional designs, often coloring them arbitrarily. Plants may be endowed with animal features, and human heads can appear in the midst of almost any pattern. The second consistent feature of the arabesque is that almost all arabesque designs can be analyzed and described more easily in abstract terms—dark or light, full or void, symmetrical or repetitive—than in terms of their concrete details.

By dematerializing the visible world and by substituting artificial principles of composition for natural forms, Muslim art succeeded in achieving something remarkably contemporary. It demonstrated that everything can be made beautiful and exciting and that an almost infinite number of transformations can be attached to any one motif. This development has frequently been interpreted as another example of a Muslim proclamation of God as the only creator. Whether this is correct or not, the result has been a striking freedom for Muslim artists to create an especially rich world of forms. And it is probably correct to seek meanings in these forms beyond their purely decorative value. As late as the fifteenth century, Arabic texts constantly refer to the *lifelike* quality achieved in successful artistic creativity. If this judgment is mystifying to non-Muslims, if it seems contradicted by their own experience as they look at Muslim works of art, it is perhaps because these monuments and objects reflect a reality beyond the obvious.

Egalitarian Aspects of Islamic Art

At the time of the European Middle Ages, Islamic objects were prized throughout the world and especially in the West. Bodies of Christian saints were wrapped in Near Eastern textiles, and several schools of ceramicists, ivory makers, and metalworkers in Europe tried for centuries to imitate Islamic techniques.

It is indeed true that Islamic objects display great technical variety and inventiveness. Ceramicists developed luster, glazes, and a host of other techniques to extend the possibilities of design and color. They sought ways to imitate the qualities of expensive gold and silver objects in cheaper clay. As a result, artisans and patrons did not feet constricted by technical limitations: Although it is a subject of much debate, the first examples of these new techniques probably appeared in Iraq in the second half of the eighth century. More or less the same pattern of development occurred in metalwork, glass, and textiles, although each medium obviously exhibits its own peculiarities.

Why did the Muslim world value the art of the object so highly? What is the meaning of the whole phenomenon? The key point is that, much earlier than any other society in the Middle Ages, Islamic culture combined egalitarian ideals and urban values. This synthesis led to the extensive development of beautiful objects that could serve formal purposes in the relationships between men as well as the needs of daily life. These objects were produced inexpensively enough to permit as many levels of society as possible to enjoy them. There is indeed a deeply democratic aspect to the creativity of Islamic art.

The most obvious kind of object used in social and personal relations—textiles—has not been well preserved or studied. We do know that the state strictly controlled the manufacture of textiles through a complicated system of private and public enterprises. Robes and cloth were given as gifts, and they indicated or symbolized honors, ranks, and achievements. They were carefully stored in private houses, and royal treasuries contained thousands of them. Although masses of textile fragments exist today, scholars are not yet able to relate them to the precise ceremonies and uses documented in literary sources. Because textiles were easily transported, they were major carriers of Arab-Islamic taste, and quite frequently the movement of textiles explains the appearance of Arab-Islamic styles and motifs in remote areas.

Gold and silver objects were also obvious gifts and symbols of importance, and a surviving description of the Fatimid[5] treasure in Cairo provides us with a tantalizing list of magnificent works, none of which exists today. It is only through their occasional impact on later, humbler works of art and through a small number of royal ivories from Spain that we can begin to imagine what these luxurious objects might have been like.

5. ruling dynasty in Egypt

If we are not on very secure ground in defining the official and royal objects used by rulers and presented as princely gifts, we do have a somewhat better understanding of the utilitarian art available at the lower social level of the urban world. Exquisite pottery and elaborately decorated bronzes demonstrate a considerable variety of characteristics within a single technique and indicate a wide breadth of taste in traditional Islamic culture. The mass production of artistically fine utensils transformed daily life and daily activities— eating, drinking, serving water or food, washing—into pleasing and attractive events. The introduction of sensuous pleasure into routine settings and the practice of conspicuous consumption reflect the strikingly modern attitude toward the functions of art that was so characteristic of the traditional Muslim world.

The growth of an art devoted to the creation of individualized, personal objects, as opposed to huge paintings and sculptures, indicates the emphasis the Muslim culture placed on the private world. As in any culture, there was, of course, a tendency toward sameness of taste and design at any one time. Yet no matter how repetitive any technique became, unique objects frequently were produced in the Muslim world. These original creations are the great works of art of the culture, but they came into being only because of the consistently high level of technical accomplishment within the culture as a whole. The superb "Baptistère de St. Louis" in the Louvre (actually a bronze basin inlaid with silver made for a Mamluk prince) and the *Maqamat* manuscript illustrated by al-Wasiti in 1237 are among the crowning achievements of a tradition that had existed for centuries. They were made for personal, private enjoyment. It is perhaps the greatest distinction of Islamic art that, almost from its inception, it found aesthetically brilliant ways to satisfy individual needs and desires.

The Arab World Under Assault

Amin Maalouf

Amin Maalouf explains that the Arab world in the thirteenth century was under assault by two powerful enemies: the French and the Mongols. The first incursion of Mongols into Islamic territory occurred in Syria between 1218 and 1221. Many ruling dynasties were overthrown and uprooted, including the Khwarazmian Turks. According to Maalouf, the fleeing Turks regrouped and began themselves to conquer Syrian cities, finally taking Jerusalem from the Franks who had controlled the city. Maalouf explains that another threat to Islamic lands appeared in 1249 when the king of France, Louis IX, launched an attack on Egypt. But the French, called the Franj in colloquial Arabic, were defeated by a combination of Muslim and Mamluk Turks at Mansura in 1250. With that victory, Maalouf states, the Turks believed that they had saved Egypt and accordingly claimed more authority and leadership. They were rebuffed, but took control of Egypt anyway under the leadership of a brilliant Turkish officer named Baybars.

Maalouf reports that the western Arab world came under a renewed Mongol assault headed by a grandson of Genghis Khan, Hülegü, who had brutally attacked and slaughtered the population of Baghdad and killed the caliph. Hülegü and the Mongols pushed farther into Islamic lands, ultimately advancing on Cairo. The Mamluk Turks who controlled Cairo quickly mobilized the Egyptian army under the leadership of Qutuz. Maalouf argues that the Mongols were weakened by the absence of Hülegü, who retreated to his homeland with a sizable portion of his army to maintain power after the death of the Supreme Khan. Qutuz surprised the remaining Mongols in

Excerpted from Amin Maalouf, *The Crusades Through Arab Eyes.* Copyright © 1984 Al Saqi Books. Reprinted with permission from Schoken Books, a division of Random House, Inc.

a decisive battle near Damascus on September 3, 1260. The Arabs were liberated from the scourge of the Mongols.

Amin Maalouf is a writer, journalist, and the editor-in-chief of the weekly magazine *Jeune Afrique*.

If one day you are told that the earth has never known such calamity since God created Adam, do not hesitate to believe it, for such is the strict truth. Nebuchadnezzar's massacre of the children of Israel and the destruction of Jerusalem are generally cited as among the most infamous tragedies of history. But these were as nothing compared to what has happened now. No, probably not until the end of time will a catastrophe of such magnitude be seen again.

Nowhere else in his voluminous *Perfect History* does Ibn al-Athir[1] adopt such a pathetic tone. Page after page, his sadness, terror, and incredulity spring out as if he were superstitiously postponing the moment when he would finally have to speak the name of the scourge: Genghis Khan.

The Threat of Genghis Khan

The rise of the Mongol conqueror began shortly after the death of Saladin,[2] but not until another quarter of a century had passed did the Arabs feel the approach of the threat. Genghis Khan first set about uniting the various Turkic and Mongol tribes of central Asia under his authority; he then embarked on what he hoped would be the conquest of the world. His forces moved in three directions: to the east, where the Chinese empire was reduced to vassal status and then annexed; to the north-west, where first Russia and then eastern Europe were devastated; to the west, where Persia was invaded. 'All cities must be razed', Genghis Khan used to say, 'so that the world may once again become a great steppe in which Mongol mothers will suckle free and happy children.' And prestigious cities indeed would be destroyed, their populations decimated: Bukhārā, Samarkand, and Herat, among others.

The first Mongol thrust into an Islamic country coincided with the various Frankish invasions of Egypt between 1218 and 1221. . . . This was undoubtedly part of the explanation for al-Kāmil's[3] conciliatory attitude over the question of Jerusalem. But Genghis Khan finally abandoned any attempt to venture west of Persia. With his death in 1227 at the age of sixty-seven, the pressure of the horsemen of the steppes on the Arab world eased for some years.

---

1. Arab chronicler 2. Arab sovereign in the twelfth century 3. Arab sultan

In Syria the scourge first made itself felt indirectly. Among the many dynasties crushed by the Mongols on their way was that of the Khwarazmian Turks, who had earlier supplanted the Seljuks from Iraq to India. With the dismantling of this Muslim empire, whose hour of glory had passed, remnants of its army were compelled to flee as far as possible from the terrifying victors. Thus it was that one fine day some ten thousand Khwarazmian horsemen arrived in Syria, pillaging and holding cities hostage and participating as mercenaries in the internal struggles of the Ayyubids.[4] In June 1224, believing themselves strong enough to establish a state of their own, the Khwarazmians attacked Damascus. They plundered the neighbouring villages and sacked the orchards of Ghūta. But then, since they were incapable of sustaining a long siege against the city's resistance, they changed their target and suddenly headed for Jerusalem, which they occupied without difficulty on 11 July. Although the Frankish population was largely spared, the city itself was plundered and put to the torch. To the great relief of all the cities of Syria, a fresh attack on Damascus several months later was decimated by a coalition of Ayyubid princes.

The French Attack Egypt

This time the Frankish knights would never retake Jerusalem. Frederick,[5] whose diplomatic skill had enabled the Occidentals to keep the

Louis IX of France

flag of the cross flying over the walls of the city for fifteen years, was no longer interested in its fate. Abandoning his Oriental ambitions, he now preferred to maintain more amicable relations with the Cairene[6] leaders. In 1247, when Louis IX of France planned an expedition against Egypt, the emperor sought to dissuade him. Better still, he kept Ayyūb, son of al-Kāmil, regularly informed of the preparations of the French expedition.

Louis arrived in the East in 1248, but he did not immediately head for the Egyptian border, for he felt it would be too risky to undertake a campaign before spring. He therefore settled in Cyprus and spent these months of respite striving to realize the dream that was to haunt the Franj[7] to

4. Arab dynasty 5. Frederick II, Holy Roman Emperor 6. Egyptian leadership 7. Arabic word for Westerners and the French in particular

the end of the thirteenth century and beyond: the conclusion of an alliance with the Mongols that would trap the Arab world in a pincer movement. Emissaries thus shuttled regularly between the camps of the invaders from the East and the invaders from the West. Late in 1248 Louis received a delegation in Cyprus that put forward the tempting possibility that the Mongols might convert to Christianity. Entranced by this prospect, he hastily responded by dispatching precious and pious gifts. But Genghis Khan's successors misinterpreted the meaning of this gesture. Treating the king of France as they would a mere vassal, they asked him to send gifts of equivalent value every year. This misunderstanding saved the Arab world from a concerted attack by its two enemies, at least temporarily.

Thus it was that the Occidentals alone launched their assault on Egypt on the fifth of June 1249, although not before the two monarchs had exchanged thunderous declarations of war, in accordance with the customs of the epoch. *I have already warned you many times,* wrote Louis, *but you have paid no heed. Henceforth my decision is made: I will assault your territory, and even were you to swear allegiance to the cross, my mind would not be changed. The armies that obey me cover mountains and plains, they are as numerous as the pebbles of the earth, and they march upon you grasping the swords of fate.* To bolster these threats, the king of France reminded his enemy of a number of successes scored by the Christians against the Muslims in Spain the year before: *We chased your people before us like herds of oxen. We killed the men, made widows of the women, and captured girls and boys. Was that not a lesson to you?* Ayyūb replied in similar vein: *Foolish as you are, have you forgotten the lands you occupied which we have reconquered, even quite recently? Have you forgotten the damage we have inflicted upon you?* Apparently aware of the numerical inferiority of his forces, the sultan found an appropriately reassuring quotation from the Koran: *How often has a small troop vanquished a great, with God's permission, for God is with the good.* This encouraged him to predict to Louis: *Your defeat is ineluctable. Soon you will bitterly regret the adventure on which you have embarked.*

At the outset of their offensive, however, the Franj scored a decisive success. Damietta, which had resisted the last Frankish expedition so courageously thirty years before, was this time abandoned without a fight. Its fall, which sowed disarray in the Arab world, starkly revealed how weak the legatees of the great Saladin had become. Sultan Ayyūb, who was immobilized by tuberculosis and unable to take personal command of his troops, preferred to adopt the policy of his father al-Kāmil rather than lose Egypt: he proposed to Louis that Damietta be exchanged for Jerusalem. But the king of France refused to deal with a defeated and dying 'infidel'. Ayyūb then decided to resist, and had himself transported by litter-bearers to the city of Mansūra, 'the victorious', which had been built by al-Kāmil on the very spot at which the previous Frankish invasion had been defeated. Unfortunately, the sultan's health was sinking fast. Racked by fits of coughing so severe that it seemed that they would never end, he fell into a coma on 20 November, just as the Franj, encouraged by the receding waters of the Nile, left Damietta for Mansūra. Three days later, to the great consternation of his entourage, the sultan died.

How could the army and the people be told that the sultan was dead while the enemy was at the gates of the city and Ayyūb's son Tūrān-Shāh was somewhere in northern Iraq, several weeks' march away? It was then that a providential personality intervened: Shajar al-Durr, or 'Tree of Pearls', a female slave of Armenian origin, beautiful and crafty, who for years had been Ayyūb's favourite wife. Gathering the members of the sultan's family together, she ordered them to keep silent about his death until the prince arrived, and even asked the aged emir[8] Fakhr al-Dīn, Frederick's old friend, to write a letter in the sultan's name summoning the Muslims to *jihād*.[9] . . .

The battle raged around Mansūra throughout the long winter months. Then on 10 February 1250 the Frankish army, aided by treason, penetrated the city by surprise. Ibn Wāsil, who was then in Cairo, relates:

> The emir Fakhr al-Dīn was in his bath when they came and told him the news. Flabbergasted, he immediately leapt into the saddle—without armour or coat of mail—and rushed to see what the situation was. He was attacked by a troop of enemy soldiers, who killed him. The king of the Franj entered the city, and even reached the sultan's palace. His soldiers poured through the streets, while the Muslim soldiers and the inhabitants sought salvation in disordered flight. Islam seemed mortally wounded, and the Franj were about to reap the fruit of their victory when the Mamluk Turks arrived. Since the enemy had dispersed through the streets, these horsemen rushed bravely in pursuit. Everywhere the Franj were taken by surprise and massacred with sword or mace. At the start of the day, the pigeons had carried a message to Cairo announcing the attack of the Franj without breathing a word about the outcome of the battle, so we were all waiting anxiously. Throughout the quarters of the city there was sadness until the next day, when new messages told us of the victory of the Turkish lions. The streets of Cairo became a festival.

In subsequent weeks, from his post in the Egyptian capital, the chronicler would observe two sequences of events that were to change the face of the Arab East: on the one hand, the victorious struggle against the last great Frankish invasion; on the other, a rev-

8. a Turkish title for a military commander 9. holy war

olution unique in history, one that was to raise a caste of officer-slaves to power for nearly three centuries.

The Mamluk Turks Revolt

After his defeat at Mansūra, the king of France realized that his military position was becoming untenable. Unable to take the city, and constantly harassed by the Egyptians in a muddy terrain criss-crossed by countless canals, Louis decided to negotiate. At the beginning of March he sent a conciliatory message to Tūrān-Shāh,[10] who had just arrived in Egypt. In it he declared that he was now prepared to accept Ayyūb's proposal to abandon Damietta in exchange for Jerusalem. The new sultan's response was not long in coming: the generous offers made by Ayyūb should have been accepted during Ayyūb's lifetime. Now it was too late. At this point, the most Louis could hope for was to save his army and get out of Egypt alive, for pressure was mounting on all sides. In mid-March several dozen Egyptian galleys inflicted a severe defeat on the Frankish fleet, destroying or capturing nearly a hundred vessels of all sizes and removing any possibility of the invaders' retreating towards Damietta. On 7 April the invading army tried to run the blockade and was assaulted by the Mamluk battalions, swelled by thousands of volunteers. After several hours of fighting, the Franj had their backs to the wall. To halt the massacre of his men, the king of France capitulated and asked that his life be spared. He was led in chains to Mansūra, where he was locked in the house of an Ayyubid functionary.

Curiously, the new sultan's brilliant victory, far from enhancing his power, brought about his downfall. Tūrān-Shāh was engaged in a dispute with the chief Mamluk officers of his army. The latter believed, not without reason, that Egypt owed its salvation to them, and they therefore demanded a decisive role in the leadership of the country. The sovereign, on the other hand, wanted to take advantage of his newly acquired prestige to place his own supporters in the major posts of responsibility. Three weeks after the victory over the Franj, a group of these Mamluks met together on the initiative of a brilliant 40-year-old Turkish officer named Baybars, a crossbowman, and decided to take action. A revolt broke out on 2 May 1250 at the end of a banquet organized by the monarch. Tūrān-Shāh, wounded in the shoulder by Baybars, was running towards the Nile, hoping to flee by boat, when he was captured by his assailants. He begged them to spare his life, promising to leave Egypt forever and to renounce any claim to power. But the last of the Ayyubid sultans was finished off mercilessly. An envoy of the caliph[11] even had to

10. son of Sultan Ayyūb 11 . spiritual commander of the believers

intervene before the Mamluks would agree to give their former master a proper burial. . . .

The coup d'état in Cairo did not alter the fate of the king of France. An agreement in principle reached during the time of Tūrān-Shāh stipulated that Louis would be released in return for the withdrawal of all Frankish troops from Egyptian territory, Damietta in particular, and the payment of a ransom of one million dinars. The French sovereign was indeed released several days after the accession to power of Umm Khalīl, but not before being treated to a lecture by the Egyptian negotiators: 'How could a sensible, wise, and intelligent man like you embark on a sea voyage to a land peopled by countless Muslims? According to our law, a man who crosses the sea in this way cannot testify in court.' 'And why not?' asked the king. 'Because', came the reply, 'it is assumed that he is not in possession of all his faculties.'

The last Frankish soldier left Egypt before the end of May.

The Sack of Baghdad

Never again would the Occidentals attempt to invade the land of the Nile. The 'blond peril' would soon be eclipsed by the far more terrifying danger of the descendants of Genghis Khan. The great conqueror's empire had been weakened somewhat by the wars of succession that had flared after his death, and the Muslim East had enjoyed an unexpected respite. By 1251, however, the horsemen of the steppes were united once again, under the authority of three brothers, grandsons of Genghis Khan: Möngke, Kubilay, and Hülegü. The first had been designated uncontested sovereign of the empire, whose capital was Karakorum, in Mongolia. The second reigned in Peking. It was the ambition of the third, who had settled in Persia, to conquer the entire Muslim East to the shores of the Mediterranean, perhaps even to the Nile. Hülegü was a complex personality. Initially interested in philosophy and science, a man who sought out the company of men of letters, he was transformed in the course of his campaigns into a savage animal thirsting for blood and destruction. His religious attitudes were no less contradictory. Although strongly influenced by Christianity—his mother, his favourite wife, and several of his closest collaborators were members of the Nestorian[12] church—he never renounced shamanism, the traditional religion of his people. In the territories he governed, notably Persia, he was generally tolerant of Muslims, but once he was gripped by his lust to destroy any political entity capable of opposing him, he waged a war of total destruction against the most prestigious metropolises of Islam.

His first target was Baghdad. At first, Hülegü asked the 'Abbasid caliph, al-Musta'sim, the thirty-seventh of his dynasty, to recognize

---

12. followers of the doctrine of Nestorius, patriarch of Constantinople, 428–431

Mongol sovereignty as his predecessors had once accepted the rule of the Seljuk Turks. The prince of the faithful, overconfident of his own prestige, sent word to the conqueror that any attack on his capital would mobilize the entire Muslim world, from India to north-west Africa. Not in the least impressed, the grandson of Genghis Khan announced his intention of taking the city by force. Towards the end of 1257 he and, it would appear, hundreds of thousands of cavalry began advancing towards the 'Abbasid capital. On their way they destroyed the Assassins'[13] sanctuary at Alamūt and sacked its library of inestimable value, thus making it almost impossible for future generations to gain any in-depth knowledge of the doctrine and activities of the sect. When the caliph finally realized the extent of the threat, he decided to negotiate. He proposed that Hülegü's name be pronounced at Friday sermons in the mosques of Baghdad and that he be granted the title of sultan. But it was too late, for by now the Mongol had definitively opted for force. After a few weeks of courageous resistance, the prince of the faithful had no choice but to capitulate. On 10 February 1258 he went to the victor's camp in person and asked if he would promise to spare the lives of all the citizens if they agreed to lay down their arms. But in vain. As soon as they were disarmed, the Muslim fighters were exterminated. Then the Mongol horde fanned out through the prestigious city demolishing buildings, burning neighbourhoods, and mercilessly massacring men, women, and children—nearly eighty thousand people in all. Only the Christian community of the city was spared, thanks to the intercession of the khan's wife. The prince of the faithful was himself strangled to death a few days after his defeat. The tragic end of the 'Abbasid caliphate stunned the Muslim world. It was no longer a matter of a military battle for control of a particular city, or even country: it was now a desperate struggle for the survival of Islam.

Mongol Advance into Egypt

How far would the Tartars go? Some people were convinced that they would go all the way to Mecca, thus dealing the *coup de grâce* to the religion of the Prophet. In any event they would reach Jerusalem, and soon. All Syria was convinced of this. Just after the fall of Damascus, two Mongol detachments quickly seized two Palestinian cities: Nablus in the centre of the country, and Gaza in the south-west. When Gaza, which lies on the edge of Sinai, was overrun in that tragic spring of 1260, it seemed that not even Egypt would escape devastation. Even before his Syrian campaign had ended, Hülegü dispatched an ambassador to Cairo to demand the unconditional surrender of the land of the Nile. The emissary was received, spoke his piece, and was then beheaded. The Mamluks were

13 . secret Muslim order

not joking. Their methods bore no resemblance to those of Saladin. These sultan-slaves, who had now been ruling for ten years, reflected the hardening, the intransigence, of an Arab world now under attack from all directions. They fought with all the means at their disposal. No scruples, no magnanimous gestures, no compromises. But with courage and to great effect.

All eyes were now turned in their direction, for they represented the last hope of stemming the advance of the invader. For twelve months, power in Cairo had been in the hands of an officer of Turkish origin named Qutuz. Shajar al-Durr and her husband Aybeg had governed together for seven years, but had finally killed each other. There have been many conflicting versions of the end of their rule. The one favoured by popular story-tellers is a mix of love and jealousy spiced with political ambition. The sultana, it says, was bathing her husband, as was her custom. Taking advantage of this moment of détente and intimacy, she scolded the sultan for having taken a pretty 14-year-old girl slave as his concubine. 'Do I no longer please you?' she murmured, to soften his heart. But Aybeg answered sharply: 'She is young, while you are not.' Shajar al-Durr trembled with rage at these words. She rubbed soap in her husband's eyes, while whispering conciliatory words to allay any suspicion, and then suddenly seized a dagger and stabbed him in the side. Aybeg collapsed. The sultana remained immobile for some moments, as if paralysed. Then, heading for the door, she summoned several faithful slaves, who she thought would dispose of the body for her. But to her misfortune, one of Aybeg's sons, who was fifteen at the time, noticed that the bath-water flowing through the outside drain was red. He ran into the room and saw Shajar al-Durr standing half-naked near the door, still holding a bloodstained dagger. She fled through the corridors of the palace, pursued by her stepson, who alerted the guards. Just as they caught up with her, the sultana stumbled and fell, crashing her head violently against a marble slab. By the time they reached her, she was dead.

However highly romanticized, this version is of genuine historical interest inasmuch as it is in all probability a faithful reflection of what was being said in the streets of Cairo in April 1257, just after the tragedy.

However that may be, after the death of the two sovereigns, Aybeg's young son succeeded to the throne. But not for long. As the Mongol threat took shape, the commanders of the Egyptian army realized that an adolescent would be unable to lead the decisive battle now looming. In December 1259, as Hülegü's hordes began to roll across Syria, a coup d'état brought Qutuz to power. He was a mature, energetic man who talked in terms of holy war and called for a general mobilization against the invader, the enemy of Islam.

With hindsight, the new coup in Cairo could be said to represent a genuine patriotic upheaval. The country was immediately placed on a war footing. In July 1260 a powerful Egyptian army moved into Palestine to confront the enemy.

Qutuz was aware that the Mongol army had lost the core of its fighters when Möngke, Supreme Khan of the Mongols, died and his brother Hülegü had to retreat with his army to join in the inevitable succession struggle. The grandson of Genghis Khan had left Syria soon after the fall of Damascus, leaving only a few thousand horsemen in the country, under the command of his lieutenant Kitbuga.

Sultan Qutuz knew that if the invader was to be dealt a decisive blow, it was now or never. The Egyptian army thus began by assaulting the Mongol garrison at Gaza. Taken by surprise, the invaders barely resisted. The Mamluks next advanced on Acre, not unaware that the Franj of Palestine had been more reticent than those of Antioch towards the Mongols. Admittedly, some of their barons still rejoiced in the defeats suffered by Islam, but most were frightened by the brutality of the Asian conquerors. When Qutuz proposed an alliance, their response was not wholly negative: although not prepared to take part in the fighting, they would not object to the passage of the Egyptian army through their territory, and they would not obstruct supplies. The sultan was thus able to advance towards the interior of Palestine, and even towards Damascus, without having to protect his rear.

Kitbuga was preparing to march out to meet them when a popular insurrection erupted in Damascus. The Muslims of the city, enraged by the exactions of the invaders and encouraged by the departure of Hülegü, built barricades in the streets and set fire to those churches that had been spared by the Mongols. It took Kitbuga several days to reestablish order, and this enabled Qutuz to consolidate his positions in Galilee. The two armies met near the village of 'Ayn Jālūt ('Fountain of Goliath') on 3 September 1260. Qutuz had had time to conceal most of his troops, leaving the battlefield to no more than a vanguard under the command of his most brilliant officer, Baybars. Kitbuga arrived in a rush and, apparently ill-informed, fell into the trap. He launched a full-scale assault. Baybars retreated, but as the Mongol gave chase he suddenly found himself surrounded by Egyptian forces more numerous than his own.

The Mongol cavalry was exterminated in a few hours. Kitbuga himself was captured and beheaded forthwith.

On the night of 8 September the Mamluk horsemen rode jubilantly into Damascus, where they were greeted as liberators.

Africa and the Americas

PREFACE

In the thirteenth century three major powers emerged in Africa and the Americas: the Mali Empire in western Africa, the Aztec migration in Mesoamerica, and the Indians at Cahokia in North America. All three of these civilizations were able to overcome the challenges of their environment by first gaining political and military control and then by developing prosperous means of production through sedentary farming and trade.

Like the indigenous Berbers of North Africa, the Malinke people of the Mali Empire in western Africa were influenced by the spread of Islam. The Muslims not only brought their religion, but inspired literacy and stimulated trade. The Mali Empire arose from the collapse of the warring people of Ghana. The Malinke, a tribe that had once been part of Ghana, gained control of the gold-producing area in the savannah region of the Upper Niger River around 1230. Sundiata, the powerful leader of the Malinke, organized fractious clans and subsequently assumed the position of head mansa, the one powerful guardian of the all-important ancestor spirits. Although most of the Mali leadership outwardly expressed Muslim beliefs, they never abandoned their traditional religion based on agricultural spirits and ancestor worship. The Mali Empire grew powerful, sustaining its strength with two primary sources: abundant agricultural production from the fertile soil of the Upper Niger River savannah and the extensive and rich gold trade with Islamic and European merchants. Mali society sustained a wealthy and elite class of professional traders who extended the influence of the Malinke throughout the known world.

Like the Mali, the Indians at Cahokia sustained a thriving empire built on agriculture and trade. In 1250 these North American Indians reached a peak of civilization centered at Cahokia, a magnificent city located on the current site of East St. Louis, Illinois. The city was distinguished by 120 huge earthen pyramids built for rituals that remain unknown today. Archaeologists believe that the rise of the Indians of Cahokia corresponded with the introduction of the hoe and new types of maize, beans, and other agricultural products from Mexico. In addition to farming, the Cahokia Indians conducted a vast and successful trading enterprise, made possible because their location straddled a major nexus on the Mississippi River. Hence, an extensive water network provided easy travel in almost any direction for trade, commerce, and communication. Moreover, Cahokia was the point at which the three indigenous language families of North America converged: Muskogean, Iroquoian, and Siouan.

At the time that the Indians at Cahokia were peaking, a new civilization in Mexico—the Aztec—was emerging. Over the course of several generations beginning at the outset of the thirteenth century, numerous groups of Aztecs migrated to central Mexico. Accounts of this migration vary; some historians suggest that these Aztec people came from a savage and primitive people called the Chichimecs and other accounts claim that they came from a more civilized group called the Toltecs. Soon the Aztecs, poor and warlike, assimilated the indigenous people of the Valley of Mexico around Lake Texcoco, a shallow lake surrounded by swamps and fertile farmland. The unification of the various groups in the valley was expedited by the fact that they spoke the same language, Nahuatl, and shared a common core of gods, ceremonies, and beliefs. Like the Indians at Cahokia, the Aztecs built great pyramids used for religious rituals. To please their gods, the Aztecs practiced human sacrifice. By 1325 all the migrating groups had settled and the Aztecs flourished into a great civilization.

All three of these civilizations—the Mali, the Aztecs, and the Indians at Cahokia—prospered with similar strengths: the development of efficient sedentary farming, the acceptance of a unifying religion, the building of flourishing cities, and the establishment of a solid base of commerce through trade. It is important to remember, however, that these civilizations did not arise with the same cultural traits as Old World civilizations. The Aztecs and the Indians at Cahokia, for example, rose to power without Old World advances in technology and without the same understanding of progress. Grounded in different customs, beliefs, politics, morality, and worldviews than the Western world, these cultures established themselves as striking and advanced civilizations.

The Mali Empire of Western Africa

Kevin Shillington

Kevin Shillington describes the rise of the great Mali Empire during the thirteenth century. The Mali emerged from the twelfth-century African Berbers who had conquered northern Africa and, after they embraced Islam, spread literacy through West Africa. Moreover, the Berbers increased trade, particularly in gold, with Christian Europe. Late in the twelfth century a new source of gold was discovered in the savannah country of the upper Niger River, a land first conquered by a Sosso leader, Sumaguru. According to Shillington, in 1235 Malinke armies organized and led by the great Mali leader Sundiata ultimately defeated Sumaguru. Under Sundiata, the Mali flourished and became the most influential African power of the thirteenth century.

Mali religion was traditional, based largely on agricultural spirits that could be contacted through the spirits of ancestors. Regional religious leaders eventually transferred their power to Sundiata who became the powerful sole guardian of the ancestors, called the *mansa*. Shillington argues that although most of the Mali *mansas* after Sundiata were Muslim, they never entirely abandoned their traditional agricultural/ancestor religion. According to Shillington, the Mali economic structure was based on two primary sources: the gold trade and agriculture, which produced abundant crops on the fertile land of the southern savannah. The trade of gold and goods generated great wealth and gave rise to a class of professional traders who sustained and extended the influence of the Mali Empire.

Kevin Shillington, a professor of African history, taught in Zambia

Excerpted from Kevin Shillington, *History of Africa*. Copyright © 1989 Kevin Shillington. Reprinted with permission from St. Martin's Press.

and Botswana. He is the author of *The Colonisation of the Southern Tswana* and *A Junior Certificate History of Zimbabwe.*

In their[1] northern empire of Morocco and southern Spain the former nomads of the desert were soon corrupted by the wealth and power of a settled existence. Their corruption and loss of religious piety provoked reaction among the Berbers[2] of north Africa. In the 1140s this reaction erupted in a *jihad* against the Almoravids themselves. It was led by Abd al-Mu'min who united the north African Berbers, overthrew the Almoravid Sanhaja and founded the Almohad state. In effect the Almohad *jihad* continued the work of the Almoravids in unifying the whole of the Maghrib.[3] This was complete by the end of the twelfth century. During this period the north African Berbers became more thoroughly Islamised and immigrant Arab nomads extended the Arabic language and culture into the rural areas.

One of the most important consequences of this was the spread of literacy through the Muslim world of north and west Africa. Literacy, usually in Arabic, was spread through the teaching of the Quran.[4] The mosques thus became centres of learning. In this way the peoples of northern and western Africa were exposed to and contributed to the intellectual achievements of the Muslim world. These achievements were considerable, especially in the fields of mathematics and science. It was people from this vast Muslim-Arab world who developed our modern numeral system based on counting from 1 to 10. They invented algebra and the use of the decimal point. They developed physics and astronomy. They studied chemistry and were the first people to separate medicine from religion and develop it as a secular science. . . .

The political unity of the Maghrib collapsed in the thirteenth century as the Almohad empire split into three rival states. At the same time Muslims were pushed out of Spain and into north Africa by the advancing armies of the Christian kingdoms of Aragon, Castile and Portugal. In 1415 the Christian Portuguese extended their 'Reconquista' to north Africa with the capture of the coastal fortress of Ceuta. In the century that followed, Spain and Portugal established a number of trading ports along the north African coast.

The Almoravid and Almohad states of north Africa gave a great boost to the trans-Saharan gold trade. Like the Fatimids of Egypt in the tenth and eleventh centuries, the Almoravids and Almohads of the eleventh to thirteenth centuries minted their own gold coins. With increasing trade between Christian Europe and Muslim north

1. Almoravid Sanhaja, a body of strict Islamic followers 2. indigenous people of northwestern Africa 3. territories of northwestern Africa 4. Koran

Africa and Asia, Europe too by the thirteenth century began experiencing an economic revival. European kings and princes turned increasingly from silver and copper to gold for minting their coins. And most of that gold came from south of the Sahara. It has been estimated that as much as two-thirds of the gold circulating in Europe and north Africa in the fourteenth century came from trade with the western Sudan. . . . The Almoravid unification of the Saharan Berbers and the spread of Islam among west African rulers in fact did much to stabilise and expand the trans-Saharan trade in gold. . . . New sources of gold were opened up and Ghana lost its domination of the trade. This opened the way for the rise of new west African states, and in particular the rise of Mali.

Rise of the Mali Empire

The main new source of gold was at Bure in the savannah country of the upper Niger river. This brought the southern Soninke[5] and Malinke-speaking peoples of the savannah more thoroughly into the great Sudanese trading network. The first to take full advantage of this were the Sosso, a branch of the southern Soninke. Under the leadership of Sumaguru of the Kante clan the Sosso quickly established a new and separate state, independent of Ghana. The Sosso state was built mainly on raid and conquest, killing rulers and seizing tribute. During the early 1220s Sumaguru's army raided the Malinke to his south and then attacked the northern Soninke of Ghana, sacking their capital in about 1224 AD.

A Malinke survivor of the Sosso raids, Sundjata of the Keita clan, set about organising Malinke resistance. He brought a number of Malinke chiefdoms into an alliance under his authority. In 1235 he led a Malinke army against the Sosso of Sumaguru whom he defeated in battle at Kirina near modern Bamako. With the defeat of Sumaguru, Sundjata took control of all the Soninke peoples recently conquered by the Sosso, including much of former Ghana.

Within a very few years Sundjata had built up a vast empire, known to us as Mali. The capital was built at Niani in the southern savannah country of the upper Niger valley near the goldfields of Bure. Even in Sundjata's lifetime the empire of Mali extended from the fringes of the forest in the southwest through the savannah country of the Malinke and southern Soninke to the Sahel of former Ghana. Awdaghust remained in the hands of the Sunhaja, but by then the more easterly town of Walata had become the main southern desert 'port' for the trans-Saharan trade. And whereas Ghana at its height had barely reached the upper Niger delta, Sundjata's successors extended the empire's boundaries to include Timbuktu and the

5. people of ancient Ghana

middle Niger bend. At its height in the fourteenth century the empire of Mali stretched from the Atlantic south of the Senegal to the Songhay capital of Gao on the east of the middle Niger bend. In the south it reached the forest and included the goldfields of Bure and Bambuk while in the north it stretched across the Sahel to include the southern Saharan 'ports' of Walata and Tadmekka.

Religion of the Malinke

The traditional religion of the Malinke was like that of many west African agricultural peoples. The core of their belief was that it was the 'spirits of the land' who ensured the success of their crops. The earliest farmers to have settled in a particular region were believed to have made a deal with the spirits to ensure the successful production of their crops. And it was through spiritual contact with their ancestors that the people of the present were able to keep in touch with the original settlers and thus with the 'spirits of the land'. The village head or chief, the *mansa* in Malinke, was the person most directly descended from the earliest farmers. He was the most direct link with the 'spirits of the land' upon whom continued production of their crops depended. The *mansa*, as guardian of the ancestors, was thus both religious and secular leader of his people.

When Sundjata formed his Malinke alliance against the Sosso, he persuaded the other Malinke *mansas* to surrender their titles to him. He thus became the sole *mansa*, religious and secular leader of all the Malinke people and in due course of the whole of the empire of Mali. As the power of the *mansa* increased, so did his religious significance. The *mansa*'s central religious role within the empire was crucial to the people's survival and he was thus treated with exaggerated respect. He lived apart from his subjects, who approached him on their knees. He was surrounded by displays of great wealth and ceremonial regalia. This emphasised his power and dignity and no doubt helped instil respect and obedience to his rule. But despite the misunderstanding of outsiders, he was not a 'divine king' as it was understood in Ancient Egypt.

Most of the rulers of Mali after Sundjata were Muslim, some more firmly so than others. A number made pilgrimage to Mecca, the most famous being the huge and lavish pilgrimage of Mansa Musa in 1324–5. Traders and court officials in the towns, those most detached from the traditional values of the land, accepted Islam more willingly and thoroughly than the bulk of rural commoners. The latter, most of whom were peasant farmers, were still closely dependent on the goodwill of the 'spirits of the land'. Though the rulers of Mali accepted Islam, they never totally rejected their national traditional religion. To have done so would have lost them the support of their largely pagan farming subjects.

Political and Economic Structure of Mali

The political organisation of Mali was in many ways similar to that of Ghana. A number of literate Muslims were employed at court as scribes and treasurers to carry out most of the administrative work. In the outlying districts of the empire, traditional rulers were left in place provided they collected and forwarded tribute to the capital. The *mansa* kept a large standing army and the battalion commanders were among the more important officials at the royal court. Each army battalion consisted of a small elite corps of horsemen and a large body of footsoldiers armed with bows and spears. The army was used to protect the empire from outside attack, to patrol trading routes and to ensure that district chiefs paid their tribute to the king. The main source of royal income besides tribute was a tax on trade. As with the kings of Ghana, the *mansa* of Mali levied a tax on all goods passing in, out of and through the empire.

The main economic basis of the empire was the agricultural production of the rural areas. In this respect Mali was far better situated than its predecessor Ghana. It is significant that Niani, the capital of Mali, was centred in the south of the country in the heart of some of the most productive land within the empire. Unlike Sahelian Ghana, the empire of Mali stretched right across the southern savannah where rainfall was adequate to produce regular food surpluses. Different areas specialised in different crops. The main savannah crops were sorghum and millet with rice being produced in the Gambia valley and around the upper Niger floodplain. This left the more northerly and drier Sahelian grasslands for the specialist grazing of camels, sheep and goats. Food was traded from one district to another and in particular from the savannah and Niger floodplain to the trading towns of the Sahel. Most of the empire's food was produced by independent peasant farmers living fairly close together in small family villages. They paid a proportion of the surplus to their traditional district chief who kept a portion and forwarded the rest to the government. At the same time the *mansa* and his army commanders controlled their own 'state' farms where slaves were organised to produce food for the army and the court.

The main economic activity observed by outsiders was of course the gold trade. And control of this, as we have seen, was a major stimulus behind the founding of the state. But though the rulers of Mali taxed the trade that passed through the empire, they did not exercise direct control over the mining of gold. The peoples of the goldfields were particularly anxious to maintain their independence. They were prepared to send tribute of gold nuggets to the *mansa* and to pay a tax on their imports of salt. But whenever the rulers of Mali tried to interfere directly with their mining, the miners themselves simply ceased their production. They even ceased production when the *mansa* of Mali tried to convert them to Islam, so the project was abandoned.

There developed within the Mali empire a class of professional traders called Wangara in the west and Dyula in the east. They were Malinke, Bambara or Soninke in origin and were usually practising Muslims. They carried the trade of the empire to the furthest corners of west Africa. They penetrated the forest to trade for kola nuts and they carried these and the food, shunting produce and gold of west Africa to the trading towns of the Sahel: Walata, Tadmekka, Timbuktu and Gao. It was Dyula traders from Mali who in the late fourteenth century penetrated south to the Akan forest of modern Ghana. From there they brought a whole new field of gold production into the trans-Saharan network. The opening of the Akan goldfields shifted the centre of the gold trade further eastwards enabling Timbuktu and Jenne to replace Walata as major 'ports' of exchange.

Sometime during the fourteenth century cowrie shells from the Indian Ocean were introduced as currency into the internal trade of the western Sudan. This appears to have been a deliberate move encouraged by the government. It improved the collection of taxation and eased the internal exchange of food and other goods. But gold dust and salt remained the main mediums of exchange in the long-distance trade of the Sahara.

The Rise of Aztec Civilization

Michael E. Smith

Michael E. Smith argues that the rise of the great Aztec civilization was more an evolution of advanced ancestral central Mexican cultures than a rags-to-riches story of simple nomads turned glorious conquerors. The Aztecs came to central Mexico from their original home, called Aztlan. According to Smith, scholars do not know the exact location of Aztlan or even if it existed at all. The migration of the Aztecs occurred over several generations, with the first groups arriving at the beginning of the thirteenth century and the last, the Mexica, in 1250. Smith writes that accounts vary concerning the sophistication of the migrants. Some histories depict the Aztecs as descending from a savage and primitive nomadic people called the Chichimecs, while other accounts support descent from a more civilized group called the Toltecs.

Smith reports that the indigenous people living in central Mexico were quickly assimilated into the Aztec groups. Settlements grew rapidly into towns and cities and soon all of central Mexico was a dynamic network of city-states. Despite frequent small-scale warfare between city-states, a common Aztec culture emerged. Smith suggests that this happened quickly because the people shared a language, Nahuatl, as well as a common core of gods, ceremonies, rituals, and beliefs. Eventually they developed a distinctive new style of temple building characterized by twin temples and double stairways. By 1325 all the migrating groups were settled and the Aztecs flourished into a great civilization.

Michael E. Smith is an archaeologist who has written extensively about the Aztecs. His articles have appeared in numerous periodicals, including the *Journal of Field Archaeology*.

The evolution of Aztec civilization is partly a rags-to-riches story of the sudden rise of the Nahuatl speakers from obscurity to power and partly a chronicle of continuity in the cultural achievements of central Mexican civilizations. These two themes were important elements in Aztec native historical accounts, and they loomed large in the Aztecs' own sense of identity and heritage. The rags-to-riches theme centers on the Mexica people, following them from their origin as a simple nomadic tribe in the northern desert, through the founding of Tenochtitlan, and on to their rise to power as the lords of the Aztec empire. Native historical accounts of this story suggest that the rise of Aztec civilization was due to the genius and accomplishments of the Mexica and their leaders.

In contrast to the rags-to-riches story, the theme of cultural continuity stresses the debt that the Aztecs (Mexica and others) owed to both their Toltec ancestors and the still earlier Teotihuacan culture. The last in a series of advanced urban civilizations, the Aztecs inherited much of their culture from these earlier peoples. Although the progress of the Mexica people may make a more exciting story, most scholars today find the theme of cultural continuity provides a more satisfactory account of cultural evolution in Postclassic central Mexico. The rise of Aztec civilization was due less to the genius and success of one small group (the Mexica) than to the larger social forces that had shaped the rise and fall of central Mexican civilizations over the centuries. . . .

Aztec Migration

According to native historical accounts, the Aztecs migrated into central Mexico from an original home in a place called Aztlan. Some scholars believe that Aztlan was a real place and argue over its exact location (opinions range from just north of the Valley of Mexico to the southwestern United States). Others argue that Aztlan was a mythical place with no precise location on the map. The term Aztlan, meaning "place of the herons," is the origin of the word "Aztec," a modern label that was not used by the ancient peoples themselves. Whether or not there ever was a place called Aztlan, scholars agree that the Aztec peoples migrated into central Mexico from the north.

Setting out from Aztlan, the migrants visited Chicomoztoc, or "place of seven caves." A number of sources describe seven tribes at Chicomoztoc although they disagree over the identity of these tribes. When all of the native histories are compared, no fewer than seventeen ethnic groups are listed among the original tribes migrating from Aztlan and Chicomoztoc. . . . The southward migration of these groups took several generations to complete. The migrants were led by priests, and they stopped periodically to build houses and temples, to gather or cultivate food, and to carry out rituals.

The historical accounts of the Aztlan migrations may vary widely in the content of their lists of the migrating groups and the precise order in which they travelled, but there is consistency in the overall timing of three contingents of migrants. The first groups to arrive in central Mexico settled throughout the Valley of Mexico. The groups that formed part of this initial contingent were the ancestors of the major Nahuatl ethnic groups to be found in the Valley of Mexico in the sixteenth century; they included the Acolhua, Tepaneca, Culhua, Chalca, Xochimilca, and several other groups.

The second contingent of migrants arrived to find the Valley of Mexico settled, so they moved on to occupy the surrounding valleys of central Mexico. These groups included the Tlahuica of Morelos, the Tlaxcalteca and Huexotzinca of Tlaxcala and Puebla, the Matlatzinca of the Toluca Valley and the Malinalca of Malinalco. Historical dates for the arrival of the Aztec migrants fall around AD 1200 for the Valley of Mexico groups and around 1220 for the groups in the surrounding valleys. The last to arrive, around AD 1250, were the Mexica, who found all of the good land occupied and were forced to settle in an undesirable, desolate area of the Valley of Mexico called Chapultepec, "grasshopper hill" or "place of the grasshopper." Far more details are available about the Mexica migration than about the other groups simply because more Mexica-based histories have survived. These sources tell us that the Mexica were guided by their patron god, Huitzilopochtli, whose image was carefully carried from Aztlan to the Valley of Mexico. We know the names of the places where the Mexica stopped on their journey, and some of the events that happened along the way.

Native historical descriptions of the Aztlan migrants contain contradictory information on the cultural sophistication of these peoples. In some accounts they are said to have lived in caves, made their living by hunting with bows and arrows, and wore animal skins for clothing. These traits describe peoples known as Chichimecs (barbaric peoples from the north), and the Mexica and other groups claimed to have been Chichimecs before they settled down and became civilized in central Mexico. The Chichimec notion was a major part of the rags-to-riches theme of Aztec origins.

Contrasting with this picture of the migrants as barbaric Chichimecs are descriptions of complex economic and cultural activities such as the planting of maize, the construction of temples, and the use of the ancient Mesoamerican 52-year calendar. Nomadic hunter/gatherers of the north Mexican desert did not have these practices, which suggests that the migrants had experience with Mesoamerican civilization long before they arrived in central Mexico. The presence of these contradictory traits among the Aztlan migrants is part of the dual conception of the cultural origins of the Aztecs, who believed themselves descended from both savage Chichimecs and civilized Toltecs. . . .

Growth of City-States

The Aztlan migrants arrived in central Mexico during the Early Aztec period. The countryside was far from empty and the settlers avoided existing settlements to found their own sites. Most of the indigenous non-Nahuatl-speaking peoples were eventually assimilated into Aztec culture, although some groups, such as the Otomi, managed to retain their separate ethnic identity within Aztec civilization. Many of the new settlements were successful and grew rapidly into towns or cities with regional political and economic significance. Nearly all of the major Aztec cities and towns extant at the time of Spanish conquest were founded during this time period.

Central Mexico became the arena for a dynamic system of interacting city-states. The rulers of these small polities were petty kings called *tlatoque* (sing. *tlatoani*,) who endeavored to establish genealogical links to the Toltec kings through marriage ties with their descendants or through invention. Like systems of city-states in other ancient cultures, the polities of Early Aztec central Mexico interacted intensively with one another in both friendly and antagonistic fashions. Alliances between dynasties and trade between city-states were accompanied by warfare and aggression.

The native histories are full of accounts of battles among the city-states. During the first century or so after initial settlement, small-scale warfare among the new city-states was frequent, but because of shifting alliances and the small scale of most conflicts, no individual polity succeeded in establishing a tributary empire. Among the more active and influential polities at this time were the cities of Azcapotzalco, Coatlinchan, Culhuacan, Tenayuca, and Xaltocan in the Valley of Mexico, and Cuauhnahuac, Tollocan, Cholula, and Huexotzinco in surrounding areas.

During the Early Aztec period a common Aztec culture emerged among the new settlers of the central Mexican highlands. The use of the Nahuatl language and the acknowledgement of a common Aztlan origin were at the foundation of this widespread culture. The intensive interactions among city-states, particularly through trade and noble marriage alliances, kept far-flung peoples in touch. An important component of this widespread culture was religious ritual. Although individual gods and ceremonies varied slightly from region to region, a common core of ritual and belief united most of the central Mexican peoples. This religion received concrete material expression in a distinctive new style of temple pyramid. In con-

The cities and temples built during the early Aztec period were immense and elaborate.

trast to earlier Mesoamerican pyramids with a single temple on top and a single stairway up the side, the pyramids built by the Early Aztec peoples had twin temples and double stairways. Impressive examples of such pyramids have been excavated and restored at the Early Aztec sites of Tenayuca in the northern Valley of Mexico and Teopanzolco, in the modern city of Cuernavaca, Morelos. This style was later adopted by the Mexica for the central temple of Tenochtitlan, the Templo Mayor.

Native historical accounts provide increasing detail about political events in the Valley of Mexico in the thirteenth and fourteenth centuries. In the context of an unstable city-state system, the story of the Mexica peoples stands out since the vast majority of the surviving native histories come from the Mexica tradition.

Evolution of the Mexica

By the time the Mexica arrived in the Valley of Mexico around 1250, most of the land was already claimed by the city-states of the earlier immigrants groups. The Mexica settled initially in Chapultepec, a hill adjacent to a swamp, because the land was empty and barren. Nearby groups, such as the Tepaneca and Chalca, were wary of the newcomers. A young warrior named Copil, son of a Mexica sorceress who had been exiled during the migration, stirred up opposition to the Mexica among their neighbors. War broke out and the allied armies forced the Mexica to flee Chapultepec (although they did manage to kill Copil and throw his heart into the swamp).

The Mexica convinced the reluctant king of Culhuacan to let them settle in an isolated, snake-infested part of his realm called Tizaapan. Culhuacan was an ancient town southeast of Chapultepec that had been settled by both Toltecs and Aztlan migrants, and the Culhua nobles and peoples considered the Mexica newcomers barbaric. The Culhua ruler Coxcoxtli said to his advisors that for the Mexica, Tizaapan "is good, for they are no true people, but great villains, and perhaps they will perish there, eaten by the serpents, since many dwell in that place." Rather than perish, the Mexica flourished on a diet of snakes and lizards, prompting Coxcoxtli to later exclaim to his court, "See what rascals they are; have no dealings and do not speak to them." The king's attitude soon changed as the Mexica became good subjects and neighbors of the Culhua. The Mexica began to trade in the Culhuacan market and soon were intermarrying with the Culhua people. The Culhua called on the Mexica to come to their aid in a fierce battle with the Xochimilca, and the arrival of Mexica troops turned the tide in favor of the Culhua. This victory was important, for it previewed the later military success of the Mexica as vassals of the Tepanecs.[1]

The Mexica managed to turn the Culhua against them, however. According to the semi-mythical accounts of native history, their god Huitzilopochtli ordered the Mexica to obtain a Culhua princess to be worshipped as a goddess. The Culhua king agreed and sent them his favorite daughter. Some time later, he and the other Culhua lords were invited to witness ceremonies and sacrifices to the new Mexica goddess. On Huitzilopochtli's orders the Mexica had killed and flayed the princess, and a Mexica priest donned her skin to dance in public. When the Culhua king saw what the Mexica had done, he ordered his nobles and troops to attack, and the Mexica were driven from Tizaapan by force. This was all part of the god Huitzilopochtli's divine plan, however.

The Mexica fled into the wilderness of swamps that ringed the salty lakes of the Valley of Mexico, where they wandered for weeks. Huitzilopochtli appeared in a vision to one of the priests and told the Mexica that they would soon find their promised homeland, in a place where an eagle lived atop a tall nopal cactus. This was a sacred place, for the cactus had grown from the heart of Copil after his

1. Aztec ethnic group

death in the Mexica's first battle. When the Mexica saw the eagle and cactus on a small island in the swamp, they were overjoyed and proceeded to found the site of Tenochtitlan, "place of the cactus fruit," in the year 2 House, AD 1325.

The fourteenth century was a time of rapid and far-reaching transformation among the Aztecs. One of the most striking changes was an unprecedented population explosion. Many new settlements were founded, existing villages grew into towns, and towns grew into cities; the overall population of central Mexico increased by a factor of five or more. Major modifications were made to the landscape in order to intensify agricultural production to feed the growing number of people. Another dramatic change was the emergence of the first true empire since Teotihuacan.

The North American Indians of Cahokia

Jack Weatherford

Jack Weatherford writes that the Indians at Cahokia, once located in the area St. Louis occupies today, numbered over twenty-thousand at the city's peak in 1250. The Cahokians built massive earthen flat-topped pyramids. Of the original 120 pyramids built by the Cahokian Indians, the largest, called Monk's Peak, served as a site of unknown rituals. Just outside of Cahokia archaeologists have discovered a large circle that once consisted of poles, called Woodhenge, which served as a giant solar calendar. Surrounding Cahokia were ten other large urban populations spreading along the Mississippi River.

According to Weatherford, the origins of these Mississippian Indians coincided with the introduction of the hoe and new strains of maize, beans, and other agricultural products from Mexico. In addition to farming, the Cahokia Indians conducted a vast trading enterprise. The city's location straddles a major nexus on the Mississippi River providing an ideal location for trade, commerce, and communication. Cahokia was the center of a vast water network from which Indians could travel by river in almost any direction.

Weatherford reports that no original records or writing have been found at Cahokia, but artifacts from distant parts of North America unearthed there indicate that Cahokia was a center for a widespread trading empire. Three major indigenous language families also converged in this area: Muskogean, Iroquoian, and Siouan. Weatherford speculates that the demise of the Cahokian civilization may have been caused by early contact with the white man, fluctuations in climate, or a shift of the Mississippian culture to the Gulf states.

Jack Weatherford is a professor of anthropology at Macalester College in St. Paul, Minnesota. He is the author of *Tribes on the Hill* and *Indian Givers*.

A climber ascending the worn slope of the great pyramid sees the river plain slowly stretching out to the horizon. The top of the pyramid soars a hundred feet in the air, the equivalent of a ten-story building, and provides the highest viewpoint on the plain. Unlike the pointed top of the Egyptian pyramid, this truncated pyramid is capped by a massive field large enough to host a football game.

On each side of the pyramid, lumps in the earth mark the sites of smaller pyramids, burial mounds, large open plazas, or perhaps markets and other buildings that surrounded the main pyramid. Faint traces remain visible in the soil showing the line of a stockade that surrounded the entire ceremonial complex.

The Pyramids of Cahokia

With more than twenty thousand residents, Cahokia was the largest city in America north of ancient Mexico. During its most prosperous period, around A.D. 1250, Cahokia was larger than London and ranked as one of the great urban centers of the world. Even the colonial cities founded by European settlers across North America did not surpass ancient Cahokia's population until the eighteenth century, when Philadelphia grew to twenty thousand inhabitants.

From the top of the great pyramid at Cahokia, one can see the river to the east, just beyond which loom modern skyscrapers surrounded by residential areas. Gleaming on the distant bank of the river rises the great arch of St. Louis, which seems small and barely visible from the top of the Cahokia pyramid.

Cahokia lies in southern Illinois, just across the river from St. Louis, Missouri. Of all the great pyramids built in the world—in Egypt, Mexico, Guatemala, and Peru—this is the most northerly. Cahokia and the other earthen pyramids of the United States are the world's only pyramids built in a temperate zone.

Climbing any of the world's great pyramids is much the same experience. The climbers mostly watch their feet and the immediate area, searching for the next firm foothold. On some pyramids, such as those of Egypt, it is a little harder because the pyramid was not made for climbing. On others, such as at Cahokia, or at Teotihuacán in Mexico, the climb is a little easier because the pyramid comes equipped with stairs or ramps for that purpose. What varies from one pyramid to the next is not the climb to the top, but what the climber sees from the top. . . .

Monk's Mound, the largest of the Cahokia pyramids, covers 16 acres; it rests on a base 1,037 feet long and 790 feet wide, with a total volume of approximately 21,690,000 cubic feet, a base and total volume greater than that of the pyramid of Khufu (or Cheops), the largest in Egypt. The pyramid of Khufu is 756 feet on each side (an area of 571,536 square feet), but the base of the Cahokia pyramid is nearly 250,000 square feet larger than the Egyptian pyramid. In all the world, only the pyramids at Cholula and Teotihucin in central Mexico surpass the Cahokia pyramid in size and total volume. No other structure in the United States approached the size of the Cahokia pyramid until the building of airplane hangars, the Pentagon, and skyscrapers in the twentieth century.

The top of Monk's Mound served as the place for now-unknown ancient rituals and as the home of a chief or priest, but it was clearly an uncomfortable place to live. In the summer the sun shines directly onto the top of the mound without the mitigating effects of trees or hills. Standing on top of the pyramid in August is like standing in the middle of a large, desolate parking lot. The wind merely redistributes the stifling heat without offering relief. At the end of a long, hot day, storm clouds frequently blow overhead and cast giant shadows across the pyramids like rapidly moving ink blots.

In the cooler months, icy winds swoop down from the north and blast the top of the mound. Nothing stands between the top of the mound and the Arctic but the long, flat plains of the North American interior. Thick air from the Gulf of Mexico brings enough moisture to make the area around Cahokia very humid, but it does not bring enough tropical warmth to defeat the winter cold. Only a few minutes in that wind can leave one with an earache, a runny nose, and small particles of ice dangling from eyelashes and hair ends.

The ruins of approximately 45 smaller pyramids and burial mounds still stand clustered around Monk's Mound; these alone survive from the 120 originally constructed by the Indians. For decades, European-American settlers used the mounds as quarries for dirt, and obliterated 75 of them. Farmers slowly cut down the pyramids through repeated years of tilling the soil. Especially the horseradish farmers have loosened and damaged the archaeological remains by cutting into the earth the eighteen inches that they need for their deep-root crop.

Despite the losses and degradation of the site, Cahokia still ranks as the largest collection of pyramids ever constructed in one place anywhere in the world. In addition to Cahokia, ten other large urban areas occupied this stretch of the Mississippi River, and scattered between them were another fifty smaller villages. The present city of St. Louis now occupies the site of one such suburb of ancient Cahokia. The white settlers of St. Louis nicknamed their settlement "Mound City" in recognition of the twenty-six Indian mounds they found there, but those mounds have since been cleared away to make room for the modern city.

Origins of Cahokia

Little is known about the people who made this city. Even the name *Cahokia* comes from the name of the Indians living in the area when the French arrived in the eighteenth century. For lack of a more accurate name, anthropologists generally call the people who built it "Mississippian," and the site of Cahokia is in a twenty-five-mile stretch of the river called "American Bottom" in anthropological literature. The name of the largest pyramid, Monk's Mound, derives not from ancient Indian priests who lived on it, but from Christians, namely the Trappist monks who owned it and farmed it in the nineteenth century.

The city plan of Cahokia closely followed a common pattern of urban Mississippian sites, but Cahokia achieved a scale that surpassed all others. A collection of temple pyramids, mounds for chiefs' houses, and burial mounds bordered an open, rectangular plaza that was probably used for religious and civic ceremonies as well as athletic events and markets. The cities and towns that we now call Mississippian were concentrated along the Mississippi, Ohio, and Arkansas Rivers in the central part of the United States and across the entire width of the Southeastern United States from St. John's River along the Atlantic Coast of Florida and Ocmulgee in the uplands of Georgia to Spiro, Oklahoma.

Archaeological investigations reveal that settlement began between A.D. 600 and 800 at Cahokia and grew steadily to its greatest size a few centuries before the arrival of the Europeans. The city started before the foundation of the Holy Roman Empire and persisted through the time of the Middle Ages and the Renaissance in Europe.

In the 1960s, archaeologists made an unexpected discovery when a freeway was about to be built within a half-mile of Monk's Mound. They found a large circle that had once consisted of a series of large poles, which they named Woodhenge after its similarity to England's Stonehenge. The ancient Cahokians erected Woodhenge about A.D. 1000. The circle measures 410 feet in diameter, with the largest post in the center. The structure apparently served as a giant solar calendar for determining the solstices and equinoxes of the year, important information for an agricultural civilization.

The origins of the Mississippian culture coincide with the introduction of the hoe, which replaced the smaller digging stick in the eighth century, and with the introduction of new types of maize from

Mexico around the tenth century, and it seems to have been steadily reinforced by the introduction of new types of beans and the domestication of native plants. A great variety of squashes, maize, and beans formed the "three sisters" that typified agriculture throughout North America. Indian cooks knew how to make virtually every corn dish that we know today, including corn on the cob, hominy grits, stew, and cornmeal. They also grew pumpkins, Jerusalem artichokes, nuts, persimmons, sunflowers, marsh elder, and a number of seed plants that now grow wild in the Mississippi area.

Even though today we do not know who the people were who founded Cahokia, we can easily imagine why they located it where they did; it was a transportation, trade, and communications hub, the evidence and noise of which still deafens visitors. From atop Monk's Mound today, one can hardly escape the noise of the surrounding area. Planes fly overhead, going into and out of St. Louis International Airport. Automobile traffic on Collinsville Road seems reasonably light between rush hours, but the trains that crisscross it frequently stop the cars until they form queues even longer than the passing trains. The trains connect the city north to Chicago, south to New Orleans, and east and west to the Atlantic and Pacific coasts.

Barges churn up and down the Mississippi River, but the constant whine of cars on the adjacent freeways drowns out the comparatively silent engines of even the largest chain of barges. No matter in which direction one looks from the top of Monk's Mound, one sees a freeway. Three cross-country freeways and a major urban loop intersect, leaving Cahokia marooned on an island in the middle of them. Interstate 55 passes Cahokia on its path from Chicago to New Orleans; Interstate 70 joins it there in its run from Pennsylvania to Denver and out into the middle of Utah. Interstate 64 terminates there after starting at Norfolk, Virginia. Interstate 255 circles the site as part of the outer loop around the greater St. Louis area.

Location of Cahokia

Ancient Cahokia arose where it did for much the same reason that St. Louis arose, because both straddle a major nexus on the Mississippi River, halfway between its origins in Minnesota and its effluence from Louisiana into the Gulf of Mexico. Cahokia sits at the continental hub of North America. It was an ideal place for trade, commerce, and communication.

Whether measured by length, width, volume of water, or size of the total area drained, the Mississippi River ranks as one of the great rivers of the world. Its tributaries, including the Missouri, Arkansas, and Ohio, would be major rivers in their own right if they stood alone in another part of the world. With a length of 3,740 miles, the Mississippi-Missouri system is the fourth-longest river, since it is a few hundred miles shorter than the Nile, Amazon, and Yangtze. But if we examine the total drainage area, only the Amazon and the Congo surpass the 1,255,000 square miles drained by the Mississippi system. This dwarfs the 733,400 square miles of the Nile system or the 454,000 square miles of the Yangtze. The Mississippi and its tributaries drain an area equal in size to India, or more than one and a quarter times the size of the Mediterranean Sea.

The builders of Cahokia selected their city just to the south of where the Missouri and Illinois rivers empty into the Mississippi and to the north of where the Meramec River drains into the Mississippi from the Ozark Mountains. Only 150 miles south of Cahokia, the Ohio joins the Mississippi at Cairo, where the modern states of Kentucky, Illinois, and Missouri converge. Virtually no other spot on this planet can claim a more favorable location for long-distance travel by river in every direction.

Travelers along the waterways of the Mississippi can reach the southern areas of what are now Alberta and Saskatchewan provinces in Canada. They could reach Montana and Idaho in the northwest, or New Mexico in the southwest. Toward the east, the Ohio and Tennessee rivers lead to the edge of the Appalachian Mountains and the borders of Pennsylvania and the Carolinas. In addition to this massive area drained by the rivers, the Mississippi and several of its tributaries reach within only a few miles of the Great Lakes, providing easy access into the largest freshwater lakes in the world, and from there into the St. Lawrence River system, the next largest in North America.

At its southern terminus, the river spills into the Gulf of Mexico, which is virtually an inland sea surrounded by land on all sides except where it opens into the Atlantic Ocean and the Caribbean Sea with a line of islands stretching across the open water between the peninsulas of the Yucatán and Florida. In the midst of all this stood Cahokia, at the center of a water network stretching effectively from the Caribbean to Hudson Bay and uniting peoples with vastly different cultures, economies, and languages.

Cahokia's Trading Empire

Even though we have no ancient writing from the city of Cahokia, no carved friezes, no illustrated manuscripts or records, we do know, from the trade items found in their burials, that the citizens of Cahokia utilized the full diversity of this area through trade. Archaeologists have found rolled sheets of copper imported from the Great Lakes, arrowheads made from the black chert of Oklahoma and Arkansas, ornamental cutouts of mica from North Carolina, worked shells from the Gulf of Mexico, salt from southern Illinois, lead from northern Illinois, and worked stone from around what is now Yellowstone National Park in Wyoming. Cahokia itself probably controlled the entry into this network of chert deposits that were mined extensively in nearby quarries and controlled a major source of salt.

Cahokia united a trading empire larger than the combined area of France, the United Kingdom, Spain, Germany, Austria, Italy, Belgium, the Netherlands, Ireland, Greece, Denmark, Romania, Switzerland, Czechoslovakia, Yugoslavia, Portugal, Luxembourg, and Bulgaria. Its trade stretched along routes longer than from London to Constantinople, from Madrid to Moscow, or from Paris to Cairo. We have no evidence that Cahokia controlled a political empire, but it certainly controlled the nexus of a trade empire that surpassed in geographic size the empires of ancient Rome and Egypt.

Another interesting fact about Cahokia emerges when we examine the distribution of North American languages at the time of European contact. We find that Cahokia straddled the boundary of the three great language families of eastern North America. The southern Muskogean languages of the Gulf Coast, the eastern Iroquoian languages, and the western Siouan languages all converged in this area. In this regard, Cahokia may have played an important intermediary role as a channel of trade, information, and the regulation of social or political relations among these three major groups.

We know very little about the civilization of Cahokia. The Indian record was not written, and no European explorer ever saw Cahokia at its height and lived to record it. By the time the explorers arrived at Cahokia, the area had already suffered two centuries of Old World diseases that traveled overland much faster than did the European explorers. The civilization of Cahokia had already withered and died. Some evidence points to destruction from indirect contact with the whites, while other evidence indicates that with a fluctuation in climate, the focus of Mississippian culture shifted to southern sites in the Gulf states from Louisiana to Georgia. . . .

Even though today we no longer share Columbus's folly of thinking that we are in Asia, we still do not adequately know where we are. We have built cities and cleared farms across the continent, but we do not know the story of the land on which we live. We take nourishment from this soil, but because we cannot see our roots down deep in the American dirt, we do not know the source of that nourishment.

Our cultural roots as a modern people lie buried in Cahokia and a thousand similar historical sites and surviving Indian reservations across the continent. These ancient and often ignored roots still nourish our modern society, political life, economy, art, agriculture, language, and distinctly American modes of thought.

Document 1: Papal Bull Issued by Pope Boniface VIII

In 1296 Pope Boniface VIII (1294–1303) issued a papal bull that prevented the taxation of clergy by lay powers, including the French king Philip IV, who tried to levy taxes on the church. In the thirteenth century bitter conflicts arose between the church and state as the two institutions struggled for ascendancy.

The history of olden times teaches, and daily experience proves, that the laity have always felt hostile to the clergy and have constantly striven to overstep their bounds by wickedness and disobedience. They do not reflect that all power over the clergy, over the persons and property of the Church, is denied them. They lay heavy burdens on prelates, churchmen and both regular and secular clergy, crush them with taxes, taking sometimes half, at other times a tenth or a twentieth or some other portion of their revenues, trying to reduce them to slavery in a thousand ways. In the bitterness of our souls we must add that certain prelates and other ecclesiastical persons, fearful when there is nothing for them to fear, seek fugitive peace, and dread a temporal majesty more than the eternal. They may lend themselves to these abuses less through temerity than imprudence, but without obtaining due faculty and authorization from the Holy See.[1] . . . To cut short these abuses we, in accord with the cardinals and by virtue of our apostolic authority, ordain the following: all prelates and in general all persons belonging to the Church, monks, or secular clergy who, without the consent of the Apostolic See, pay or promise to pay to laymen any imports, taxes, tithes, or half tithes or even a one-hundredth part or any portion whatsoever of their revenues or of the goods of their church by way of a subvention, loan, gift, subsidy, etc., as also emperors, kings, princes, barons, rectors, etc., who levy the same, who exact such taxes or receive them or who even put their hand on valuables placed in the church or who co-operate in this sort of act, all these persons *ipso facto* incur excommunication. We interdict anyone who preaches in defense of these condemned acts. Under the penalty of deposition, we order prelates and all Christians not to permit these taxes to be collected without the express consent of the Holy See.

1. the pope's authority

From J.H. Robinson, *Readings in European History,* Harry E. Wedeck, ed., *Putnam's Dark and Middle Ages Reader: Selections from the 5th to 15th Centuries.* New York: G.P. Putnam's Sons, 1964.

Document 2: A Letter to Oxford University

The development of European universities in the twelfth and thirteenth centuries allowed a select group of medieval men to earn prominent careers both within the church and in the cities. In his letter to the Masters of Oxford University in 1283, the bishop of Worcester not only asks for an expansion of the-

ology study but also expresses the thirteenth-century enthusiasm for learning.

> To the venerable men and beloved in Christ, Sir. . . . Chancellor and the University of Masters of Oxford, Godfrey, by divine permission minister of the church of Worcester, fulness of health and eternal happiness.

The high vicar of Christ in the church thought that the study of theology should be increased, so that by enlargement of the space of its tent it might make its ropes longer, and lo we hear of the laudable and divinely inspired devotion of the brethren of the abbey of St Peter's Gloucester, in our diocese, specially adhering to the same vicar of Christ, who are now disposed to put aside ignorance, the mother of error, and to walk in the light of truth, that they may become proficient in learning to the augmentation of their merits.

We therefore, helping all we can their so healthful purpose, put our earnest prayers before your University, asking you with all affection to permit and grant that in the house they possess in Oxford they may have a doctor in the sacred page to attend them, so that the way of learning may lie open to those thirsting for wisdom, and so at last they themselves becoming learned may be able to instruct the people in righteousness to the honour of God and the church.

May the most Highest always direct you in perfect love and the light of His love.

Dated at Henbury 9 April in the year aforesaid [1283].

Catherine Moriarty, ed., *The Voices of the Middle Ages in Personal Letters, 1100–1500.* New York: Peter Bedrick Books, 1989.

Document 3: Roger Bacon's Vision of Technology

In the thirteenth century the spirit of scientific inquiry was exemplified by one of the most enlightened scientists of the age, Roger Bacon. Bacon (c. 1214–1294) was a prolific writer on mathematics, philosophy, science, and the scientific method. In his work De Secretis Operibus *Bacon explores the possibilities of technology and unlimited human ingenuity.*

I shall therefore now describe first of all works of skill and marvels of nature, in order to designate afterward their causes and characteristics. There is no magic in them, so that all the power of magic seems inferior to these mechanisms and unworthy of them. And first, through the shaping and planning of skill alone. Instruments for navigation can be made without rowers, so that the largest ships, both on river and on sea, are steered by one man only in control at a greater speed than if they were filled with men. Similarly, carts can be made to move without animals at an incalculable velocity, as we think the chariots with scythe blades attached must have been in which the ancients fought. Similarly, flying machines can be made so that a man sits inside the machine rotating some ingenious contraption by means of which the wings, artfully arranged, beat the air like a bird flying. So, a machine, small in size, can be made, for raising and lowering weights almost infinitely, a most useful device in an emergency. For with an instrument three fingers high and the same in width and less in size, a man could escape with his companions from every danger of imprisonment and raise and lower himself. Also an instrument could easily be devised whereby a single man could draw a thousand men forcibly toward him against their own will, and so with attracting other objects. Also instruments can be made for walking in the sea or rivers right down to the bottom without any physical risk. Alexander the Great used such instruments to probe the secrets of the ocean, according to the stories of Ethicus the astronomer. These things were done in antiquity and in our own day as well, and this is unquestionable; except a flying machine, that I have not seen or known anyone who did. But I know quite well the adept who thought out this device. And an infinite number of such objects is possible: such as bridges over rivers, without columns or any support; and machines, and unheard-of ingenuities.

Harry E. Wedeck, ed., *Putnam's Dark and Middle Ages Reader: Selections from the 5th to 15th Centuries.* New York: G.P. Putnam's Sons, 1964.

Document 4: The Sacred Stigmata of St. Francis

The story of St. Francis (1182–1226) is recorded in a biography written by the thirteenth-century historian and theologian St. Bonaventura (1221–1274). St. Bonaventura writes of St. Francis receiving the stigmata, the bodily marks matching the wounds of the crucified Christ.

When, therefore, by seraphic glow of longing he had been uplifted toward God, and by his sweet compassion had been transformed into the likeness of Him Who of His exceeding love endured to be crucified—on a certain morning about the Feast of the Exaltation of Holy Cross, while he was praying on the side of the mountain, he beheld a Seraph having six wings, flaming and resplendent, coming down from the heights of heaven. When in his flight most swift he had reached the space of air nigh the man of God, there appeared betwixt the wings the Figure of a Man crucified, having his hands and feet stretched forth in the shape of a Cross, and fastened unto a Cross. Two wings were raised above His head, twain were spread forth to fly, while twain hid His whole body. Beholding this, Francis was mightily astonied, and joy, mingled with sorrow, filled his heart. He rejoiced at the gracious aspect wherewith he saw Christ, under the guise of the Seraph, regard him, but His crucifixion pierced his soul with a sword of pitying grief. He marvelled exceedingly at the appearance of a vision so unfathomable, knowing that the infirmity of the Passion doth in no wise accord with the immortality of a Seraphic spirit. At length be understood therefrom, the Lord revealing it unto him, that this vision had been thus presented unto his gaze by the divine providence, that the friend of Christ might have foreknowledge that he was to be wholly transformed into the likeness of Christ Crucified, not by martyrdom of body, but by enkindling of heart. Accordingly, as the vision disappeared, it left in his heart a wondrous glow, but on his flesh also it imprinted a no less wondrous likeness of its tokens. For forthwith there began to appear in his hands and feet the marks of the nails, even as he had just beheld them in that Figure of the Crucified. For his hands and feet seemed to be pierced through the midst with nails, the heads of the nails showing in the palms of the hands, and upper side of the feet, and their points showing on the other side; the heads of the nails were round and black in the hands and feet, while the points were long, bent, and as it were turned back, being formed of the flesh itself, and protruding therefrom. The right side, moreover, was—as if it had been pierced by a lance—seamed with a ruddy scar, where from ofttimes welled the sacred blood, staining his habit and breeches.

St. Bonaventura, *Life of St. Francis,* Norton Downs, ed., *Readings in Medieval History.* Princeton, NJ: D. Van Nostrand, 1964.

Document 5: The Last Baghdad Caliphate

The Arabic chronicler Abu'l-Faraj records the attitude of al-Musta'sim, the last Baghdad caliphate (successor of Muhammad and the head of the Islamic state). In 1258 the Mongols (Tatars) sacked Baghdad and destroyed the caliphate and the old Islamic order.

In the year 640 [1242] allegiance was sworn to al-Musta'sim on the day when his father al-Mustansir died. He was devoted to entertainment and pleasure, passionately addicted to playing with birds, and dominated by women. He was a man of poor judgment, irresolute, and neglectful of what is needful for the conduct of government. When he was told what he ought to do in the matter of the Tatars, either to propitiate them, enter into their obedience and take steps to gain their goodwill, or else to muster his armies and encounter them on the borders of Khurāsān before they could prevail and conquer Iraq, he used to say, "Baghdad is enough for me, and they will not begrudge it me if I renounce all the other countries to them. Nor will they attack me when I am in it, for it is my house and my residence." Such baseless fancies and the like prevented him from taking proper action, and so he was stricken by calamities which he had never imagined.

Abu'l-Faraj, *Ta'rikh Mukhtasar al-duwal,* Bernard Lewis, ed. and trans., *Islam: From the Prophet Muhammad to the Capture of Constantinople.* New York: Walker and Company, 1974.

Document 6: The Egyptian
Defeat of the Mongols at Ayn Jalut

An envoy of the attacking Mongols led by the great Tatar general Hülegü delivered the following demand for surrender to the Egyptian sultan al-Malik al-Muzaffar Qutuz. Although the Mongols generated great fear, the sultan beheaded the four members of the envoy, rallied his troops, and drove the Tatars out of Egypt at the pivotal battle of Ayn Jalut in 1260.

From the King of Kings in the East and the West, the mighty Khan:
    In your name, O God, You who laid out the earth and raised up the skies.
    Let al-Malik al-Muzaffar Qutuz, who is of the race of mamlūks who fled before our swords into this country, who enjoyed its comforts and then killed its rulers, let al-Malik al-Muzaffar Qutuz know, as well as the amirs of his state and the people of his realms, in Egypt and in the adjoining countries, that we are the army of God on His earth. He created us from His wrath and urged us against those who incurred His anger. In all lands there are examples to admonish you and to deter you from challenging our resolve. Be warned by the fate of others and hand over your power to us before the veil is torn and you are sorry and your errors rebound upon you. For we do not pity those who

weep, nor are we tender to those who complain. You have heard that we have conquered the lands and cleansed the earth of corruption and killed most of the people. Yours to flee; ours to pursue. And what land will shelter you, what road save you; what country protect you? You have no deliverance from our swords, no escape from the terror of our arms. Our horses are swift in pursuit, our arrows piercing, our swords like thunderbolts, our hearts like rocks, our numbers like sand. Fortresses cannot withstand us; armies are of no avail in fighting us. Your prayers against us will not be heard, for you have eaten forbidden things and your speech is foul, you betray oaths and promises, and disobedience and fractiousness prevail among you. Be informed that your lot will be shame and humiliation. "Today you are recompensed with the punishment of humiliation, because you were so proud on earth without right and for your wrongdoing" [Qur'ān, xlvi, 20].[1] "Those who have done wrong will know to what end they will revert" [Qur'ān, xxvi, 227]. Those who make war against us are sorry; those who seek our protection are safe. If you submit to our orders and conditions, then your rights and your duties are the same as ours. If you resist you will be destroyed. Do not, therefore, destroy yourselves with your own hands. He who is warned should be on his guard. You are convinced that we are infidels, and we are convinced that you are evil-doers. God, who determines all, has urged us against you. Before us, your many are few and your mighty ones are lowly, and your kings have no way to us but that of shame. Do not debate long, and hasten to give us an answer before the fires of war flare up and throw their sparks upon you. Then you will find no dignity, no comfort, no protector, no sanctuary. You will suffer at our hands the most fearful calamity, and your land will be empty of you. By writing to you we have dealt equitably with you and have awakened you by warning you. Now we have no other purpose but you. Peace be with us, with you, and with all those who follow the divine guidance, who fear the consequences of evil, and who obey the Supreme King.

> *Say to Egypt, Hülegü has come,*
> *with swords unsheathed and sharp.*
> *The mightiest of her people will become humble,*
> *he will send their children to join the aged.*

1. Koran, collection of revelations by Muhammad

Bernard Lewis, ed. and trans., *Islam: From the Prophet Muhammad to the Capture of Constantinople.* New York: Walker and Company, 1974.

Document 7: The Reed Flute

Jalaluddin Rumi, often called "the Master," is one of the finest Persian poets of the thirteenth century. In many of his poems and teachings he uses the reed to symbolize the soul, which has been separated from God and longs to return.

Listen to the story told by the reed,
of being separate.

"Since I was cut from the reedbed,
I have made this crying sound.

Anyone separated from someone he loves

understands what I say.

Anyone pulled from a source
longs to go back.

At any gathering I am there, mingling
in the laughing and the grieving,

a friend to each, but few
will hear the secrets hidden

within the notes. No ears for that.
Body flowing out of spirit,

spirit up from body. We can't conceal
that mixing, but it's not given us

to see the soul." The reed flute
is fire, not wind. Be nothing.

Hear the love-fire tangled
in the reed notes, as bewilderment

melts into wine. The reed is a friend
to all who want the fabric

torn and drawn away. The reed is
hurt and salve combining.

Intimacy and longing for
intimacy in one song.

A disasterous surrender,
and a fine love, together.

The one who secretly hears this
is senseless.

A tongue has one customer,
the ear.

The power of a cane flute comes
from its making sugar in the reedbed.

Whatever sound it has
is for everyone.

Days full of wanting, let them go by
without worrying that they do.

Stay where you are, inside
such a pure, hollow note.

Document 8: A Lesson from *The One Thousand and One Nights*

During the thirteenth century folklore literature, compilations of stories and fairy tales, spread over the Arabic-Islamic world. One of the best compilations is The One Thousand and One Nights. *The stories, like the one included here about an ass and an ox, not only entertain, but deliver lessons on how to live.*

Once a merchant with abundance of wealth and property was favored by God with understanding the animals' speech. In his country home, he had an ass and an ox. One day the ox visited the ass and found the latter's place swept and clean with plenty of barley and straw in the manger. The merchant was there and heard the ox say to the ass, "How lucky you are! You live comfortably in this well-attended place while I work hard at the plough and the mill with very little to eat." The ass then said to the ox, "When you go to the field next time and the yoke is put upon your neck, fall down and lie on the ground as if you were sick. If they give you even beans to eat, refuse food for a day or two until you rest." Having overheard and understood this conversation, the merchant told the attendant to leave the ox alone since it was sick, and to take the ass in its place. Toward the end of the day, the ox thanked the ass for his kindness in letting him rest for a day. Yet the ass did not respond to the ox and regretted very much having given such advice. On the following day again the ass was taken to work instead of the ox; and by the day's end the ass returned to the barn feeling tired with a lacerated neck. When the ox offered its thanks again, the ass remarked to itself, "I was living in peace and comfort, and nothing gave me trouble except my own imposition." He then said to the ox, "I would like to give you a brotherly advice. This morning, I overheard our master say that should the ox continue to be sick for another day, it would be sold to the butcher for meat. I am therefore worried about you and want only to warn you for your own safety." Upon hearing this, the ox thanked the ass, rose up immediately and began to eat. The following morning, when the attendant came to take the ass to work, he was surprised to see the ox eating and drinking with all signs of health and strength. He took the ox to work and left the ass to rest.

The One Thousand and One Nights, Wilson B. Bishai, *Humanities in the Arabic-Islamic World.* Dubuque, IA: Wm. C. Brown, 1973.

Document 9: Marco Polo and the Sack of Baghdad

In 1271 Marco Polo traveled with his merchant father to China and the court of Kublai Khan. For the next seventeen years Polo served as an emissary of Kublai Khan, traveling with unprecedented freedom across the Mongol Empire. His account of his journeys, entitled The Travels of Marco Polo, *inspired future explorers, including Christopher Columbus. One of his journeys took him to the magnificent city of Baghdad, captured by the Mongols in 1255.*

Baghdad is a huge city where the Caliph of all the Saracens[1] lives, just as the head of the Christian world lives in Rome. It is built on a large river which flows into the Indian Sea, and up and down which traders travel with their goods. It takes some eighteen days to reach the sea by river and merchants on their way to India sail down to the city of Kais where they come into the open sea. On the river, between Baghdad and Kais, is another city called Basra, in the woods around which the best date palms in the world can be found. In Baghdad itself a great variety of materials are worked—cloth of gold, silk, damask, brocade and cramoisy, embroidered with many different designs of animals. Most of the pearls imported from India into Christendom are pierced in Baghdad, and the city is a centre for the study of the laws of Mohammed, of necromancy, physics, geomancy and physiognomy. It is the most important and largest city in that part of the world.

It must be explained how it was discovered that the Caliph of Baghdad[2] owned the greatest collection of gold, silver and precious objects ever to belong to one man.

In the early days of their power, the Tartar lords consisted of four brothers; the eldest, Mongu, was the Great Khan. They had already subjected Cathay to their rule, but this was not enough. They planned to conquer the world. So they divided it into four parts: one of them was to subjugate the Orient, another the south and the two others were to divide the rest. In about 1255, Hulagu, one of the four brothers, raised an enormous army and came to conquer Baghdad. It was a tremendous undertaking because there were in Baghdad over 100,000 cavalrymen, not to mention the infantry. Once he had taken the city, Hulagu discovered that the Caliph owned a tower full of gold, silver and precious objects such as had never been seen in one place. When Hulagu saw so much treasure, he was amazed and summoned the Caliph to his presence.

He asked the Caliph: 'Why have you amassed so much treasure? What were you planning to do with it? Didn't you realize that I was your enemy and that I would attack you with a large army in order to take your throne? And if so, why didn't you use your treasure to enlist more soldiers and to defend your city?'

The Caliph had no answer, so Hulagu went on to say: 'Since you are so fond of your treasure, I will make you eat it.' He then had the Caliph locked up in the tower and ordered that under no circumstances should he be given anything to eat or drink.

'You may eat your treasure to your heart's content since you like it so much,' Hulagu told the Caliph, 'and remember, you will never have anything else to eat again.'

The Caliph died in the tower after four days; he was the last of the Caliphs.

There is much more that could be said about the people of Baghdad, their affairs and their way of life, but it would take too long to tell.

1. Arabs 2. successor of Muhammad, prophet of Islam

Marco Polo, *The Travels of Marco Polo*, trans., Teresa Waugh. New York: Facts On File, 1984.

Document 10: Sundiata's Victory: The Beginning of the Mali Empire

From 1235 to 1240, Sundiata Keita, the ruler of the Malinke, a people inhabiting the savannah country of the upper Niger River, attacked and defeated King Sumaguru, ruler of the Sosso, a branch of the Soninke, clans of ancient Ghana. This battle marks the beginning of the great Mali Empire. The account of Sundiata's victory is recorded in an anonymous Arabic manuscript.

As Sundiata advanced with his army to meet Sumanguru, he learned that Sumanguru was also coming against him with an army prepared for battle. They met in a place called Kirina [not far from the modern Koulikoro]. When Sundiata turned his eyes on the army of Sumanguru he believed they were a cloud and said: "What is this cloud on the eastern side?" They told him it was the army of Sumanguru. As for Sumanguru, when he saw the army of Sundiata, he exclaimed: "What is that mountain of stone?" For he thought it was a mountain. And they told him: "It is the army of Sundiata, which lies to the west of us." Then the two columns came together and fought a murderous battle; in the thick of the fight, Sundiata uttered a great shout in the face of the warriors of Sumanguru, and at once these ran to get behind Sumanguru; the latter in his return uttered a great shout in the face of the warriors of Sundiata, all of whom fled to get behind Sundiata. Usually, when Sumanguru shouted, eight heads would rise above his own head.

When they had done this, Sundiata said to Sangaran Danguinia Konnté: "Have you forgotten the taboo?" [A reference to an earlier prophecy of Sumanguru's imminent downfall, and the manner of its bringing about.] As soon as Sangaran Danguinia heard Sundiata's question he came to the front of the army, halted, grasped the arrow (spear?) armed with the spur of a white cock, and threw it at Sumanguru. As soon as it had struck Sumanguru, Sangaran said: "This is the arrow of him who knows the ancient secrets. . . ." While he was saying this, Sumanguru vanished and was seen no more. Now he had had a gold bracelet on his wrist, and this fell on that spot [i.e., at Kirina]; a baobab tree grew out of it and carries the mark to this day. [Fifty years ago, it is said, the people of Kirina would still show their visitors a baobab tree which they held to be the same one as grew there on the day of Sundiata's famous victory.]

. . . As for Sundiata, he defeated the army of Sumanguru, ravaged the land of the Susu and subjugated its people. Afterwards Sundiata became the ruler of an immense empire [Mali].

Anonymous, trans., Maurice Delafosse, *Traditions Historiques et Legendaires du Soudan Occidental*, in Basil Davidson, *The African Past: Chronicles from Antiquity to Modern Times*. Boston: Little, Brown, 1964.

Document 11: The Arrival of the Mexicas in the Valley of Mexico

During the thirteenth century the many city-states that emerged in the Valley of Mexico would eventually form the great civilization of the Aztecs. One group, the Mexicas, migrated to the valley from the plains in the north. They spoke Nahuatl and were guided by their faith in their god, Huitzilopochtli. Nahuatl texts recount the troubles the Mexica encountered as they entered the Valley of Mexico.

Immediately, the Mexicas began their march toward here,
they exist, they are painted [in the codices],
the places through which the Mexicas passed,
are noted in the Nahuatl language.
And when the Mexicas approached,
truly they wandered without direction,
they ended up being the last to arrive.

Upon arriving,
when they were following their path,
they were not received anywhere.

Everywhere they were reprehended.

No one knew their face.
Everywhere they were told:
"Who are you?
Where do you come from?"

Thus they were unable to settle anywhere,
they were only cast out,
everywhere they were persecuted.
They went to Coatepec,
they went to Tollan,
they went to Ichpuchco,
they went to Ecatepec,
then to Chiquiuhtepetitlan,
then immediately to Chapultepec,
where many people came to settle.

And a dominion already existed in Azcapotzalco,
in Coatlinchan,
in Culhuacan,
but Mexico did not yet exist.
There were still bulrushes and reedbeds
where Mexico is now.

Miguel Leon-Portilla, *The Aztec Image of Self and Society*. Salt Lake City: University of Utah Press, 1992.

CHRONOLOGY

632
Muhammad dies; caliphate begins

1150
Toltec empire in Mesoamerica ends, early groups move into the
    Valley of Mexico

1181–1226
Life of Francis of Assisi

1192
Yoritomo Minamoto gains the title of shogun

1198–1216
Papal rule of Pope Innocent III (Lothair of Segni)

1200
Rise of the Mali Empire; Mississippian Indians at Cahokia flourish

1201
A master of schools is appointed at Oxford University in England

1202–1204
The Fourth Crusade and the sack of Constantinople

1206
Dominican order is founded; Genghis Khan takes power

1211–1215
Genghis Khan invades China

1214–1292
Life of Roger Bacon

1215
King John signs the Magna Carta; Fourth Lateran Council

1216
Pope Innocent III dies

1218–1221
Fifth Crusade against Egypt

1219
Genghis Khan takes Peking

1220
Mongols attack eastern Islamic lands; construction of Amiens Cathedral in France begins

1225–1274
Life of Thomas Aquinas

1227
Genghis Khan dies

1233
Arab historian Ibn al-Athir dies

1235–1255
Sundiata rules the Mali Empire

1237–1240
Mongols conquer Russia

1240
Malians capture the gold trade in western Africa; Sundiata conquers Ghana

1241
Lübeck and Hamburg form an alliance to protect trade interests

1244
University of Rome is founded

1248–1254
Sixth Crusade against Egypt

1250
Zenith of Cahokia; last of the Aztec groups migrate into the Valley of Mexico; Mamluk Turks rule in Egypt

1257
Sorbonne founded in Paris

1258
Baghdad and the caliph fall to the Mongols

1259
Kublai Khan overthrows the Song dynasty in southern China and establishes his Yuan dynasty

1260
Sundiata dies; Turk and Arab forces defeat Mongols at Ayn Jalut; Thomas Aquinas writes *Summa Theologica*

1265–1321
Life of Dante

1267
Mongols launch a sea attack against Japan; Giotto is born (dies in 1337)

1275–1292
Marco Polo travels to China and serves in Kublai Khan's court

1277
Mongols launch a second sea attack against Japan

1290
Jews are expelled from England

1294
Kublai Khan dies

FOR FURTHER READING

Africa and the Americas

Basil Davidson, *Africa in History: Themes and Outlines*. New York: Macmillan, 1991.

Nigel Davis, *Aztec Empire: Toltec Resurgence*. Norman: University of Oklahoma Press, 1988.

Peter Farb, *Man's Rise to Civilization: The Cultural Ascent of the Indians of North America*. New York: Penguin, 1968.

Robert July, *A History of the African People*. New York: Charles Scribner's Sons, 1970.

Miguel Leon Portilla, ed., *The Broken Spears: The Aztec Account of the Conquest of Mexico*. Boston: Beacon Press, 1992.

Carl Sauer, *Man in Nature: America Before the Days of the White Man*. Berkeley, CA: Turtle Island Foundation, 1975.

R. Silverberg, *The Mound Builders*. Athens: Ohio University Press, 1986.

Lois Warburton, *Aztec Civilization*. San Diego: Lucent, 1995.

Arabs-Islam

Carl Brockelmann, *History of the Islamic Peoples*. New York: Capricorn, 1960.

Albert Hourani, *A History of the Arab Peoples*. Cambridge, MA: Belknap Press of Harvard University Press, 1991.

Robert Ernest Hume, *The World's Living Religions*. New York: Charles Scribner's Sons, 1931.

Bernard Lewis, *The Arabs in History*. New York: Harper & Row, 1960.

J.J. Sanders, *A History of Medieval Islam*. London: Routledge, 1965.

G.E. von Grunebaum, *Medieval Islam: A Study in Cultural Orientation*. Chicago: University of Chicago Press, 1953.

China and Japan

Peter Duus, *Feudalism in Japan*. New York: Knopf, 1969.

Patricia Buckley Ebrey, *Chinese Civilization and Society: A Sourcebook*. New York: Free Press, 1981.

Elizabeth Endicott-West, *Mongolian Rule in China*. Harvard-Yenching Institute Monograph Series, No. 29. Cambridge, MA: Harvard University Press, 1989.

L. Frederic, *Daily Life in Japan at the Time of the Samurai*. London: Allen and Unwin, 1972.

Valerie Hansen, *Changing Gods in Medieval China, 1127–1276*. Princeton, NJ: Princeton University Press, 1990.

G. Sansom, *A History of Japan to 1334*. Stanford, CA: Stanford University Press, 1958.

H.F. Scherman, *The Economic Structure of the Yuan Dynasty*. Cambridge, MA: Harvard University Press, 1956.

Richard Wilhelm, *A Short History of Chinese Civilization*. New York: Viking, 1929.

Europe

Norman F. Cantor, ed., *The Encyclopedia of the Middle Ages*. New York: Viking, 1999.

Robert De Clari, trans. Edgar Holmes McNeal, *The Conquest of Constantinople*. Toronto: University of Toronto Press, 1997.

Umberto Eco, *Art and Beauty in the Middle Ages*. New Haven, CT: Yale University Press, 1988.

Hans-Werner Goetz, trans. Albert Wimmer, *Life in the Middle Ages: From the Seventh to the Thirteenth Century*. Notre Dame, IN: University of Notre Dame Press, 1997.

Michael Haren, *Medieval Thought: The Western Intellectual Tradition from Antiquity to the Thirteenth Century.* Toronto: University of Toronto Press, 1993.

C.H. Haskins, *The Rise of Universities.* New York: P. Smith, 1940.

Friedrich Heer, *The Medieval World: Europe 1110–1350.* New York: World, 1961.

David Knowles, *Evolution of Medieval Thought.* New York: Random House, 1962.

C.W. Previt-Orton, *The Shorter Cambridge Medieval History.* Cambridge, England: Cambridge University Press, 1952.

Jean Richard, trans. Jean Birrell, *The Crusades, c. 1071–1291.* Cambridge, England: Cambridge University Press, 1999.

Brian Tierney, *The Crisis of Church and State: 1050–1300.* Englewood Cliffs, NJ: Prentice-Hall, 1966.

Lynn White Jr., *Medieval Technology and Social Change.* Oxford, England: Oxford University Press, 1966.

Jews

Israel Abrahams, *Jewish Life in the Middle Ages.* New York: Athenaeum, 1969.

Jeremy Cohen, *The Friars and the Jews: The Evolution of Medieval Anti-Judaism.* Ithaca, NY: Cornell University Press, 1982.

Jacob Marcus, *The Jew in the Medieval World.* New York: Athenaeum, 1972.

Ellis Rivkin, *The Shaping of Jewish History.* New York: Charles Scribner's Sons, 1971.

Robert M. Seltzer, *Jewish People, Jewish Thought.* New York: Macmillan, 1980.

Mongols

Peter Brent, *The Mongol Empire.* London: Weidenfeld and Nicolson, 1976.

F. W. Cleaves, *The Secret History of the Mongols*. Cambridge, MA: Harvard University Press, 1960.

Editors of Time-Life Books, *The Mongol Conquests: Timeframe AD, 1200–1300*. Alexandria, VA: Time-Life Books, 1989.

Michael Gibson, *Genghis Khan and the Mongols*. London: Wayland, 1973.

J.J. Sanders, *The History of the Mongol Conquests*. London: Routledge and Kegan Paul, 1971.

INDEX

Africa. *See* Mali; North Africa
agriculture
  and Cahokia Indians, 194,
    212–13
  and Malinke people, 194, 200
Albigenses, the, 107
Alexius III (Byzantine emperor),
  90, 91
Alexius IV, 91, 93
Almohad Empire, 162, 197
Almoravids, 161–62
Almoravid Sanhaja, 197
Americas. *See* Aztecs; Cahokia
  Indians
Amiens Cathedral, 84–85
Angelu, Isaac, 91, 93
Aquinas, St. Thomas, 18–19, 35,
  52
  criticism of, 50–51
  existential unity of, 50
  logical system of, 48–49
  on the physical world, 49–50
  on proof of God's existence,
    53–54
  on the state, 50
  youth of, 47–48
Arab-Muslims, 19–22
  achievements of, 197
  attack on Khwarizm, 120–21,
    185
  and Christianity, 20, 21–22
  creation of new civilization,
    20–21, 158–59
  crusades against, 38–39, 90–95,
    155
  major developments of, 166
  and Mali, 194, 199
  Mongol invasions, 184–85
  Mongols converted to, 170
  in North Africa
    acculturation process, 160

Almoravids in, 162–63
Berber resistance, 159–60
decline of, 162–63
flourishing cities in, 160–61
tolerance of, 158
philosophical influences, 46
rise and decline of, 155
sack of Baghdad, 14, 24–25,
  123–24, 156, 166, 168–69,
  189–90
threats to, 155–56
see also art, Islamic; Egypt
architecture. *See* cathedrals
Aristotle, 18, 46, 48
art, 19, 36
  Chinese, 115, 136
  Gothic cathedrals, 82–85
  international style, 86–87
  Islamic, 156
    arabesque, 180
    attitude toward
      representational, 176–77
    calligraphy, 179–80
    egalitarian aspects of,
      180–82
    use of representational,
      177–79
  Italian painting, 86
  Japanese, 117, 146
Athir, Abn al, 24, 125, 184
Augustine, Saint, 46–47
Avignon, France, 43
Aybeg, 170, 191
Ayyub, Sultan, 185, 186–87
Aztecs, 14, 28, 30, 195
  cultural sophistication of,
    204–205
  development of city-states by,
    205
  and the Mexica, 206–208
  migration, 203–204